PLOUGHSHARES INTO SWORDS? : IS
DS 126.5 S452 1991

P9-DXM-289

Ploughshares Into Swords?

Ploughshares Into Swords?

Israelis and Jews in the Shadow of the Intifada

Colin Shindler

I.B. Tauris & Co Ltd
Publishers
London · New York

Published in 1991 by
I.B.Tauris & Co Ltd
110 Gloucester Avenue
London NW1 8JA

175 Fifth Avenue
New York
NY 10010

Distributed in the United States of America
and Canada by
St Martin's Press
175 Fifth Avenue
New York
NY 10010

A CIP record for this book is available from the British Library
US Library of Congress Catalog Card Number: 90–071577
A full CIP record is available from the Library of Congress

ISBN 1–85043–324–0

Cover photo courtesy of BIPAC, London

Printed and bound in Great Britain by
WBC Print Ltd, Bridgend, Mid Glamorgan

For Sara, Joshua, Ruthie and Miriam

Who is the bravest hero?
He who turns his enemy into a friend

Avot d'R. Nathan, 23

Contents

Acknowledgements

This book was written during 1989–90 in Jerusalem, where I was a Visiting Research Fellow at the Hebrew University's Harry S. Truman Research Institute for the Advancement of Peace. In Jerusalem I was able to witness at first hand the deteriorating situation between Israeli and Palestinian. I met many fine people, Jews and Arabs, who were struggling against tremendous odds to keep their extremists at bay and to maintain the hope that one day the two peoples will live peaceably side by side. I remain conscious of the fact that I am not an academic outsider, nor an intermediary in a distant quarrel, and I hope that sense of involvement permeates the book.

A general idea of writing a book about Israel and its problems was developed after talking to David Cesarani and Simon Louvish. I must also thank Jonny Zucker for allowing me to make use of his thesis on the Israeli Peace Movement. My good friend Jerry Lewis helped me in a variety of ways as usual. My neighbour in Jerusalem, Martin Gilbert, proffered the excellent advice that I should actually type straight on to the word processor rather than first write the text out longhand.

I must thank the many people who generously gave up their time to see me and to answer my questions, both during the last year and in the past. They included Morale Bar-On, Avrum Burg, Dafna Golan, Galia Golan, Yosef Heller, Arthur Hertzberg, Reuven Kaminer, David Kretzmer, Yechezkel Landau, Rabbi Jeremy Milgrom, Moshe Negbi, Rabbi Isaac Newman, Ehud Shprinzak, David Tal, Shmuel Toledano and Debbie Weisman.

I am grateful to Michael Lerner, editor of *Tikkun* magazine, for his comments on the chapters concerning the Diaspora, and to Rabbi Isaac Newman for his remarks on chapter 3, 'Inheriting the Land'. Dan Leon, senior editor of *New Outlook* magazine, and John Cecil took the trouble to read a draft of the entire manuscript and made pertinent and valuable points. I must also thank Ruth Cohen for her observations and my friend Edy Kaufman for his continuous goodwill and advice.

Rabbi Jonathan Wittenberg helped to ensure consistency in the transliteration of Hebrew. The system which I have employed is designed for the convenience of the English reader rather than the precise demands of the scholar.

The library staffs of the Truman Institute for the Advancement of Peace at the Hebrew University and the Institute of Jewish Affairs in London were always helpful.

I wish to thank Anna Enayat and Emma Sinclair-Webb of I. B. Tauris, and my copy-editor Brenda Thomson, for their kindness and professionalism in helping this book on its odyssey. Any errors of fact or interpretation are mine alone.

Finally, my gratitude to my wife, Jean, without whom this entire venture would have been impossible.

I write these words from the greyness of Finchley, but I can still feel the warmth of Jerusalem despite the tension there. A few days ago three Israelis were knifed to death outside the communal centre in Baka, where I took my children almost every day. This followed the Temple Mount killings. The two events are symbolic of the reality which Israelis and Palestinians face – a reality which no book can convey.

Colin Shindler
Finchley, London
October 1990

ושפט בין הגוים
והוכיח לעמים רבים
וכתתו חרבותם לאתים
וחניתותיהם למזמרות
לא ישא גוי אל גוי חרב
ולא ילמדו עוד מלחמה

ישעיה ב :ד

And He shall judge between the nations
And shall decide for many peoples
And they shall beat their swords into ploughshares
And their spears into pruning-hooks
Nation shall not lift up sword against nation
Neither shall they learn war any more.

Isaiah 2:4

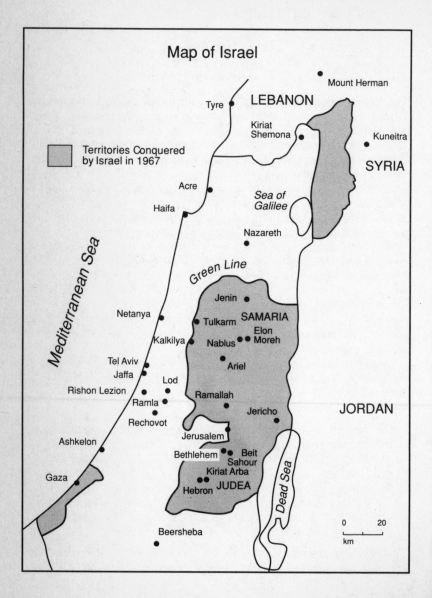

Map of Israel

Territories Conquered
by Israel in 1967

Mount Herman

LEBANON

Tyre

Kiriat
Shemona

Kuneitra

SYRIA

Acre

Sea of
Galilee

Haifa

Nazareth

Green Line

Mediterranean Sea

Jenin

SAMARIA

Netanya

Tulkarm

Elon
Moreh

Kalkilya

Nablus

Tel Aviv

Ariel

Jaffa

Lod

Rishon Lezion

Ramallah

JORDAN

Ramla

Jericho

Rechovot

Jerusalem

Ashkelon

Bethlehem

Beit
Sahour

Gaza

Kiriat Arba

Hebron

JUDEA

Dead Sea

0   20

km

Beersheba

Introduction

The formation of a narrow right-wing administration in Israel led by Yitzhak Shamir in June 1990 unnerved Western governments. They believed that the chances for peace in the Middle East and for an Israeli–Palestinian dialogue had been relegated to a rhetorical oblivion. Diaspora Jews were similarly aghast. Generally liberal in inclination owing to their status as a minority, their dreams of an enlightened Jewish State – a light unto the nations – did not concur with the reality of an Israeli government in which Ariel Sharon was a dominant figure. A government had been formed in which the right wing of Likud and the smaller parties of the Far Right had gained ascendancy.

Although this government wisely refrained from controversial statements during the Iraqi invasion of Kuwait in 1990, it also tried hard to capitalize on its improved status as Iraqi President Saddam Hussein's implacable enemy and thus a moral ally of the military forces in the Gulf States. The Palestine Liberation Organization (PLO)'s folly in courting Saddam throughout 1990 and then, by default, finding itself entrapped politically by the invasion of Kuwait, lent credibility to the government's hardline approach.

In the face of the vengeance threatened by the Iraqi leader, Shamir's patriotic resolve was comforting to a nervous population. One week after the invasion of 2 August 1990 he told a graduation ceremony at the National Defence College that

> the history of the people of Israel has won it a reputation for stubbornness and adherence to its beliefs, for devotion to its forefathers' homeland, for its moral level, and for the indefatigable aspiration for excellence in all fields of human endeavour. The combination of these characteristics has given our nation a power to withstand and endure because of which we shall not fear or flinch from the bullies and enemies who threaten and plot against us time after time.[1]

This appeal to the national tradition of the Jews to triumph over their enemies was directed at Iraq. But its unspoken sentiment was that

Israel would also stand firm against any attempt to force it to come to terms with Palestinian nationalism.

Yet Israel benefited little from the Gulf crisis. Attempts to seek a reward for the PLO's alignment with Saddam Hussein failed. US Secretary of State James Baker reminded Israel of its commitment to the Shamir initiative to stage elections in the Terrorities and its often repeated willingness to participate in a dialogue with the Palestinians.

The riot on the Temple Mount, Jerusalem, in October 1990, in which almost a score of Palestinians died, brought the issue back into sharp focus. The tardy official reaction to the tragedy and the government's failure to establish an official judicial inquiry under the aegis of the Supreme Court of Justice seemed indicative of its ideological somnambulism.

In 1990 Israel seemed to lurch from one political controversy to another. If it was not quiet government funding for the purchase of St John's Hospice in the Christian quarter of the Old City of Jerusalem, then it was the studied procrastination over the Baker Plan. The precipitous deterioration of US–Israeli relations caused both Yoram Ettinger, the Israeli liaison man with Congress, and Moshe Arad, the Israeli Ambassador in the United States, to send long secret telegrams to Jerusalem detailing the erosion of congressional support and the disillusionment of the Jewish community.[2]

A politically divided Israel, however, did not view the formation of the new Shamir government with the same sense of despondency. A telephone poll of over 500 Israelis on the eve of a vote of no-confidence in the previous government had shown that a slender majority preferred a narrow Likud-led government over a narrow Labour-led one.[3] Whilst Yitzhak Shamir was uninspiring as a leader, for many Israelis he held at bay the possibility of negotiating with the PLO. He was a lacklustre politician, but he was also viewed as an archetypal stiffnecked Jew. Moreover, historically, Israel had always dwelt alone amongst the nations. The present situation confirmed the legacy of the past. There was nothing new under the sun.

In Europe and the United States, however, perceptions were entirely different. While Yasser Arafat and the PLO were hardly viewed through rose-tinted spectacles, there was a profound sense of official indignation with Israeli government policy and in particular with the figure of Yitzhak Shamir, who was considered untrustworthy by the White House. Many of Israel's admirers asked how the Jewish State had reached such an impasse after the heroic early years. Why had Israel changed? Were the original ideals of Zionism just too utopian and thus unattainable? Many non-Jews asked how such an intelligent people as the Jews could suffer a leadership which could enact such seemingly unintelligent policies.

It was, however, the Intifada – the Palestinian civil uprising in the Territories – which became the supreme symbol of Mr Shamir's unwillingness to come to grips with the Palestinian issue. Israeli soldiers who were trained to defend their country against hostile neighbours were now asked to perform the role of a riot control squad. Despite the aim of Zionism to create a just society based on the vision of the Hebrew Prophets, young armed Israelis were now confronting angry and dangerous crowds of stone-throwing youngsters and women.

Three years of the Intifada brought its inevitable results. According to B'Tselem, the Israeli Information Centre for Human Rights in the Occupied Territories, 712 residents of the Territories, including 161 children, were killed by the Israel Defence Forces (IDF) from the beginning of the Intifada (9 December 1987) up to the end of October 1990. Amongst Jews in the Diaspora, there was a feeling that Israel was forfeiting its unique status as a Jewish State and was changing into a mere state of the Jews – like any other state. Many had warned – both publicly and privately – that it was

> manifestly absurd to maintain military rule over a million Palestinians as if it was a well-thought-out recipe for harmony and stability. It has had a divisive and corrosive effect on Israeli society and created an unjust system of double standards for Jew and Palestinian. It was inevitable that sooner or later the frustrations of the downtrodden would overcome their fears . . . and now the post-1967 generation of Palestinians have stirred the cauldron and it has boiled over.[4]

Whilst Jewish commitment to the State of Israel did not lessen, many people – Jews and non-Jews alike – began to ask why this process of regression had taken place? Was it simply the Palestinian problem and the inability of their leaders to reach a *rapprochement* with Israel? Was it the unimaginative leadership of successive Israeli governments? Or were these developments unavoidable – inevitable in the context of the Israeli-Palestinian struggle? Were the changes within Israeli society an inevitable transformation, a normal evolutionary process in the life of a new nation-state? Or was today's reality a temporary aberration?'

The answers to such questions are neither easy nor simple. This book seeks merely to provide some food for thought. In one sense, it records the history of the Jewish State; but, more important, it attempts to elucidate Israel's political evolution and the problems that have arisen in the course of that odyssey. It aspires to throw some light on why Israel is like it is today.

The Baal Shem-Tov (1700–60) commented that 'Forgetfulness leads to exile, while remembrance is the secret of redemption'. It is my hope that the information and analysis contained within these pages will help lead to a reclaiming of 'remembrance' and an eradication of 'forgetfulness'.

Part I

A People That Dwells Alone

1

The Origins of Zionist Radicalism

The triumph of the Far Right

The road which led to the government of June 1990 began decades ago, but 1984 appropriately proved to be the year of foreboding for the State of Israel. In that year, the election of the late Rabbi Meir Kahane to the Knesset on behalf of the Kach party symbolized the emergence of the Far Right in Israel. Its appearance and rapid growth during the 1980s were indicative of Israeli society's broad movement towards a position politically right of centre. Although the Far Right acquired on average ten out of a total of 120 Knesset seats in both elections in the 1980s, its influence was disproportionate to the numbers elected. The effect, however, was to bolster the position of the hardliners within Likud and to cement a more hawkish stance within the party in general. In the public arena, they initiated and thereby legitimized open debate on hitherto taboo subjects such as transfer and deportation – a sensitive area of public discourse which had previously been considered the prerogative of the politically extreme and eccentric.

In the West, by utilizing the figleaf of a demogogic Kahane and highlighting his message of menacing reductionism, the Far Right was caricatured more often than not as essentially a religious phenomenon. This accorded with the popular view of the advance of religious fundamentalism in the Muslim world. Yet while the antics of Kahane's juvenile followers made news, they also served to divert attention from the growing influence of the Far Right on Israeli public opinion. In reality, the manic behaviour of Kach paradoxically sanitized and made respectable fellow travellers who were both more articulate and more rational in advocating Kahane's ideas. The Rabbi's sensationalism certainly induced a sharp reaction to his public behaviour, but his crystallization of clear-cut approaches during a period of political stagnation and immobility struck a resonant chord within Israeli society. Kahanism effected a psychological breakthrough which permitted some citizens to perceive the Israel–Palestine conflict as one which was not complex at all but on the contrary lent itself to easy, straightforward solutions. While Kahane was deemed publicly untouchable, others emerged to promote quietly and respectably the tenets of his canon – and this proved acceptable to the Israeli political establishment, which moved to ban Kahane from standing in the 1988 election.

The emergence of the Far Right was not a consequence of Rabbi Kahane's emigration to Israel (from the United States) in the early 1970s. Its ideological antecedent was undoubtedly Revisionist Zionism during the formative inter-war years, but its contemporary genesis lies in the rejection of the Camp David Accords (negotiated by Menachem Begin in 1979) by a loose coalition of long-term maximalists on the question of the Territories. Moreover, it was not only adherents of Likud and the National Religious Party (NRP) which opposed Camp David, but also ideological socialists such as the Ein Vered circle from within the Labour movement. The growth of the Far Right was assisted and enhanced by the profound insecurity and uncertainty generated by the débâcle of the war in Lebanon in 1982 and the advent of the Intifada in 1987.

The legacy of Jabotinsky

For decades the mantle of ultra-nationalism in the Jewish state rested safely on the shoulders of Menachem Begin. As a charismatic disciplinarian, a strong and principled leader of the Herut movement, he was perceived by friend and foe alike as the first keeper of the Revisionist Zionist faith passed down to him by its founder, Ze'ev Jabotinsky. Until the schismatic effect of the Camp David Accords, the fundamentalists within Likud had lauded Begin and expressed their deep conviction in his ability to maintain the heritage of Revisionism. The Far Right's confidence in Begin as its standard-bearer was not misplaced, for his world outlook and his advocacy of 'shlemut ha'moledet (the "completeness" of the homeland)' significantly did not stem from the mainstream of Revisionism but instead from its radical right wing, personified by its youth movement, Betar.

Betar, significantly, came into existence before Ze'ev Jabotinsky created the Revisionist Zionist Organization in 1925. A number of school students established the first group in Riga in 1923. Its name was taken from the last Jewish fortress to hold out against the Romans, but more importantly it commemorated the life and times of the soldier–pioneer Joseph Trumpeldor who had been killed by Arab marauders at the distant outpost of Tel Hai, near the border with Lebanon, in 1920. Betar was the abbreviation of Brit Yosef Trumpeldor (the Covenant of Joseph Trumpeldor). The martyred Trumpeldor, who was actually a socialist, provided Jabotinsky with an important icon for his new youth movement. In his song of the prisoners of Acre, Jabotinsky romanticized the legend of the one-armed Trumpeldor and the heroes of Tel Hai who guarded the Land at its very edge: 'From generation to generation, no holier blood was shed, than the blood of the tillers of Tel Hai'.[1] Jabotinsky was imprisoned in Acre, north of Haifa, in 1920–1, and wrote the poem on hearing about Trumpeldor's death. Other Jews were also imprisoned by the British at that time.

But Betar actually pursued a separate development from the main Revisionist organization, even though they were technically linked. Both Betar and the Irgun *Zva'i Le'umi* (National Military Organization), which Begin later commanded in the revolt against the British, were in reality segregated entities which owed allegiance only to the figure of Jabotinsky and not to the Revisionist Organization as such. Jabotinsky jealously protected Betar from the Revisionist hierarchy. He allowed the movement the space to flourish and to evolve within his own conceptual framework. But such individualism inevitably spawned independent policies. Moreover, the young people naturally adopted a more radical posture than their elders. Indeed, when the moderate wing of the party split with Jabotinsky in 1933 over his increasingly authoritarian approach, a referendum showed that nearly 94 per cent of Betar voters supported him, even though he was a minority in his own executive.[2]

Jabotinsky's personal magnetism and intellectual brilliance attracted the poor and downtrodden, the unworldly and the undereducated from the Jewish ghettoes and townships of Eastern Europe in the 1920s and 1930s. At its inception in 1923–4, many young Jews enrolled in Betar out of a sense of disillusionment with the Bolshevik revolution. Menachem Begin was, himself, a one-time member of the Polish branch of Hashomer Hatzair, the Marxist–Zionist youth group. In contrast to the drabness of their own lives, Jabotinsky painted for the young people a bright picture of a future Jewish homeland, a beacon of national salvation where Jews could live as a free people, their heads held high and beholden to no one; a place where Jews could determine their own destiny; a completely Jewish homeland, free of anti-semites, where the Jew would be the master. He told them that they were extremely fortunate to have been born during that period of history when the Third Jewish State would be built by Jewish endeavour. Jabotinsky lauded the common man. He bestowed upon his followers a self-image of heroic proportions. Even the ordinary were extraordinary. They were the heirs to the ancient kingdom of David and had a duty to participate in the coming struggle to liberate the homeland. His romantic vision of heroism and sacrifice, untrammelled by complex realities, radiated an aura of irresistibility.

His secular invocation of the precept of *sha'atnez* (a religious prohibition on the mixing of wool and linen in clothes) within the context of political Zionism manifested itself in the doctrine of 'monism' – Jews should be subservient to only one ideal, to the purity of Zionism and not to a hybrid mixture of Socialism and Zionism which then dominated the movement. The emphasis on particularism in the cause of establishing a Jewish homeland overshadowed any universalist sentiment. Socialism was deemed to be un-Jewish and a foreign influence.

Betar's formation and style were also clearly conditioned by the emergence of newly independent nation-states and their youth movements in Eastern Europe following the break-up of the Austro-Hungarian and German Empires in 1918. In particular, the example of Czechoslovakia's President, Thomas Masaryk, influenced Jabotinsky. He worked zealously to mould the stereotype of a confident, determined Jewish youth, ready to fight and to die for the cause of Israel. It was symbolized in the Irgun emblem: in the background, a map of Eretz Israel stretching across both sides of the Jordan; in the foreground, a hand clutching a gun with the Hebrew slogan '*Rak Kach*' (Only This Way!)'. Such imagery was naturally condemned by the Labour-dominated Zionist mainstream as a dangerous mixture of extreme nationalism peppered with crude militarism.

Others found the fervour which Jabotinsky generated distasteful and illusory. Nahum Sokolov, the Hebrew writer and President of the World Zionist Organization, 1931–5, described Revisionism as '*Shabbetai Zevi-ism*' after the false messiah whom many Jews had followed with disastrous results during the seventeenth century.[3] Labour Zionists opposed Jabotinsky's repeated plan to move millions of Jews to the Yishuv, the Jewish settlement in Palestine, within a short time without an infrastructure to accommodate them. The plan to bring in everybody indiscriminately further undermined the commitment of 'selective Zionism' such that only those committed to building a new society and to the radical transformation of the Jewish people should participate in the Zionist experiment. One modern critic termed it an historical 'big bang' true to the Revisionist craving for an absolutist heroic solution. Yet the essential difference between mainstream Zionism and Jabotinsky's philosophy remained a perception of what was possible and what was not: 'The Revisionist movement was intoxicated by the strength of the will. In their view, the bold will can shatter the fetters of reality and overcome all obstacles. The strength of subjective desire can overcome objective facts . . . Reality is ephemeral, no more a force to be reckoned with than clay in the hands of a potter'.[4]

While the Left shared the intense determination to reverse history, it regarded the future Jewish State as something far more revolutionary than simply a haven for the persecuted. It invoked a clean break with the past and the narrowness of a particularism which they believed had prevented the Jewish people from determining their own destiny. Zionism was integral to the age of socialism as the movement of national liberation of the Jewish people. Zionism was the political leap from the static periphery of history into its moving centre.

With the rise of Nazism, left-wing critics found a ready-made model in Betar for their resentment of Revisionism and, not unexpectedly, many condemned Jabotinsky's creation as akin to Jewish facism. Even Rabbi Stephen Wise, a leader of American Zionism sympathetic to Revisionism, was disconcerted by the emerging parallelism. 'For the Revisionist as for the Fascists, the state is everything and the individual nothing,' he commented.[5] Yet like the success of communism amongst Jewish youth in Europe, Betar's reaction to the deteriorating situation in Europe provided a sharp focus and attracted many new members.

Although worshipped by his young followers, Jabotinsky was a product of another age. He was a conservative politician and not a militant of the radical Right. A romantic and a poet, given to formidable displays of appealing rhetoric, a *fin de siècle* intellectual who could turn his mind to a multitude of subjects, he came from an assimilated, secular, upper-middle-class background. All this was in complete contrast to the cultural environment of the Betarim, who were typical products of the traditional world of East European Jewry. Begin and his contemporaries were completely at home in this milieu – Diaspora Jews in every sense, despite themselves. Jabotinsky, although their mentor and their symbol, was paradoxically an outsider, owing to both his background and his wider experience of the world. While he instilled in them a belief in themselves and a certainty in their ideological mission, Jabotinsky himself could operate on different levels. He was never a believer in unchallengable absolute truths and immutable doctrines which later became a hallmark of the Herut movement. He never renounced the vestiges of nineteenth-century liberalism to which he had always been committed. His concept of morality was rooted in an earlier epoch and this distanced him from his adolescent acolytes. Even in the late 1930s, when the dangers facing the Jewish people were increasingly apparent, he still maintained the belief that 'what rules the world is conscience'.[6] Like Chaim Weizmann, then President of the World Zionist Organization, and unlike Begin, he believed that a solution lay in a political accommodation with the British and not in a military uprising. When the Irgun commenced a policy of retaliating against Arab acts of terror in 1937, Jabotinsky was privately aghast when their actions violated his norms of moral behaviour: 'How can your Irgun people throw bombs in Arab quarters at random, indiscriminately

8   PLOUGHSHARES INTO SWORDS?

killing women and children? You must at least warn them.' Yet publicly he maintained a studied silence.[7]

Jabotinsky's distaste for 'adventurism' was clear even in the early 1930s when a proto-fascist group, *Brit Ha'Biryonim* (the Union of Zealots), was active in Palestine. The radical poet Uri Zvi Greenberg compared them to the Second Temple period Sicarii, Jewish extremists whose declared enemies were not only the Romans but also Jews who advocated moderate policies. In an article entitled 'The Meaning of Adventurism', published in the Revisionist movement's periodical, *Russviet*, Jabotinsky wrote, 'I categorically and firmly deny the ideology of sansculottism; it is no good, and if "adventurism" might sometimes be of use, it does not mean that 'adventurism' is everything or the main thing. Not at all. It is neither everything nor the the most essential thing.'[8]

Given the situation in Europe and the lack of progress in establishing a Jewish State, such subtle admonitions did not ring true for those in Betar and the Irgun who perceived events in a clear-cut, uncomplicated manner. Towards the end of his life, Jabotinsky's encouragement of organizational autonomy for Betar and for the Irgun began to conflict with his spiritual control of these movements. Youthful zeal had produced a radical golem. On the one hand, he opposed the official Zionist policy of *havlaga* (self-restraint) and its acceptance of the partition of Eretz Israel into Jewish and Arab states. On the other hand, he was unable to constrain his followers within the logic of political feasibility. To be sure, he gradually began to lose control of his movements. In July 1938, at a private session with Eliahu Golomb, Commander of the Hagana (the official Jewish Defence Force), he was asked to use his authority to curb the independent retaliatory attacks of the Irgun. 'Do you think that those who are engaged in such action would obey my orders?' he replied.[9]

The Irgun in Palestine was rapidly losing faith in the efficacy of diplomacy and had even undermined Jabotinsky's authority by unofficially conscripting members of Betar in Poland. Avraham Stern, then a member of the Irgun, referred to Jabotinsky as 'Hindenberg' – an aged relic from a past era. Jabotinsky did not even consider that war in Europe was imminent. Even for those who were totally loyal to his person, it was clear that he only dimly perceived the historical process taking place. When he died in New York in 1940, Jabotinsky had already passed into history. Within a few weeks, the Irgun split when Avraham Stern led discontented members from the organization to form a splinter movement, later known as Lehi – Lochamei Herut Israel (Fighters for the Freedom of Israel).

Freedom fighters

The seeds of dissent within the nationalist camp were sown at an early stage. Jabotinsky's conservatism and his belief in the British was increasingly regarded as anachronistic by his young followers in Betar. Together with the Irgun, they wanted to commence a revolt against the British which Jabotinsky adamantly refused to initiate. Frustration with the lack of movement against the British authorities in Palestine and the worsening situation in Europe unglued Jabotinsky's balancing act as the spiritual head of the Revisionist movement, Betar and the Irgun. At Betar's Third World Conference in Warsaw in 1938, the confrontation between nineteenth-century conservatism and the radicalism of the Far Right manifested itself in a clash between Jabotinsky and the youthful Begin. The elder statesman rejected the concept of 'military Zionism' and told Begin that if he did not believe in appeals to the conscience of the world, he should join the communists or 'throw yourself into the Vistula'. The conference gently rejected Jabotinsky's approach.

Although Jabotinsky has been depicted by Revisionists as the 'Father of the Revolt' against the British, the Irgun concentrated on putting bombs in Arab marketplaces at that time rather than attacking the British. It was only on the eve of the Second World War that the Irgun killed two CID men, Ronald Barker and Ralph Cairns, and the bomb-disposal expert Fred Clarke. The killings were viewed as reprisals for British actions against the Irgun. Cairns was head of the CID's Jewish section and had a reputation for torturing his prisoners. Before any dramatic moves could be initiated, the war intervened and the Irgun formally co-operated with the British against the Nazis. Indeed, the commander of the Irgun, David Raziel, was killed during a military mission on behalf of the British.

Avraham Stern was in the gallery at the Betar conference in Warsaw and witnessed Jabotinsky's refusal to adopt a policy of armed struggle against the British. The hanging of the young Revisionist Shlomo Ben-Yosef in 1938 and the final straw of the British White Paper of 1939, however, convinced Stern that the time had finally come to commence the revolt.

Stern had been politically inactive for many years after his arrival in Palestine from Poland in 1925. As a thinker and a writer, he never accepted the framework of a movement and therefore never formally joined the Revisionists. As chief of foreign relations and indoctrination for the Irgun, he gradually reached a position whereby 'the fate of Eretz Israel would be determined by the sword'. Whilst Jabotinsky was a central influence in the formation of his ideological approach during this period, Stern was also swayed by the radical right-wing views of the poet Uri Zvi Greenberg and the 'Canaanite' Yonatan Ratosh. But an even more important influence was that of Abba Achimeir, the leader of Brit Ha'Biryonim. Intellectually he facilitated Stern's connection with the rising tide of European – and in particular Italian – fascism. Stern's appreciation for Mussolini deepened when he went to study classical languages and literature in Italy in the early 1930s. Between 1928 and 1933, before the Duce's adoption of an anti-semitic policy in 1938, at least 10 per cent of Rome's Jews were members of the Fascist Party[10] and leaders of the Italian Revisionists gave the fascist salute at their conferences. In a letter to a friend in Palestine, Stern mentioned that he was enrolling Italian Blackshirts in support of the Revisionists.

Stern had also been influenced by the Easter Rebellion in Dublin in 1916 and read a lot of IRA literature; his translation of P. S. O'Hegarty's *The Victory of Sinn Fein* into Hebrew was published in 1941. The nineteenth-century Russian anarchists, the Narodnaya Volya, also interested Stern, as did Jewish national heroes such as Bar-Kochba, leader of second revolt against the Romans in AD 132–5. Stern's *nom de guerre* was 'Yair' after Elazar Ben-Yair, a leader of the Jewish fighters at Masada, who committed suicide rather than surrender to the Romans. The name also betrayed a certain death-wish beyond pure romanticism which permeated Stern's personality. His early poetry was symptomatic of this tendency:

> And we shall believe in the day of the shadow of death
> A time when the rifle will sing its battlesong
> We shall wrestle with God and death
> And welcome Zion's redeemer
> We shall welcome him. Our blood will be
> A red carpet on the streets
> And upon this carpet – our brains
> Like white roses. [11]

Stern documented eighteen principles of national revival which became the 'constitution' for members of Lehi ('the Stern Gang'). It advocated the forging of pacts with anyone who would assist Lehi – which in due course was to become 'the Hebrew Army of Liberation'. Education would be predicated on the basis that the Jews had independently to defend their State and could not rely on outsiders. Stern urged the revival of the approach that 'the sword and the book came bound together from heaven' (Midrash Vayikra Rabba 35:8). He envisaged Israel as a strong military power in the Middle East and proposed continual war against those who opposed it. Stern believed in *Malchut Israel* – a Jewish homeland which stretched from 'the River of Egypt unto the great river, the river Euphrates' (Genesis 15:18) and in the conquest of the homeland from foreign rule and its eternal possession. The problem of the non-Jewish population in the Land and their claims to sovereignty would be solved through an exchange of populations. His final principle proclaimed the building of the Third Temple in Jerusalem as 'a symbol of the new epoch of complete redemption.'

Stern was imprisoned in Mazra prison between February and June 1940 and then, amazingly, set free by the British. As history records, the Stern Gang then attempted to act as a revolutionary underground, carrying out bank robberies and attacks on the military until Stern met his death when British policemen discovered his whereabouts in 1942. Yet Stern's thinking during this period exhibits an extraordinary bizarreness. Together with Begin and others who rejected Jabotinsky's approach, he believed that an uprising against the British was all-important during the course of the war against the Nazis. Jabotinsky, by contrast, had supported England in its darkest hour and had even congratulated Churchill on becoming Prime Minister. Stern and his followers believed the struggle for independence was paramount. The World War, in their eyes, was 'a conflict between Gog and Magog and Israel should have no part in it'.[12]

Stern's conclusion that the end justifies the means led him to advocate an alliance with Hitler's Germany to defeat the common enemy. He viewed Nazi praise for the controversial 'Transfer Agreement' of 1933, which permitted German Jews to leave for Palestine with a fraction of their savings and belongings, as a precedent. He therefore put forward a plan to bring some 40,000 Jews from Europe with German help to fight the British in Palestine. Even before the war, there had been contacts with Mussolini's regime through the Italian consulate in Jerusalem. Stern also submitted a document to the Italians when their armies began to approach Egypt at the end of 1940. In return for assistance in expelling the British and facilitating Jewish emigration, he expounded the vision of a future Israel as a 'corporate state'. He further proposed continued support for Italian foreign policy and Vatican hegemony over the Old City, with the exclusion of Jewish holy sites.

Although Hitler's anti-semitic policies were well known, Stern was none the less deeply impressed by the German victories over the British in early 1940. By the end of the year his emissary had travelled to Lebanon, which was then controlled by the Vichy French, and met with a representative of the German Foreign Office. Stern solicited German help to forge a Jewish State which would be 'nationalist and totalitarian'. The Germans would provide facilities for the military training by Lehi of Jews in occupied Europe. Stern's explorations were rebuffed by the Germans – no doubt on ideological grounds.

Stern believed that German foreign policy could pragmatically be separated from Nazi racial theory. Like Jabotinsky, he adhered to the distinction drawn by Max Nordau (co-founder with Theodor Herzl of

the World Zionist Organization) between 'the anti-semitism of things'
and 'the anti-semitism of men'.[13] The Nazis, Stern believed, could be
convinced that it was to their advantage not to persecute Jews. For
Stern, Hitler fell into a historical category – he was a persecutor open
to persuasion, not an exterminator bent on elimination.[14] Moreover,
in 1940 no one believed that European Jewry was on the verge of
total destruction. For all too many leaders of the Yishuv, the struggle
for independence and the exit of the British was still of paramount
importance. Yitzhak Greenbaum, who was in charge of the Salvation
Committee of the Yishuv, commented that the fate of European Jewry
was not the only issue which concerned them. The preoccupation with
ousting the British and establishing the State was rooted in the Zionist
belief that the Jews should normalize their condition and become a
people like all others with a national struggle to secure independence.

> The normal and instinctive behaviour would have been to give
> total precedence and attention to saving helpless Jews from the
> Nazi slaughter. But this irrelevant reaction by a dedicated and
> devoted Zionist [Greenberg] demonstrates how deeply rooted
> was the Zionist concept of normalization: it remained unmoved,
> in its grotesque version, even in the face of the Holocaust.[15]

Stern was also a victim of this psychological saturation of the overriding importance of the 'normalization' of the Jewish people – albeit
before news of the Nazi extermination programme reached Palestine.
He wrote an important article entitled 'Exile and Redemption' in
response to a piece in the daily *Ha'aretz* in March 1941 about the
Warsaw Ghetto. In total ignorance of the tragedy of the Jews trapped
in the Warsaw Ghetto, he suggested that its inhabitants possessed
more autonomy than did the Yishuv in Palestine. Stern knew nothing
about the Final Solution, and indeed believed the Nazis when they said
that they would only deport Jews to Madagascar. This acceptance of
the negation of the Diaspora was so deep that Stern came to believe
in July 1939 that the Jews themselves bore some responsibility for
their adversity, since they did not grasp the opportunity to come
to Palestine to build the Jewish State. His erroneous estimation of
the Nazis depicted them as the latest pogromists in Jewish history,
bent on expelling their Jewish population. His misguided belief that
they could be persuaded to channel these Jews to fight the British
in Palestine was all too clear in Stern's document delivered to the
German Foreign Office: 'The indirect participation of the Jewish
liberation movement in the New Order in Europe already in the
preparatory stage in connection with the radical–positive solution of
the problem of European Jewry will not insignificantly strengthen the
moral bases of the New Order in the eyes of all humanity'.[16]

Following the total disarray after Stern's death, Lehi was re-established in the summer of 1943 and continued with a campaign of killings and political assassinations. The philosophy that the ends justified the means remained at the core of the group's actions, despite the demise of Avraham Stern. Yet, unlike Stern, members of the Lehi were by now beginning to grasp the full meaning of the Shoah (Holocaust). The murder in 1944 of Lord Moyne, the British Minister resident in the Middle East and a personal friend of Churchill, personified their approach. Eliahu Hakim, one of the assassins, told the court that

> we did it intentionally and with full premeditation, but we also accuse the British government of having killed intentionally and with full premeditation hundreds and hundreds of our brothers and sisters. Lord Moyne was representing this criminal policy in the Middle East. We are coming from a people educated on a book, the Bible, where it is written: 'Thou shalt not kill.' But if we took a gun to shoot, it is because we knew we were doing an act of justice. We demand to the court either we must be tried by the laws of justice and morality, or by the laws of exploitation and slavery. [17]

A central but shadowy figure in the planning of Lehi operations was Yitzhak Yezernitsky-Shamir. His *nom de guerre* was 'Michael', after the Irish revolutionary Michael Collins. This in itself signified an interest in both ideology and action. One of his close collaborators in Lehi activities, Ya'akov Eliav, later commented: 'The first thing we taught in Lehi was ideology. We put a great deal of effort into it. We maintained that a member could not fight and offer his life unless he was ideologically committed and was never going to compromise his principles.' [18]

Shamir chose the élitist Lehi rather than the amorphous Irgun, both before Begin's arrival in Palestine and after the initiation of the revolt against the British. Shamir made his first appearance in Lehi in 1941 when he was brought to a meeting of the Stern Group. Ironically it was the gathering where Stern related the German rebuttal of his proposal for co-operation against the British. Unlike two other members of the group who immediately resigned, Shamir remained within it, despite further attempts to contact the Germans, and rose to prominence in Lehi's second coming in 1943. In an unsigned article in the group's publication *He'Hazit (The Front)* in that year, the leadership asserted that the use of terror did not contradict Jewish tradition.

Later, as a revolutionary avante-garde, Lehi began to move towards a pro-Soviet position and to assume an anti-imperialist approach in the same hope of evicting the British from the Middle East. Shamir was at first surprised by this political evolution and maintained a neutral stance. Yet on one of the few occasions when he put pen to paper, he suggested that the new socialist states of Eastern Europe might prove to be a viable economic model for the new Jewish State: 'What is needed is a body which will have extensions in every sphere of life and which with its thousands of eyes and ears will prevent any attempt at sabotage and defection . . . such an example is the Communist Party in the USSR and in the Peoples' Democracies'.[19]

Following the demise of Lehi and the disappearance of his position as secretary of the Fighters' Party, Shamir vanished into the intelligence world. He then performed a series of unadventurous jobs – factory inspector, garage owner, cinema administrator – before finally applying to Herut for membership in 1970. In his Lehi days Shamir was known as a pragmatist and was somewhat disdainful of intellectuals. Significantly, in a speech to the first and last conference of the Fighters' Party in 1949, he attacked the 'intelligentsia' in the movement, including Avraham Stern himself – those 'who advocated acts which they did not possess the means to carry out. It followed that the Party could not be reduced to 'a narrow core'.[20] His sense of political realism probably prompted his application to Herut. Even though his last political utterances two decades before had a decidedly leftist tinge to them, he clearly noted the increasing support for the Herut-Liberal coalition in Israel after 1967. He was swiftly elected to the Executive Committee of Herut and in 1973 entered the Knesset. Ten years later, he became Prime Minister.

Enter Menachem Begin

Menachem Begin fortuitously arrived in Palestine a couple of months after the killing of Avraham Stern in 1942. Begin's persona and his determination to take an independent course of action were attractive to many who were rapidly losing faith in the ability of the leadership of the Yishuv to convince the British of the veracity of the Zionist case by civilized and peaceful means. Moreover, as the unimaginable enormity of the Shoah (Holocaust) began to penetrate the Yishuv without any real movement on the part of the British, the desire to react against the principle of self-restraint and rational arguments which favoured pedestrian diplomacy grew stronger. Begin, through his own personal loss of parents and family in the Shoah, and his successful struggle to reach Palestine, personified that growing tendency. His deep psychological trauma as a son of a Jewish Poland that was no more, combined with an infinite single-mindedness as the leading exponent of the radical right wing of Revisionism, made 'the Revolt' both inevitable and a necessity for him. That mixture of considerable bravery and frequent displays of military incompetence has passed into the realms of mythology. The drama has been re-enacted by hagiographer and critic alike. David Ben-Gurion, however, was equally determined not to be undermined by the highly publicized but independent actions of relatively small splinter groups. He did not recoil from using his authority to retain control and to move against those whom he considered to be acting against the Yishuv's best interests. When the Irgun rejected a government ultimatum to hand over the arms on board the *Altalena*, in June 1948, Ben-Gurion ordered the military to open fire on the ship. Ben-Gurion's action showed that he would counteract any attempt to establish rival military and political establishments in the country. Yet he was politically astute enough to maintain a direct channel of communication to Begin through an intermediary while projecting a demonic vision of the Irgun leader's intentions in order to outmanoeuvre his opponents in Mapai (Ben-Gurion's centrist Labour Party) who wished to delay the declaration of the state.

The bombardment of the arms ship *Altalena* and the deaths of a score of Irgun fighters proved to be the crossing of the Rubicon for Ben-Gurion. It sowed the seeds of a deep enmity between the Revisionists and the Labour movement for a whole generation.

An inability to perceive the 'political reality' despite an inherent courage to act on words was the basis of much of the criticism directed at Begin and his followers. Eloquent rhetoric and great deeds, it was argued, were no substitute for pragmatic action:

> Zionism succeeded and Israel exists today because the Revisionist movement was shunted off to the margins. Had it come to power in the period before the establishment of the state there would certainly have been much noise and commotion, but almost certainly there would not have been a state. A state is not established by demonstrations and petitions, nor by the expectation of a redemptive event.[21]

Yet the Irgun and their supporters believed that the genteel approach would never have forced the hand of the British. In their eyes, they lit the fire and provided the symbol of the fighting Jew.

For the Labour movement, Begin also represented an attempt to pierce the imagery of a future Hebrew Socialist Republic. The legacy of Betar, with its worship of militarism and abandonment of sacred socialist icons, was anathema to those who had observed the development of the authoritarian Right in many a European country during the inter-war years. The deep bitterness and intense hatred – both in an ideological and in a personal sense – that developed during that period lasted until at least 1967 and remains an undercurrent of political behaviour in Israel today.

Begin's transition from underground fighter to party politician after 1948 did little to mollify Ben-Gurion and the Labour movement. His party, Herut, was ostracized and its adherents discriminated against by the ruling élite. Ben-Gurion gave no quarter. A personal siege was conducted against Begin and his supporters from the Irgun, *mishpachat ha'lochamim* (the 'fighting family'). Ben-Gurion would never refer to Begin by name in the Knesset, only as 'the member to the right of Dr Bader'. Such pettiness undoubtedly stiffened his followers' resolve to accept such splendid isolation in a spirit of institutionalized martyrdom. It enhanced their fundamental belief that the outside world could not be trusted – and even more so after the Shoah. Later, in government, Begin was thus used to and adept at turning his back on liberal internal critics as well as on the international community.

In the early years of the State, Begin's opposition and his often inflammatory oratory projected him as the personification of disunity. The issue of accepting reparations from the Federal Republic of Germany marked a high point of populist reaction to Ben-Gurion. In early 1952, this deeply emotive issue reached an explosive level. In his public speech and declaration before the Knesset debate, Begin egged on the crowd to such a fever-pitch that several thousand marched on the Parliament building. The ensuing violence resulted in hundreds of injuries and arrests. While Begin's speech in the Knesset was symptomatic of his own personal tragedy during the Shoah, its presentation unnerved his opponents but delighted his admirers:

> There are things in life that are worse than death. This is one of them. For this we will give our lives. We will leave our families. We will say goodbye to our children, but there will be no negotiations with Germany. Today you have arrested hundreds. Perhaps you will arrest thousands. We will sit together with them. If necessary we will die together with them, but there will be no reparations from Germany. Nations have gone to the barricades on less important issues.

The whiff of civil war on the issue of German 'blood money' may have been floated in the heat of the moment, but it also indicated the readiness of the nationalist camp to use violence when deeply held convictions were challenged.

The changes of 1967

Israel's lightning victory in the Six Day War in June 1967 was greeted by a great wave of jubilation and euphoria in the West. This extended far beyond Jewish communities in the Diaspora and traditional supporters of Israel. A second Auschwitz had miraculously been averted. The good and the great from the liberal intelligentsia hailed the military prowess of Israel's civilian army. Politicians from both Left and Right were falling over themselves in praise of Israel.

Yet the Six Day War coincided with a historical watershed. The period divided the old from the young, those who had experienced the pre-Holocaust world and those who had been born after it. In Europe and the United States, the generation which associated Israel with the struggle against Nazism, and as a haven for the remnant of a murdered people, was gradually making way for a new generation which had not been involved in the Second World War and which knew little about anti-semitism or about Zionism. Different, more urgent, issues were of immediate concern. By 1967, the post-war generation had declared its political identity in terms of the struggle of the Third World, the end of imperialism and decolonization in general.

The Six Day War marked the end of the honeymoon period for Israel and the West. In the West there was profound ignorance, and often indifference, about the Jewish question – and this was before the emergence of public awareness about the Palestinians. The Shoah was often de-Judaized and thereby universalized as a symbol for the many evils in the world. A different world-view of Israel and the Jews was forming. In 1967 General De Gaulle offered his belief that the Jews were an 'élitist, arrogant and domineering people'. The old Left, which had participated with the Jews in the struggle against fascism, was slowly subsumed by the new Left, whose superficial views on Israel and Zionism were highly coloured by the neo-Stalinist propaganda emanating from the Soviet Union.

In Israel, too, there were dramatic changes in society which estranged many longtime friends. For a number of Western intellectuals and writers whose lives had been inextricably wrapped up with the saga of the Zionist experiment, the changing face of Israel after 1967 was a source of deep disillusionment. Yet their lifelong involvement, as part of their personal odyssey through twentieth-century history, did not automatically lead to a volte-face. James Cameron, the doyen of post-war British journalists, whose views probably represented the sentiments of an entire generation, contributed a heavy-hearted piece to the *Guardian* shortly after the Egyptian President Anwar Sadat's visit to Jerusalem in November 1977:

> For twenty years I have been, and remain, what is pretentiously called a 'friend of Israel'. It does not, as is often implied, mean a non-friend of Palestine; very much on the contrary. But for thirty years Israel to me was the most stimulating and courageous of places, which is why today I am saddened by its sadness and troubled by its inflexibility and distressed

by its increasing international unpopularity. It is fair to say, yet once again, that Israel seems capable of anything, except presenting an imaginative and reasonable image of itself to others. Official spokesmen, conformist to a man, provide the clichés of righteousness, many of which have a generation's truth. The intelligent non-politicals, of whom I suppose there are still a handful in this country of critics, are in a state of exasperation not far from despair. That the first chance of peace for thirty years should founder in a sea of semantics seems perverse to the point of lunacy. To the outsider, however understanding of the dilemma, many of the issues seem both trivial and tiresome.[22]

A new generation of native-born Israelis who did not live through the epoch of the Shoah was coming of age. While survival was all-important for them, survivalism was not. The demographic complexion of the electorate was slowly changing. Jews from the East exhibited different cultural traditions from the essentially Ashkenazi Jews of Europe and the United States. But, more important, they had undergone a different historical development. The influence of the Haskalah (Enlightenment) and the French Revolution had not permeated the East and had left the Sephardim relatively untouched. In contrast, Western Jewry had been deeply affected. Indeed, the very meaning of 'Who is a Jew?' was now open to a multitude of interpretations. Thus, for many Sephardim, socialism and liberalism were alien creeds and the secular religiosity of their adherents, peculiar and incomprehensible. It was almost inevitable that before long the Sephardi immigration of the 1950s from North Africa would begin to voice its anger against the Labour élite's condescending attitudes and perceived insensitivity. This was exacerbated by the fact that the religious and the undereducated had chosen Israel whilst the cosmopolitan went to France and other countries.

There was also a generational reaction against the ageing leadership of the pre-State parties, their political infighting and their unwillingness to give way. There was a real sense of the spiritual vacuity of the brand of socialism practised by the Israeli Labour movement. The drive to make the Jews a normal people conflicted with their historic chosenness. If the tendency after 1948 had been to transform Jews into Hebrews, the Six Day War commenced a reversal of that process. The economic boom of post-1967 and the advent of materialism – albeit under the Labour government – also contrasted sharply with the efforts of the socialist pioneers of earlier years.

The 1960s generation was also uninterested in ancient arguments. The demonology surrounding the figure of Menachem Begin, which had been fostered by Ben-Gurion and his followers, became incomprehensible as well as irrelevant. It was history. By 1967, Begin was no longer considered by new voters to be beyond the pale of civilized behaviour. In part, this had been due to the tolerant policies enacted by Levi Eshkol's government, which followed Ben-Gurion's departure. For example, in 1965 it had brought Jabotinsky's body back to Israel for burial, thereby fulfilling the wishes of the Revisionist leader to be buried in 'an independent Jewish State'. Begin, too, had attempted to act less the demagogue and firebrand and more the polished parliamentarian. His standing as a bona fide participant in the political life of the country was further legitimized when the Eshkol government was forced to include him in the broad coalition formed to confront the military crisis which led to the Six Day War.

Begin had also worked hard for over a decade to expand his narrowly nationalist party into the nucleus of a right-wing bloc involving other groups. Part of the problem for Herut was that a majority of its adherents had perished in the Shoah (Holocaust) and had never reached Palestine. The Liberals at first rebuffed Herut's embrace, but their need for a charismatic leader, and their perception that their political fortunes were generally on a downward trend, persuaded them to accept Begin's offer. Herut and the Liberals fought the 1965 election as Gahal and secured twenty-six seats. Yet Gahal, like Likud later, was seen as Begin's party – a greater Herut rather than an amalgamation of two parties. Indeed, by the 1969 elections, the Liberals were quite happy to accept that the newly conquered Territories should be under Israeli sovereignty. In this way, Begin laid the foundation for the development of the Likud in the 1970s which would become the receptacle of the anti-Labour trend.

Although given to displays of mesmerizing rhetoric, from the late 1950s Begin made a conscious effort to establish himself as an accepted figure within the Jewish State – albeit with a different vision of its history and its future, in contrast with the official Mapai–inspired version. Moreover, the increase in Arab terrorism seemed to dim his past exploits and even superficial comparisons with the Irgun were frowned upon. Even Ben-Gurion in old age apparently accepted Begin as a fellow participant in the historical process. In a private letter to Begin after the Six Day War, Ben-Gurion wrote:

> I opposed your approach, sometimes strongly – both before the state and after its establishment – exactly as I would have opposed the approach of Jabotinsky. I strongly objected to a number of your actions and to your opinions after statehood and I do not regret my opposition. I was in the right; but personally I never harboured any grudge against you, and as

I got to know you better in recent years, my esteem for you grew and my Paula [Paula Ben-Gurion, David's wife] rejoiced in it.

This letter, released by Likud on Ben-Gurion's death in 1973, served to legitimize further Begin's standing as a national figure and probably helped Likud at the polls a few weeks later. It served to categorize Begin and Ben-Gurion as issuing from the same patriarchal and patriotic mould. It assisted in the dissipation of qualms which some followers of Ben-Gurion exhibited before making the transition to the ideological camp of the historic enemy. But above all, it helped Begin present himself not as a demagogue but as a strong conviction politician in the classical sense.

The 'New' Territories

Beyond all this was the significance of the acquisition of the West Bank and Gaza, with its Arab population, during the 1967 war. But Menachem Begin and his followers viewed it as the recovery of Jewish lands, of Judea and Samaria, which had been under Jordanian control between 1948 and 1967. It effectively turned the clock back to 1937 and resurrected the furious debate over partition when Ben-Gurion, Weizmann and a majority of the Jewish leadership had accepted the Peel Commission's recommendation to divide the area between the Mediterranean and the Jordan into Jewish and Arab states. Jabotinsky and his followers regarded it as a second betrayal, for the British had installed the Emir Abdullah in the eastern part of the projected Jewish State (Transjordan) in 1922. Ben-Gurion argued that it was better to have a small Jewish State as a basis for expansion later than not to have any state at all. Not only the Revisionists from the Right condemned partition; it was also vigorously opposed from the Left by Yitzhak Tabenkin and his Kibbutz movement, Ha'kibbutz Ha'meuchad, the members of which believed in the pioneering ideology of settling the whole Land. Even within Ben-Gurion's own party, Mapai, major figures such as Berl Katznelson opposed partition. The moderate leaders of American Zionism, Louis Brandeis and Stephen Wise, were also against the proposition. Jabotinsky uncompromisingly told the Peel Commission that 'our right is eternal and to the whole Land and it cannot be conceded'. Yet Nahum Goldman, a strong supporter of dividing the Land in 1937, poignantly commented in his autobiography that 'if the Zionist movement had accepted the proposal then, spontaneously and without delay, it is quite conceivable that it might have been implemented. We would then have had two years' time before war broke out and a country to which hundreds of thousands possibly millions of European Jews might have escaped.'[23]

The British eventually withdrew the plan when the Palestinian leadership proved to be as intransigently maximalist in their demands as the Revisionists. The final borders of Israel, although unrecognized, were stabilized in 1949 following the War of Independence, and this definition of size was generally accepted by the Israeli body politic, including the religious parties. Only Herut stood out against this consensus, even though Israel had expanded beyond the dimensions stipulated by the United Nations in 1947.

For most, the idea of *Eretz Israel Ha'shlema* (Greater Israel) was a nostalgic aspiration from the past which was irrelevant to the reality of early 1967. Even Herut, although not formally renouncing the Revisionist dream, co-existed with this consensus. Indeed, in 1965 it was quite willing to omit any mention of the boundaries of the Land of Israel when it forged an electoral pact with the Liberals.

The Six Day War shattered that consensus. Israel's control of the West Bank brought nearer that coalescence of the State of Israel with the historic Land of Israel. Latent but powerful sentiments were reawakened and long-buried arguments resurrected. Conventional politics were relegated to a secondary level. In its place, there was a reintroduction of fundamental but competing Zionist ideologies on the meaning of the Jewish State and its boundaries. For the maximalists who had never forsaken the idea of the Land of Israel, it was argued that 1948–67, the period of 'Little Israel', represented abnormality, a hiatus in reclaiming and settling the whole Land for the Jewish people. For those content to remain within the 1967 borders, it appeared that history had been turned on its head. The stunning victory of 1967 represented a continuation of those schismatic arguments which had all but ceased on the outbreak of the Second World War in 1939.

The desire to 'return' to the entire Land of Israel was very deep after 1967 and permeated many strata of Israeli society. Its vehicle was Tenual'ma'an Eretz Israel – the movement for the Whole Land of Israel, or, as it was referred to by its critics, 'the Greater Israel movement'. It completely cut across the dividing lines of Israeli society, embracing businessmen and poets, rabbis and kibbutzniks. S. Y. Agnon, the recipient of the Nobel Prize for literature in 1966, was an adherent, as was Ya'akov Dori, the first Chief-of-Staff of the Israel Defence Forces, and Natan Alterman, the poet. In the emotional aftermath of the war, few thought ahead to the consequences of a Greater Israel in terms of the Israel-Palestine conflict.

The Land of Israel movement was the first instrument to unite those multifarious segments of Israeli society which had always espoused a maximalist position and rejected partition. Not only did it include former members of Lehi and the Irgun, but also left-wing socialists from Achdut Avoda, who dreamed of creating in the Land of Israel a matrix of kibbutzim to cement the pioneering Zionist revolution. While the religious parties were overjoyed to be reunited with biblical Judea and Samaria, secular intellectuals such as the poet Yonatan Ratosh seized the opportunity to develop their idea of *Eretz ha'Prat* (the Land of the Euphrates) – a confederation of Hebrewized peoples such as the Druse and the Beduin from Suez to the Tigris.[24] They wished to sever the ties between the Jewish State and the Jewish people, and favoured the ditching of the Law of Return and the downgrading of Judaism. This, they argued, would accelerate the creation of a Hebrew rather than a specifically Jewish identity and would additionally serve to throw back the tide of pan-Arabism in the Middle East.

Old ideological enemies, who a few months earlier would have refused even to speak to each other, now sat down together and discussed the prospects opened up through Israel's control of the Territories. Indeed, by 1967 the party system had ossified genuine ideological debate in the Jewish State. A certain hollowness in political life had developed, in which rehearsed arguments and personal enmities delineated the parameters of public debate. Thus the Land of Israel movement was also a revolt against the party establishments, an experiment in extra-parliamentary activity, albeit in a discreet fashion. It attracted the writer Moshe Shamir, who was fed up with the ideological rigidity and pro-Soviet attitude of the Marxist–Zionist party Mapam. The Land of Israel movement in a sense gave voice to a demand in Israeli society for an openness – a *glasnost* – which the party hierarchies across the entire political spectrum found hard to comprehend.

Indirectly, the Land of Israel movement encouraged and legitimized the move to the Right. For those in the Labour movement, to whom Begin and his followers were anathema, and who yet espoused a maximalist position and berated their own leadership for political soft-pedalling, the Land of Israel movement fulfilled an important function: 'For many the Land of Israel movement provided a transitional forum which enabled individuals for whom direct transfer of allegiance to Gahal [Begin's party] would have proved intolerable, gradually to become socialized into acceptance of a perspective in which Gahal became an available alternative.'[25]

Thus, although Begin himself did not belong to the Land of Israel movement, the espousal of its principles by sections of the Labour movement permitted a psychological breakthrough which later manifested itself in fragments of the Labour movement joining the Likud bloc. Even the unification of the various socialist parties into the Israel Labour Party in 1968 helped the move to the Right. Rafi and Achdut Avoda possessed numerous members who were not unsympathetic to the Land of Israel movement, and they were able to canvass support from within the government. They facilitated the connection between socialist–Zionist secularists and religious messianism. Thus, Yigal Allon, a member of the left-wing Achdut Avoda (a Socialist–Zionist party), then Minister of Education and later a dovish Foreign Minister, visited the first religious settlers in Hebron within a few days of their arrival in 1968.

In addition, even after the exit of Menachem Begin from the coalition in 1970, the Labour administration of Golda Meir was a decidedly conservative one in thought and deed. According to Abba Eban, 'the great obstacle was Golda . . . she was very suspicious, very defiant, and she simply didn't believe that there was a prospect for peace'.[26]

By the early 1970s, Moshe Dayan, a member of the defunct Rafi party which had broken away from Mapai, backed by Golda Meir, had embarked on a hawkish approach to the Territories. He advocated the economic integration of the West Bank, the establishment of new settlements in less-populated areas, the construction of Jewish quarters in a number of Palestinian towns and the right of Jews to purchase land. After the results of the 1977 election became known, Dayan joined the Likud government as Foreign Minister as an independent and thus left Labour.

The irresistible rise of Likud

Likud is Hebrew for 'unity'. It therefore provided a suitable name for the creation of a right-wing bloc under the leadership of Menachem Begin, who was thus able to integrate Labour splinter groups such as La'am and the State List as well as the Land of Israel movement. Although officially a confederation, it was Herut and Begin who called the shots. The dissatisfaction with Labour was Likud's central asset. Although ostensibly a workers' party, Labour was perceived as permitting areas of inequality to emerge. Its image was one of middle-class élitism in which corruption was rife. Likud's public relations, however, propagated a picture of honesty, principle, strength and respect for tradition – a party for the ordinary man who wanted to better himself. This was a projection which Ezer Weizmann and his publicity people skilfully pushed to the limit, successfully winning the 1977 election for Likud.

Since 1948 Ben-Gurion had always been very careful not to assist in the formation of a right-wing bloc, and indeed contrived to isolate Herut along with the Communists as outside the pale of recognized political behaviour. When in office he had deliberately not merged his own party, Mapai, with other socialist parties. By attracting a broad spectrum of parties into coalition government, he not only prevented the possibility of the formation of a right-wing alternative, but also created a consensus within Israeli politics moulded by his vision of the State. After his resignation, his successors, Levi Eshkol and Golda Meir, adopted the opposite approach in the belief that a left-of-centre bloc would be a political asset. Thus, Mapai soon merged with Achdut Avoda. Rafi joined to form the Israel Labour Party in 1968. The Ma'arach (the Labour Alignment) was cemented with the left-wing Mapam in the following year. In reality, the sum of the whole proved to be less than that of the constituent parts – not least because the various socialist parties had entirely different traditions regarding their ideological approach to the Territories. Maximalists from Achdut Avoda and Rafi were prepared to sleep in the same bed as the minimalist Mapam. This structural weakness proved to be the cause of political paralysis for the Israel Labour Party in both the 1970s and 1980s.

The broad Labour alignment thus presented a visible focus for grievances, real or imagined, and catalysed the growth of an alternative, the Likud, which readily welcomed all malcontents.

With the decline of the Labour Party and the inability of the Palestinians – the PLO in particular – to elicit any coherent policy which might lead to negotiations, the transformation of Israeli society from a pioneering socialist-oriented collective manifested itself in a drift to the Right on an individual level and eventually to a right-wing bloc in control of government.

In an ongoing survey, the Israeli Institute of Applied Social Research monitored this trend between 1962 and 1977 – the year in which the first Begin government was elected. When asked 'With which political tendency do you identify?', the percentage of respondents who replied 'right-wing' showed a remarkable increase

1962	1969	1973	1977
8	16	23	28

The elections to the seventh Knesset in 1969 marked the first opportunity for the post-1948 generation to vote. It was also the first election after the Six Day War when the future of the Territories occupied a place on the political agenda. In this and subsequent elections, voters showed an increasing trend to rid themselves of Labour and to support an alternative:[27]

Percentage voting Likud

Age	1969	1973	1977
under 25	36	44	51
25–39	30	44	34
40–49	25	35	29
50 plus	21	23	23

Not only was the tendency to vote Likud greater among young people, but it also increased with time. The real breakthrough for the Right came with the 1973 elections. Until then, the combined number of Knesset seats of Herut, the Liberals and the Independent Liberals had remained virtually static since 1948. The nationalist camp polled 29 per cent in 1948 and 26 per cent in 1969. In 1973 the Likud obtained thirty-nine seats – a 50 per cent increase over previous elections. Although dissatisfaction with the government's handling of the Yom Kippur War was undoubtedly a factor, for Labour the writing was on the political wall

Votes cast in elections

	1969	1973
Labour Alignment	632,035	621,183
Gahal/Likud	296,294	473,309
National Religious Party	133,238	130,349
Total votes cast	1,427,981	1,566,855

In 1948, 65 per cent of all Israelis had been born abroad and the vast majority were Ashkenazim. By the election of 1973, Herut's cultivation of the Sephardi voter was beginning to bear fruit. The second generation of native-born Sephardi Israelis looked up to Begin. By 1977 the percentage of voters in development towns who went with Likud had doubled over that of the mid-1960s. The desire of this new generation to assert themselves against the hegemony of the Ashkenazi élite and to recover what they believed had been taken from them and their parents was overwhelmingly deep. In his book *In the Land of Israel*, Amos Oz dramatically records this sense of insult which afflicted many Sephardim: 'The Mapainiks just wiped out everything that was imprinted on a person. As if it was all nonsense. And then they put what they liked into him. From that ideology of theirs. Like we were some kind of dirt. . . . we've brought Begin down on you and now you're in for it, for a long, long time.'[28]

Whilst many Sephardim warmed to a populist approach, they also had a vested interest in ensuring that the status quo remained.

After 1967 the Territories became a cheap source of labour and the Sephardim no longer found themselves on the bottom rung of the socio-economic ladder. No longer were the menial jobs purely the prerogative of the poor immigrant from North Africa. The labour force ushered into Israel each day from the Territories effectively catalysed the upward mobility of the Sephardim in Israeli society. The election of a maximalist Likud government guaranteed that there would be no return to the humiliations which their parents had endured.

The years of the Rabin government, between 1974 and 1977 were an unmitigated disaster. The open hostility between Yitzhak Rabin and Shimon Peres, rival contenders for the crown of party leadership, and the periodic corruption and reoccurring scandals were the final straw for the Israeli electorate. When a large contingent of Labour voters finally staged a revolt in the 1977 elections by supporting a new party – the Democratic Movement for Change, led by the well-known archaeologist Yigal Yadin – the Likud needed only to acquire a couple of extra seats to form a government. Menachem Begin, the standard-bearer of Betar and the radical wing of Revisionism, had waited thirty years in the political wilderness for demographic change and for Labour to be consumed by its own weaknesses. Now, at the age of sixty-four and in his eighth election as leader of Herut, he became Prime Minister.

2

The Far Right in Israel

The Camp David rebellion

While the policies of Menachem Begin's first government accentuated divisions between doves and hawks on the issue of the Territories, at the same time they travelled some considerable distance towards a peace settlement with Egypt. Sadat's visit to Jerusalem and the final Camp David Accord were impressive achievements, contrasting dramatically with Labour's past failures. '*Rak Ha'Likud Yachol* (Only the Likud Can!)', the Likud slogan of the 1988 election, emerged from the conclusion that apparently only a strong right-wing government could secure peace with the Arabs.

By sheer procrastination and the eventual exit from the political arena of both Sadat and US President Jimmy Carter, as well as such major figures as Moshe Dayan and Ezer Weizmann from his own administration, Begin managed to sever the link between an already accomplished peace treaty with Egypt and a projected solution to the national aspirations of the Palestinians. Like some of the Labour old guard, he never recognized the concept of a Palestinian nation, only 'Palestinian Arabs' within the context of pan–Arabism. Like Golda Meir, he referred to himself as 'a Palestinian' soon after his election in 1977.

Begin offered administrative autonomy to the Palestinians but not sovereignty. They were permitted to choose between Israeli or Palestinian citizenship, but Israel would still claim sovereignty over Judea and Samaria, and Jewish settlements would proceed unimpeded. Whilst this seemed to accord with the Jabotinskyian formulation of citizenship and sovereignty as far as Begin was concerned, the practical meaning of the plan and how far it approached the Palestinian demand for national self-determination was far from clear. All discussion and definition of terms led to diplomatic dead-ends. Negotiations became bogged down in amorphous minutiae. Whether this was a preconceived initiative of artful deception or simply shallow thinking is open to conjecture. 'For Begin it was a deus ex machina, a political defense against an assault on Judea and Samaria. It is doubtful whether we shall ever know if Begin had intended from the beginning to drain the idea of autonomy of content or whether he made a policy error of grave consequence'.[1] For the maximalists, however, of all ideological origins, Camp David represented a traumatic and psychological disaster. Whatever Begin's real intentions, his credibility for the Land of Israel people and for the religious settlers plummeted dramatically. In their eyes, he had violated the sacred idea of the indivisibility of the Land and compromised fundamental principles.

The schism symbolized a deeper difference which had hitherto been submerged within the unity of the nationalist camp and the attraction of Begin's leadership. This divergence was rooted in the differing approaches of Lehi and the Irgun, which had effectively represented the Right's contribution to the struggle for Israel's independence. Lehi, which considered Avraham Stern its ideological mentor, looked back to the age of King David for its inspiration. It was both mystical and maximalist in determining the specific time at which to delineate Israel's borders. The Irgun, which relied on Jabotinsky and Begin, claimed their point of reference as the Balfour Declaration and the British Mandate of Palestine. While acknowledging the course of Jewish history, they couched their approach in the legal–constitutional framework within which the British had guaranteed a Jewish homeland in Palestine and had then reneged on their promise with the establishment of the Hashemite kingdom in 1922. Significantly, whereas Lehi and religious Jews had followed Jabotinsky in espousing the mystical term *malchut Israel* (the kingdom of Israel) as a standard for the restoration of the Jewish State, Begin and Herut, rooted in modernity, placed it in limbo.[2] Although Begin's views had coincided with the Far Right's approach in commencing a revolt against the British, in later life he clearly followed Jabotinsky in determining the boundaries of the Jewish State. Begin's attitude was thus rooted in modernity and the thought of Jabotinsky, whilst his maximalist opponents, whether religious or secular, looked to the purity of biblical times. Begin was thus able to give back Sinai to Sadat while retaining Judea and Samaria, but his opponents were unable to surrender any part of the biblical Land of Israel. Thus Begin did not espouse their slogan, *af sha'al* – 'not one inch'.

There was also considerable opposition within Likud to the Camp David Accords. Indeed, as early as 1978, immediately after Sadat's visit to Jerusalem, a number of Herut loyalists – old comrades of Menachem Begin – organized a group within the party to campaign against concessions. Their opposition centred on the autonomy plan, which they believed would lead to a Palestinian State. When details became clearer, they vigorously condemned it and together with other maximalists opposed any withdrawal from any part of the Land as envisioned by the projected return of Sinai to the Egyptians. This opposition was not limited to the fringes of the party but included Likud's major figures. Both Yitzhak Shamir, then Chairman of the Knesset, and Moshe Arens, then Chairman of the Foreign Affairs and Defence Committee of the Knesset, opposed the Camp David negotiations. In the vote in the Knesset, only twenty-nine out of the forty-three Likud Members of the Knesset (MKs) actually supported the Accords. The defection within Herut itself was even greater: only eleven out of twenty-one Herut MKs voted for the Accords.

Phrases such as 'the legitimate rights of the Palestinians', the effective 'no comment' on the final status of the Territories, and even the frequent use of the term 'West Bank' as opposed to Judea and Samaria, were anathema to Herutniks used to the taste of undiluted Jewish nationalism. And coming from the lips of Menachem Begin, the living embodiment of Revisionism and Olympian hero of the 1977 election, the effect was one of total disbelief. In the words of the dissident Likud MK, Geula Cohen, 'The Jews did not come back to Israel to make peace or even to be safe, but to build a nation on the lands given to us by the Bible'[3]. Even within the Labour Party, Yigal Allon and Yitzhak Rabin, both from a pioneering background in Achdut Avoda, were thus ideologically opposed to surrendering any settlements and initially opposed the evacuation from Sinai.

The depth of this ideological turmoil within the nationalist camp produced discussions between maximalists from different backgrounds who were united in fierce opposition to the Camp David process. Instead of yielding territory which would lead inevitably to a hostile PLO state, they argued, there should be increased settlement of the Land. Camp David effectively ruled out annexation and, ultimately, the possibility of total sovereignty over all the Land. This common denominator brought together a wide range of people – Likud MKs such as Geula Cohen, ex-Mapainiks such as Professor Yuval Ne'eman, activists of Gush Emunim (the religious settlers' movement in the Territories), Hanan Porat and Eliezer Waldman, as well as kibbutzniks and moshavniks from Rafi and Achdut Avoda. The writer Moshe Shamir, originally from the Marxist Mapam, joined with veteran Lehi ideologist Israel Eldad to determine what could be done. Within weeks of the signing of the Camp David Accords, Banai (the Covenant of Eretz Israel Loyalists) was established. The group's objective was to coerce the leadership of both the Likud and the National Religious Party to return to the path of truth. Begin did not heed the advice. Instead, he signed an official peace treaty with Sadat. The crossing of the Rubicon came when Banai transformed itself into a new political party, Techiya (Renaissance), in June 1979. Significantly, this had been the term used by Avraham Stern in delineating his eighteen principles which had guided Lehi both during his lifetime and even more so after his death.

Although there was widespread resistance to Camp David, few Likud MKs were actually prepared to defect. Like all ideological splits, it created antagonism and bitterness between these rivals for the nationalist vote and over the purity of its Zionism. Likud was concerned because Techiya represented a broad front of former Labour people and the respectable Right, religious and secular. It was not a party of rabble-rousers, but numbered amongst its members businesspeople, academics, lawyers and poets – respectable members of Israeli society. It was a reaction against the ideological unreliability of both the Likud and the National Religious Party. In effect, the post-1967 Land of Israel movement had now also moved into the parliamentary arena.

Mindful of the split in Labour in 1977 when the Democratic Movement for Change had captured fifteen seats and let in Menachem Begin, Likud played raucously to the nationalist crowd during the 1981 election. It was a campaign marked by sloganing, demagoguery and violence. The militant Likud campaign and the prominence of Menachem Begin as its symbol turned the vote around. Begin played on his prestige as a peacemaker. Paradoxically, as 'the party of peace', Likud was now able to adopt a much more hawkish stand than during the actual Camp David negotiations. Dayan resigned from the government at the end of 1979 and Weizmann in 1980. They were replaced by the more hawkish Yosef Burg of the National Religious Party. Begin rose to the occasion and rejuvenated both himself and his party's campaign. From the real possibility of an electoral trouncing a few months before, his style resulted in a second government under his premiership. In part, the militancy was designed to ensure that the nationalist vote stayed solid regardless of the reaction of liberal Israelis to the violence – they would be unlikely to vote Likud in any case.

The strategy worked, since Likud not only ran level with Labour in the number of Knesset seats obtained, but also reduced the rebellion on the Far Right. Techiya, in its first election, polled 44,700 votes, 2.3 per cent of the electorate, and returned only three Members to the Knesset. The great Camp David rebellion had failed miserably, proving once more the innate conservatism of the Israeli voter.

A number of lessons for the Far Right emerged from the election of the second Begin government in 1981. First, the election of Likud in 1977 was not a flash in the pan, not an exception but the acceptance of new policies and an alternative vision of the Jewish State by large numbers of Israelis. Second, 1981 confirmed all the demographic trends that were already appearing in 1977. Third, the election campaign widened the boundaries of acceptable political behaviour and thought. Finally, it indicated to the maximalists that a change in attitudes should also be pursued through means other than success at the ballot box.

In April 1979, the Modi'in Ezrachi Institute characterized the average Likud voter as young, the offspring of parents of oriental origin, evoking respect for religious tradition, a low educational attainment and low income.[4] Thus Likud did better in newer *moshavim* than in old ones. It polled highly in the poorer areas of cities. For example, Mamila, a working-class district of Jerusalem, gave 57.8 per cent of its vote to Likud, more than twice as much as its middle-class neighbours in Rehavia.[5]

Techiya, the new party of the radical Right, failed to make any impact in either urban cities or new development towns in Israel. Its strength was totally in the Territories, where it polled ten times as many votes as in Israel itself. Only in the West Bank settlements did it take votes from both Likud and the National Religious Party.

The politics of violence and intolerance

The authorized withdrawal by the Begin government from the verdant town of Yamit in 1982, and its reversion to Egypt as part of the Camp David Accords, had considerable symbolic value for the supporters of a Greater Israel. At Yamit, the Far Right confronted the power of the elected representatives of the people – albeit a right-wing government – and challenged its credentials. Soldiers faced taunts and insults from hundreds of people who believed that not one inch of the historic Land should be surrendered. Settlers from the Territories used the memory of the Shoah to deter the soldiers by donning yellow Stars of David. The Begin government seriously feared that there would be violence and bloodshed, especially if the resisters succumbed to a Massada complex to kill themselves. Rabbi Levinger, a founder of Gush Emunim, preached a Sabbath sermon to a congregation in Yamit, reminding them that, although suicide was forbidden in Judaism, it was permissible to make sacrifices for the Land of Israel. Yamit's own rabbi, Israel Ariel, who also served as a rabbi in the Northern Command, ordered soldiers to disobey their officers. Despite all the threats, in the end nothing happened except a continuing civil disobedience. But the spectacle of physical resistance from the maximalist camp induced conflicting emotions within the country. On the one hand, it represented an attack on the democratically elected government and the forces of law and order as represented by the Israel Defence Forces. On the other, the surrender of conquered land and the product of years of effort even to a former enemy was hard to take. The Minister of Defence Ariel Sharon, who actually supported the Camp David Accords, ensured that Sinai was handed back to the Egyptians in accordance with the terms of the agreement. Yamit was razed to the ground and only the synagogue was left standing. The resistance at Yamit showed what was possible. Religious settlers with their families had moved there *en bloc* from the Territories to prevent the evacuation from Sinai, literally in the certitude that God would provide. Whilst the betrayal at Camp David extinguished any allegiance to the government, however democratically elected, the defeat at Yamit diminished any lingering respect for the rule of law. To be sure, the maximalists confidently adhered to a higher authority, whether religious or secular. Moreover, they were supported by the Techiya MKs – all of whom decided to settle in Yamit and to resist the army.

Techiya members were quite willing to supervise the breaking and bending of the law in pursuit of their political goals. Yuval Ne'eman, for example, strongly defended the Jewish underground's bombings of the West Bank mayors. The members of Techiya 'introduced a new doctrine which implied that illegal extraparliamentarianism just as legal parliamentarianism was a legitimate avenue of action'.[6] The failure to retain Yamit was psychologically devastating for the religious settlers from the Territories. Unlike the pragmatic members of Techiya, the lack of success at Yamit had the measure of a spiritual crisis since the settlers believed deeply that God would not permit the town to be evacuated and destroyed. Until the last moment they and their families had conducted a normal lifestyle in the belief that the government would succumb. They also refrained from violent opposition to the government, as they were convinced that it too was a holy instrument in God's plan to bring about the redemption and the institution of *malchut Israel.* There was also a strong belief that one Jew should not fight another, which historically stemmed from the murderous civil war conducted within the walls of Jerusalem while the Romans laid siege. They, above all, knew that the outcome of that internecine conflict was the destruction of the Temple and the Holy City itself.

The polarizing effect of the evacuation of Yamit was cemented by the trauma of the war in Lebanon a few months later in June 1982. Although much has been written about the growth of the peace movement during the Lebanon War, the policy of the Likud government was strongly applauded – and not only by its supporters and those on the Far Right. Sharon's Clausewitzian belief that the war in Lebanon was politics by other means was heartily endorsed by the Far Right.[7]

In the early days of the war, the vast majority of Israelis believed the conflict to be justified. A Modi'in Ezrachi poll in the third week of the war showed that a minuscule 4.6 per cent opposed it. Likud MKs sailed with the tide and called for the banning of all peace rallies and demonstrations. The peace movement was depicted as little more than a fifth column. The government not only propagated a great deal of internal propaganda aimed at the Israeli public, but also made it clear that it would definitely brook no dissent. Full-page advertisements signed by hundreds of Likud supporters appeared in the Israeli press. Even when it eventually became all too obvious that there was no absolute consensus for the war, the government pretended one existed and came down on anyone who thought otherwise. An advertisement in the *Jerusalem Post*, 2 July 1982, called upon the citizens of Israel 'to join us in this indictment against the slanderers at home and abroad who divide and weaken the people, some for narrow personal or party interests, thereby aiding the enemy, prolonging the war and endangering the lives of our sons and comrades who are defending the Jewish people'.

Moreover, the government was able to command the attendance of nearly a quarter of a million people during a demonstration in July 1982. Techiya put aside its fundamental disagreement over Camp David to enter the Begin administration during the war, for the government was perceived as the mainstay of nationalist endeavour. It had to be defended against the Left. It had to be bolstered and influenced from within. For example, Yuval Ne'eman of Techiya advocated the annexation of southern Lebanon to include the Litani River. Yet there were some, such as Zvi Shiloah, one of the original Land of Israel ideologists, who were unable to contemplate an alliance with the Likud. They resigned from Techiya and re-emerged some years later as the prime movers behind Moledet, the party of 'transfer'.

The war in Lebanon, although a devastating verdict on Likud policy, forced the ordinary citizen to take sides. Instead of a verdict of political bankruptcy, the war produced a laager effect within the nationalist camp by creating a wall of solidarity to contain the assault from both home and beyond. In hindsight, many came to view the war as ill-conceived and a needless waste of life and resources. It may not have strengthened the Right within the country, but it did increase the influence of the Far Right within the nationalist camp in that they now had access to a much more receptive, albeit insecure, audience.

When Begin departed in 1983, a broken man, he was essentially the last of the architects of the Camp David Accords. Those who had entered government with him in 1977 were either dead or sojourning in the political wilderness. The Likud administration of 1983–4, in the aftermath of the débâcle of the war in Lebanon, was far from making a genuine assessment of why things had gone wrong. No sense of accountability was ever voiced by the Cabinet. Its very composition mitigated against self-inspection. It consisted of Camp David rejectionists (Shamir and Arens), Techiya maximalists (Yuval Ne'eman) and tarnished survivors of the grand design for the war in

Lebanon (Ariel Sharon). It was very much a government of the radical Right. Indeed, there was unrestricted settlement in the Territories. But the receptacle for such disillusionment was not the Labour Party, whose leaders remained discredited through past conduct. Thus it was not surprising that the 1984 election showed a redivision of the nationalist vote. Some 100,000 voters deserted the Likud. No doubt some were disillusioned Sephardim who preferred to vote for their own ethnic religious parties, Shas and Tami, but a considerable percentage had switched to the Far Right. As Likud lost seven seats, Techiya increased to five. But the sensation of 1984 was that a sufficient number of voters had elected Rabbi Meir Kahane for the Kach movement. Kach received nearly 26,000 votes, 2.5 per cent of the soldiers' vote going to Kahane.

Attacks on the Peace Movement

Kahane's election was also indicative of the early 1980s as a time when passions ran high and violence was on the increase. The elevation of Meir Kahane from electoral oblivion in 1981 to the Knesset in 1984 was made possible by the attitude of the radical right-wing government of Yitzhak Shamir in 1983–4. Likud itself had moved closer to the Far Right, as was manifest in the vehemence of its attacks on those Israelis who had opposed it during the war in Lebanon. There was a great sense of bitterness in the nationalist camp against those whom they believed had stabbed them in the back, when they themselves had always done their patriotic duty in supporting the government of the day during wartime. Those in the peace camp argued that the war in Lebanon was not like other wars where the country was forced to defend itself against Arab aggression.

More often than not, those who took part in peace demonstrations were now targeted for attack. They became the focus of resentment as liberal do-gooders, representatives of the Ashkenazi élite. Even though many in the peace movement actually disagreed with the conservative policies of Peres and Rabin, they became their surrogate representatives for many supporters of Kahane and the Far Right. In 1983, the Peace Now movement held a march through Jerusalem to protest against Ariel Sharon's refusal to resign following the publication of the Kahan Commission's report on the massacre of Palestinians in the Sabra and Shatilla refugee camps. Towards the end of the march, a bomb was thrown and killed Emil Grunzweig, a peace activist and an officer who had just returned from reserve duty.

The Israeli writer Shulamit Ha'Even graphically depicted both the feelings of the demonstrators on that occasion and the wider *malaise* within Israeli society:

The police did not seem prepared for so much violence. Here and there a lonely policeman tried to fight off an oncoming wave of roughnecks. To my right I see a kindly policeman who looks more like the father of a big family who ought to be taking his children home from the afternoon movie than the officer of the law needed here. He tried bodily to stop the surging throng, but to no avail. Begin–Begin–Begin. PLO–PLO–PLO–PLO. Arik, King of Israel, Arik, King of Israel, Arik, Arik, Arik.

'It won't do you any good, you PLO supporters, you're trash. Your commission is rubbish, you set up a commission against Arik, a commission against Begin. We're going to kill you, we shall do a Sabra and Shatilla on you, a holocaust . . . you're trash, trash, trash. . . .'

Despite the fists, the blows and the curses, the march moves forward – a large, slow ponderous body. A sixteen-year-old boy marches next to me. He's not an Ashkenazi. He's as pale as a sheet. It's the first demonstration he has ever participated in, his first encounter with such a mob. He came to stand up for the law, as he was taught at school. The poster he is holding is torn, his shirt is torn, already he has been punched in the face. . . .

I see three goons attacking Alon, punching him in the face. Alon, who fought at Entebbe and took part in several anti-terror operations that have never been publicized, and – as the blows fall – they say, 'Have you ever been in the army, you PLO supporter? Have you done a day's army service in your life?'. . .

We pass the mall. Whenever I walk past this spot, it is a time for quiet reflection, for here, thirty-five years ago, while I was in the Hagana [Jewish Defence Force], I helped bandage people wounded in a car-bomb at this very street corner. But today, it is I who gets kicked, right at this same spot. I feel no anger, only sadness and bewilderment: Was it for this that we fought for a State? Someone near me says that tomorrow we shall all have to hand in our identity cards as citizens and stand in line to get certificates as subjects. . . .

I see a big red bruise under Alon's eye, and I know that it is only because of his iron self-discipline that he has not responded in kind. Some hours later, after the murder [of Emil Grunzweig] I hear him say 'Until now I knew that the PLO was my enemy. It was the PLO I was fighting. Now the people are fighting me. Can you explain it: Who is my enemy?'[8]

Meir Kahane's Kach movement also made a point by demonstrating at the funerals of the victims of terror. In an atmosphere of emotional tension, such sad occasions often became focuses for incitement to violence if Labour dignitaries such as Shimon Peres were present. Other groups emerged during the 1980s: Terror Neged Terror (Terror Against Terror; TNT), the Sicarii and the State of Judah. In 1989 the apartments of liberal journalists were attacked. The dovish MK Dedi Zucker, who had been very active in detailing human-rights abuses in the Territories, was attacked at his Jerusalem home by an inflamed crowd crying 'Death to Zucker'. But although Kach carried out provocative demonstrations against Arabs, with accompanying acts of petty violence, organized terrorism by Jewish settlers in the Territories was rationalized in the wake of the Camp David betrayal.

The changing face of religious Zionism

For many religious Zionists, the Six Day War marked God's re-entry into Jewish history. This reversed the idea of *hester panim*, the hiding of God's face, which was cited by Rabbi Soloveitchik as a means of theologically interpreting the Shoah.[9] The belief that God stood behind his people in 1967 further impelled many religious Zionists to surmount problems of identity as floating intermediates between secular socialist–Zionism and non-Zionist orthodoxy:

> Settlement of Judea and Samaria provided them with the oppor-
> tunity to become the vanguard of the Zionist revolution within
> a religious framework. It justified their religious upbringing vis-
> à-vis the non-religious Zionists, whom they could criticize for
> betraying the traditional ideals of Zionism such as settlement and
> security. At the same time, they felt superior to the non-Zionist
> Orthodox camp, which despite its religious beliefs, did not fulfil
> the commandment of settling the land of Israel. In short, they
> could now become the forerunners of modern Zionism, not
> despite their religious outlook but because of it.[10]

There was also the feeling that socialism had had its day and was in crisis. It had been tainted by its association with Stalinism and its subsequent inability to project an ideology in which followers could believe wholeheartedly. For many, socialism–Zionism as practised by Mapai was not an answer to the growing frustrations within Israeli society. In one sense, religious ideology gradually displaced socialist ideology in competing for the hearts and minds of many young Jews. In addition, religious Jews like the Sephardim felt aggrieved at the insensitive treatment they had received at the hands of the Mapai bureaucrats. Like the new generation of Sephardim, the youngsters of B'nei Akiva, the youth group of the NRP, were not prepared to acquiesce like their elders.

With the evolution of the two major electoral blocs of Right and Left, burning passions surfaced within the National Religious Party which, as a partner in Labour-dominated coalitions, had hitherto personified religious moderation. The interpretation of the victory of 1967 and its effect on religious Jews factionalized the NRP. Within a decade of the Six Day War, the days of the ruling moderate Lamifneh faction were numbered. Its dominance was challenged by at least three other factions: Gush Emunim, representing the settlers; the anti-Labour Young Guard, which represented both youth and the emerging professionals; and finally the Sephardim, who voiced ethnic grievances. The twelve seats which the NRP obtained in 1977 were reduced to exactly half that number by 1981. Factionalism had been transformed into schisms. The 1981 election was a disaster for the NRP. It was characterized by a plethora of internal disagreements over the direction of the party, and by a preponderance of separate religious lists, such as that of the Sephardim, Tami, which secured three Knesset seats. The NRP lost support to both Likud and Techiya, which, as far as the religious voter was concerned, projected a much more appropriate response to the question of the Territories. Many members of the religious Kibbutz Movement switched allegiance from the NRP to Techiya. On the West Bank, the vote for the NRP decreased from 48.2 per cent in 1977 to a mere 18.6 per cent in 1981.

The fragmentation of the religious vote in the aftermath of Camp David was accompanied by a political zealotry on the part of the West Bank settlers. This manifested itself through the Movement to Stop the Evacuation of Yamit in Sinai, and an emphasis on self-reliance and vigilantism. In part, this emerged out of a sense of remorse at the loss of Yamit. The settlers believed that if they had organized themselves earlier and more efficiently, they could have staved off the government's determination to evacuate Yamit. The overriding lesson was to react immediately to any sign of ideological weakness and compromise on the part of the government. The settlers appeared to have lost confidence both in the government's ability to advance their political demands and in the army's ability to protect them in the midst of an increasingly hostile environment. Anti-Arab violence became a common occurrence. Officialdom apparently turned a blind eye to Jewish attacks on Arabs, since a majority of cases investigated ended in dead-ends. The vacuum left through the non-implementation of legal norms was not filled by the government. The lack of leadership in the post-Begin era as well as in its right-wing direction tacitly encouraged the development of extra-legal behaviour.

The Jewish underground

The Camp David Accords were traumatic for many religious Jewish settlers in the Territories. They signalled a depressing postponement of the Age of Redemption. The coming of the Messiah appeared to be immobilized. How could these impediments to the unravelling of Jewish history be removed? How could the effect of Camp David be nullified? Most settlers followed the rulings of their rabbis to respect the elected representatives of the country and to observe legal norms. For others, the sense of bitterness over Camp David was so intense that they resorted to other means.

Two devout West Bank settlers, Yehuda Etzion and Menachem Livni, believed that only a profound act could return the flow of Jewish history to its natural course. They developed a sophisticated plan to destroy the Dome of the Rock in Jerusalem, one of Islam's holiest sites, which now stood where the Temple once had been. Sizeable quantities of explosives were stolen from army bases. Precision bombs were manufactured. Gas canisters and gun-silencers were purchased. The site was reconnoitred and a group of willing participants trained. The event was not meant simply to redirect the course of Jewish history but also to avert the planned withdrawal from Yamit. However, no rabbinical authority was willing to approve such a major theological decision. No one was willing to take responsibility for such an act. This was also based on a theological attitude which regarded the restoration of the Temple Mount as an act which would be carried out by God and not by mortals. The mystery and sanctity of the Temple Mount was deemed to be beyond mere human understanding. This was also the view of Rabbi Zvi Yehuda Kook, the spiritual mentor of many religious settlers. One member of the underground reputedly visited Kook sporting a photograph of the Dome of the Rock. He made gestures to indicate its destruction; Kook, however, neither reacted nor replied. No questions were ever asked directly, but only within a theoretical context of questions during *shiurim* (religious study sessions). Even Moshe Levinger, a leader of the more militant wing of Gush Emunim, demurred and suggested a further studying of the works of Zvi Yehuda Kook.

Rabbinical authorization was, however, forthcoming for retaliatory attacks on Palestinians. In May 1980, six *yeshiva* (seminary) students were killed in Hebron. Unofficial meetings at the Jewish settlement in Hebron, Kiriat Arba, subsequently resolved to use violence against the Palestinian leadership. Although a violent assault against Palestinians *en masse* was discussed, it was decided instead to implement attacks against the five leaders of the Arab National Guidance Committee, with the result that the mayors of Nablus and Ramallah were both severely crippled in car-bomb attacks. Such acts of terrorism were blessed and supported by the Kiriat Arba rabbis, albeit within the indirect and amorphous context of Jewish study sessions. Moreover, the actions of the Jewish underground were not the work of Kahane types, but often of highly educated people who were secure in their ideas. 'For these purposes, we have to choose pure people, highly observant and sinless, people with no shred of violence in them and who are disciplined to reckless action' was the advice offered to Rabbi Moshe Levinger.[11]

In July 1983, the murder of another *yeshiva* student brought revenge in the form of an attack on the students of the Islamic College in Hebron. Three were killed and thirty-three wounded. The final transition to mass terrorism almost took place in 1984 when Israeli intelligence narrowly averted a massacre of five busloads of Arab passengers. The Jewish terrorists were arrested after they had wired explosives to the buses and primed the timing device to go off late on a Friday afternoon, when few Jews would be present because of the onset of the Jewish Sabbath. Although the revelation of the network sent shock-waves through the Israeli public, and also through many settlers on the West Bank, during the trial the defendants showed no real sense of repentance or remorse but only an ideological conviction that they were living in an Age of Redemption.

Later, in prison, one of the underground's leaders, Menachem Livni, expressed repentance for his deeds. A journalist who visited Livni in Afula prison wrote, 'there is no steely vision there, no defiance. It is not the face of a beaten man but it seems a vulnerable face, the face of someone who has abandoned certitudes – someone who had once been so certain he was responding to God's will that he had taken human life'.[12]

Ehud Sprinzak, in a study of the Jewish underground, described Yehuda Etzion, another leading participant, as 'a very intelligent and educated man': 'Reading Etzion, and talking to him, reveals a unique combination of an other-worldly messianic spirit and a very logical mind, a man who talks and thinks in the language of this world but totally lives in another'. Etzion distinguished between the laws of existence and the laws of destiny. He commented that

> securing and preserving life or its preservation is an "utmost norm" for all the living nature, for humanity in general – and for us, Israel, too. This is a norm that dictates laws, and in the name of which, people go to war. But as for ourselves "our God is not theirs". Not only is our existential experience different from theirs but also from their definition. For the Gentiles, life is mainly *a life of existence* while ours is *a life of destiny*, the life

of a kingdom of priests and a holy people. We exist in the world
to actualize destiny.[13]

Sprinzak's conclusion about the phenomenon of the Jewish underground was that 'the radicalization process that finally produced
terrorism within Gush Emunim was not marginal but central'.

Rabbinical authority was a structural component of Gush Emunim.
It was a necessity for its formation and development. It was required
for the Jewish underground operations. Hence, the plan to destroy the
Dome of the Rock did not take place because no rabbinical authorization
was given, whereas it was given for other actions that were carried
through. Relatively moderate sentences were meted out and even
these were later reduced by order of President Herzog. The release
of the imprisoned members of the underground became a *cause célèbre*
for the Far Right and Techiya MKs, who were for ever petitioning for
the early release of the terrorists.

The imagery of wholesomeness projected by the Jewish terrorists
was infectious. They were friendly, young, idealistic. Their appeal was
to the very primordial essence of the Zionist pioneering enterprise –
sentiments which touched the heartstrings of many Israelis. They did
not have to be watched too carefully since the police who guarded
them knew that they would not try to escape. They were thus not
regarded as criminals in the conventional sense, and for many they
were indeed the salt of the earth. Even more significantly, opinion polls
showed that a third of the Israeli public sympathized with the actions
of the underground in that they clearly believed that the maimed and
murdered Palestinians richly deserved their fates.

The advent of the National Unity government in 1984 and the
premiership of Labour's Shimon Peres led to a withdrawal of Techiya
from the government and a curtailing of new West Bank settlements.
The border between legality and illegality became increasingly blurred
in the escalating use of direct action. Gush Emunium had travelled a
long way since its initiation of civil disobedience campaigns in the early
1970s. The use of military force as a panacea for all evils became an
ingrained tenet of faith. The war in Lebanon became a débâcle only
because of the vacillations of the government. The criticism of National
Religious Party Ministers Zevulun Hammer and Yehuda Ben-Meir,
who accused the Gush of wanting 'eternal war' after Lebanon, fell on
deaf ears. The Intifada, it was believed, could have been crushed long
ago through an overwhelming use of force. Although this confidence
emanated from Israel's victory in the Six Day War, all subsequent
setbacks – military and political – were viewed as symptomatic of the
innate weakness of the political leadership. The most hawkish member
of the Labour Party was considered to be an incorrigible leftist,

whilst hesitant Likudniks were beset with personality defects and fundamental failings. Moreover, legitimacy was not the prerogative of the elected government.

At the inception of Gush Emunim in the early 1970s, the group's mentor, Rabbi Zvi Yehuda Kook, had distinguished between the temporal legality of a government and the permanence of the biblical teachings. By 1985, theological proclamations had been transformed into dire political warnings. The Council of Settlers in Judea, Samaria and Gaza signalled Peres that an Israeli government which made territorial concessions would forfeit its legal foundations. An article in the Israeli press advocating this position went under the title 'A Prime Minister who surrenders parts of Eretz Israel will be regarded as a traitor'.[14]

The physical stand-off between the Far Right and the peace movement became increasingly fragile, not least because of the latter's unofficial contacts with the PLO. Peace Now assumed demonic proportions for many settlers. Its leaders were anti-Zionists, controllers of the media, responsible for the failure of the war in Lebanon, Arab-lovers, *Ashafists* (*Ashaf* is the Hebrew term for the PLO), anti-patriotic and traitors to the country. They were assisting in the construction of the PLO State of Palestine in Judea and Samaria. For the settlers, any interference in their perceived good works from other Jews, whether theoretical or practical, caused a determined but often irrational reaction. This polarized existing positions and there developed an increasing inability to appreciate an opposing point of view.

Menachem Livni and the two remaining members of the Jewish underground were finally released at the end of December 1990. President Herzog reduced their original life sentences to 24 years, then 15 years and, in 1989, to 10 years. A parole committee further reduced their terms by another third for good behaviour. Herzog's explanation for his actions was justified on the grounds that the prisoners had expressed 'unequivocal regret for their actions'. Livni, however, told reporters on his release that the Intifada could have been avoided if the government of the time had heeded the message behind the underground's terrorism. He further urged the government to free all imprisoned Israeli soldiers and civilians who had been interned for misdemeanours against Arabs.

Changing attitudes towards democratic behaviour

The influence of the Far Right on Israeli public opinion was indicated in several opinion polls – in terms of electoral support not so much for a particular political party, but more for a philosophy or a policy. Many observers have suggested that approximately 25 per cent of the public supported this camp. Whilst this included the hawkish wing of Likud, it also reflected the results of the 1988 election. Over 10 per cent of the electorate gave their votes to smaller parties on the secular and religious Right. The drift to the Right was not only a reaction to political events but also a comment on a shallow Likud bereft of a charismatic leadership. For many, Revisionism as a philosophy could be preached only by a Jabotinsky or a Begin.

While it is often pointed out that Israel is the most democratic country in the Middle East, with its multi-party system and its model Communist Party, the behaviour of its politicians and its political parties is not a focus of admiration. Few Israeli politicians resign as a result of political incompetence. Few are ready to stand by their principles, preferring instead to rely on political horse-trading and *protekzia*. Following the fall of the National Unity government in March 1990, the inability of the political parties to reform the electoral system, and their willingness to ingratiate themselves with potential allies through the donation of large sums of money from the public purse to religious institutions, led to a public outcry. In addition, politicians were offered tempting positions if they would renounce their positions and cross the floor of the Knesset. Right-wing politicians found that their deeply held convictions were suddenly of less importance. Small parties demanded surety guarantees if their support was required. As one wag put it, 'Israel has the best politicians money can buy!' The humour was not shared by all, and a number of high-ranking reservists of different viewpoints actually declared a hunger strike outside the Knesset to give vent to their frustrations. As in the past, this came to nothing. Whilst there was a public display of accountability on the part of the Executive, it was more a mode of riding out a political storm than of ensuring that the problem was tackled in earnest.

The roots of such aberrations of acceptable political behaviour could partially be traced back to the abnormality of the Jewish experience. When the Shoah rendered the idea of selective Zionism irrelevant, the State of Israel truly became a haven for the persecuted and the downtrodden, who more often than not knew little about democratic norms from the host societies in their former homelands. Moreover, in a difficult situation where national security was a major consideration, it was easy to revert to subconscious influences from the past.

The State had been constructed on the virtues of self-reliance and innovation. By the 1950s, a process of degeneration was under way and this was accentuated by Ben-Gurion's bitter disagreement with the Mapai Party bureaucracy. Ben-Gurion's protégés attempted to find ways around the rigidity of outdated party dogma and traditionalist thinking. The process of innovative ideas, which had characterized Zionism, lapsed into 'cutting corners' and by the 1970s had finally collapsed into a series of scandals involving outright corruption. The disappearance from the political stage of Menachem Begin – who was highly regarded even by his political opponents as a respecter of legal norms – gave *carte blanche* to many who did not possess such high ideals.

In a period of PLO intransigence and Palestinian terrorism, successive governments propagated negative images about Arabs in general. After 1977 in particular, a policy of emphasizing negative aspects while downgrading positive developments was invoked. The demonization of the Palestinians was further facilitated through ignorance and fear. At the end of 1987, the Van Leer Institute in Jerusalem published its report on an ongoing survey of the political and social positions of Israeli youth. It revealed that 60 per cent had no contact with Arabs in any social context; 50 per cent wanted to reduce the civil rights of Israeli Arabs – a position which stemmed mainly from their belief that non-service in the army was evidence of disloyalty; 40 per cent did not support the right of Israeli Arabs to vote in elections for the Knesset. This translated itself into growing support for the Far Right parties in further opinion polls of Israeli youth.

The disqualification of Meir Kahane's Kach Party from running in the 1988 election was the subject of some considerable debate in Israel. Should a party which proclaimed itself a non-believer in democracy, and which was perceived by many to be blatantly racist, be permitted to run? Should a non-democratic body be offered the fruits of democracy in order to overthrow its institutions? The Knesset Elections Committee thought not. But a survey of Israeli public opinion found that only a scant majority – around 52 per cent – agreed with the decision to ban Kach. Some 36 per cent disagreed and the rest expressed no opinion. Those in favour of Kach's participation tended to a 'rightist bias'.

The same survey asked whether 'Israel was too democratic'. Nearly 35 per cent thought that it was. When asked whether a speaker at a public meeting should be permitted sharply to criticize the State of Israel, the following breakdown was obtained:

Definitely not	30%
No	21%
Not sure	10%
Yes	23%
Definitely yes	16%

The survey further showed that religiosity, educational level and ethnic origin were prime determinants in attitudes towards democratic behaviour.

The researchers then characterized their respondents as 'traditional' – meaning 'religious, Asian–African origin, less educated' – and 'modern' – meaning 'non-religious, highly educated, Western origin'. The breakdown of the questions was as follows:

	Traditional		Modern	
	Yes	*No*	*Yes*	*No*
Israel is too democratic	52%	6%	21%	32%
Public speaker should be allowed to criticize the State	29%	62%	57%	32%

Moreover, 51 per cent of religious people interviewed favoured the participation of Kach. Such figures indicated the increasing trend towards illiberalism in Israel. The Far Right encouraged, exacerbated and profited from that tendency.

New parties

The Far Right, however, was not a uniform body and there was mobility between political parties – a phenomenon often catalysed by personality differences or by the religious–secular divide.

The emergence of Techiya as a broad front against Camp David and Kach as a personal vehicle for Kahane was followed in the early 1980s by Tsomet (Crossroad), catering for the socialist pioneering groups that had espoused a maximalist position as far as the Territories were concerned. It was headed by the former Chief-of-Staff Rafael Eitan, who had a long history as a blunt practitioner of hardline policies. He had little time for Palestinians or liberal Israelis who advocated a more moderate approach; neither did he espouse the ideology of Techiya, or the mysticism of some its supporters. Indeed, his main appeal was that of an honest, unsophisticated, simple man.

He pardoned Danny Pinto and Aryeh Sadeh, who had murdered prisoners taken in the Litani campaign in 1978. Together with Defence Minister Ariel Sharon, Eitan had been responsible for the military fiasco of the invasion of Lebanon and the siege of Beirut. The Kahan Commission, which investigated the massacre in the Sabra and Shatilla camps, severely censored him and refrained from demanding his resignation only because just a few weeks of his period of office remained. The Kahan Report stated that

> if the Chief-of-Staff [Eitan] did not imagine at all that the entry
> of the Phalangists into the camps posed a danger to the civilian

population, his thinking on this matter constitutes a serious disregard of important considerations that he should have taken into account. Moreover, considering the Chief-of-Staff's own statements quoted above, it is difficult to avoid the conclusion that the Chief-of-Staff ignored this danger out of an awareness that there were great advantages to sending the Phalangists into the camps, and perhaps also out of a hope that in the final analysis, the Phalangist excesses would not be on a large scale. This conclusion is prompted by the Chief-of-Staff's behaviour during later stages, once reports began to come in about the Phalangists' excesses in the camps.

Eitan – or 'Raful' as he was popularly known – came from a pioneering background in the left-wing Palmach. He was a no-nonsense, plain-speaking military man, given to the undiplomatic turn of phrase: 'If you catch an Arab carrying a knife, shoot him down'; or, referring to Palestinian demonstrators, 'drugged cockroaches in a bottle'. His aim was to unite those maximalists within the Labour Movement to whom any contact with Revisionists was anathema.

In October 1983, he founded the Tsomet movement as a broad alternative to Peace Now. In addition to settling the whole Land of Israel, Raful placed great emphasis on security concerns and a return to a 'true Zionism'. Tsomet's pioneering colouring strongly appealed to that section of the Labour movement. Indeed, on the eve of the 1988 election, it was estimated that Tsomet would pick up 4 per cent of the vote in Labour kibbutzim. Paradoxically, Raful echoed criticism on the Left about the use of cheap Arab labour from the Territories. He described Israel as 'a lazy, weak nation of no goods that cannot face doing its own menial labour'.[16] He advocated a return to the Zionist values of self-sacrifice and pioneering endeavour. Yet, despite a common background, he exhibited an intense detestation of the Left.

His appeal to the electorate emanated from his standing as a tough soldier who had employed strong tactics against the Palestinians. Indeed, at the very inception of Tsomet, he advocated that only those who had served in the Israel Defence Forces, both Jew and Arab, should have the right to vote in Knesset elections. His appeal to secularists was characterized by a determination to coerce the ultra-orthodox *yeshiva* students to serve in the army through cancelling their exemption from service. He strongly supported electoral reform in 1990 when the small non-Zionist religious parties effectively held the balance of power. Foreign critics were regarded as 'hypocrites' and he berated official Israeli response to instances of international condemnation as *galuti* – worthy only of those with a Diaspora mentality. Raful exhibited a bloody-mindedness that appealed to many Israelis.

Both as a soldier and as politician, he believed that 'might is right' and that force as a means of solving a conflict was a strong option: 'The Arabs have always been the enemy. But since we've had a state, we've seen to it that they can't kick us around anymore. Let's not talk about *tohar ha'neshek* [the purity of arms]'. It's meaningless anyway. A gun is for killing – it can't be pure'.[17]

Although at a Tsomet convention President Chaim Herzog referred to him as 'my friend Raful', Eitan unnerved many Israelis with the simplicity of his 'home truths'. At least one Labour MK voted to ban Tsomet from running in the 1988 election after Raful had commented that the higher birthrate of the Palestinians was unnatural and motivated by nationalism. Despite all this, during the inter-party negotiations after the 1988 elections, he was mooted as a probable Minister of Police in a Likud government. Only the coalition with Labour averted that possibility. Significantly, in June 1990, Shamir did not permit Raful to occupy any meaningful position in the narrow right-wing government which succeeded the coalition. Instead, Raful became Minister of Agriculture.

The solution of 'transfer'

Another right-wing veteran of the left-wing Palmach, Rehavam Ze'evi, also began to achieve political notoriety during the mid-1980s. Popularly known as 'Gandhi', like Raful he had held high military office and served as a special adviser on terrorism to Prime Minister Rabin in the 1970s. Gandhi's appointment as director of the Eretz Israel Museum in Tel Aviv in 1981 was in itself a matter of much discussion, since his name had allegedly been linked with organized crime and the Yemenite mafioso in particular. During his tenure at the museum, he had been at the centre of a running controversy with the Mayor of Tel Aviv over the allocation of funds. Significantly, when forming his narrow right-wing government in June 1990, Shamir refused to accede to Gandhi's request to be made Minister of Police.

Ze'evi's public contributions to the debate in Israel on the future of the Palestinian Arabs began in the year before the Intifada. He advocated a clear-cut solution to the conflict – the transfer of the West Bank Palestinians to any Arab country that would take them. Initially, his exposition of such an idea was branded as racist and for some considerable time he was barred from expounding his viewpoint from any public platform. Yet within a relatively short time, the magic of this simple solution had enchanted large sections of the Israeli public. In the absence of any real lead from the major parties, and with the onset of the Intifada, the idea of transfer had great appeal. Yet Gandhi was not the first to propose it. Meir Kahane had always advocated a total expulsion of both Israeli and West Bank Arabs. Gandhi, on the other hand, wanted only the transfer of the Palestinians from the Territories and with prior agreement between governments. He was a 'minimalist' where transfer was concerned.

The details and mechanics of the operation were always left vague. Basic questions were raised. How could such huge numbers of people be transported? What would happen if many families refused to move? What would happen if Jordan refused to accept and to absorb the refugees? How did you move 600,000 Gazans through the West Bank? What would happen if soldiers refused to carry out orders? Would the media be barred from such an operation? What would be the reaction of the international community? Would the United States intervene? Gandhi produced no answers. While some Israelis believed that he was an opportunist and his plan a recipe for civil war in Israel and untold suffering on the part of the Palestinians, opinion polls showed that a substantial minority believed that transfer was a way out of the Palestinian conundrum. In the context of the 1988 election campaign, other segments of the radical Right took up the cry of transfer both to solve the Israel–Palestine conflict and to put an end to the Intifada.

Gandhi cited other contemporary examples of population movement: the expulsion of ethnic Turks from Bulgaria; the movement of Greek Cypriots to the southern part of the island; the movement of Hungarians from Romania. International plans to solve the Palestinian problem were quoted, such as US President Hoover's suggestion in November 1945 to move the Palestinians to Iraq; or the decision of the British Labour Party's National Executive in 1944, which was even more remarkable given Ernest Bevin's policies a few years later. Read out by Clement Attlee to the Labour Party conference, it stated that

> there is surely neither hope nor meaning in a 'Jewish National Home' unless we are prepared to let Jews, if they wish, enter this tiny land in such numbers as to become a majority. There was a strong case for this before the war. There is an irresistible case now, after the unspeakable atrocities of the cold and calculated German Nazi plan to kill all the Jews in Europe. Here too, in Palestine surely is a case on human grounds to promote a stable settlement for transfer of population. Let the Arabs be encouraged to move out as the Jews move in. Let them be compensated handsomely for their land and let their settlement elsewhere be carefully organised and generously financed. The Arabs have many wide territories of their own; they must not claim to exclude the Jews from this small area of Palestine, less than the size of Wales. Indeed, we should re-examine also the

possibility of extending the present Palestinian boundaries by
agreement with Egypt, Syria and Transjordan.[18]

This highly pro-Zionist resolution hardly sparked a reaction from
the delegates at a time when the news of the Final Solution was
reaching Britain. The document, 'A Policy for Palestine', was the
handiwork of one of Labour's major figures, Hugh Dalton, who wrote
it independently, without consulting Zionist leaders. Moshe Sharett,
a future Israeli Foreign Minister who was present in Britain at the
time, was privately very concerned by Dalton's exposition on transfer
since it was not the policy of the Yishuv. Even Jabotinsky in his final
years had come out against the transfer of the Arab population – a
view which emanated from a nineteenth-century sense of fairness to
the Arab population. Yet even Jabotinsky had advocated a voluntary
transfer in his last book, *The War and the Jew*. Only Avraham Stern
had proposed population exchange in Lehi's eighteen principles of
faith. In addition to these embarrassments from the past, Gandhi
also commented that more than 100 million people this century had
been transferred from country to country to prevent internal friction.
Even the Arabs were not averse to employing the process – 250,000
residents were evicted from their Nile valley homes to make way for
the building of the Aswan Dam.

Moreover, Gandhi claimed an impeccable Zionist pedigree. His
father had been a founder of Mapai, the forerunner of the Labour
Party, and he himself had been a member of Histadrut (the Labour
Federation) since the age of seventeen. He proclaimed himself to be
a 'leftist' and his beliefs emanated from the teachings of the socialist-
Zionist theorist, Berl Katznelson and Yitzhak Tabenkin.[19] During the
1988 election, Gandhi's highest level of support came from Kibbutz
Beit Govrin outside Jerusalem.[20] Indeed, during the debate on the
no-confidence vote which eventually led to the downfall of the Shamir
government in March 1990, Ghandi peppered his pro-Likud speech in
support of the government with references to Berl Katznelson. After
he had defeated an attempt to bar his party, Moledet (Homeland) from
running for election in 1988, he proclaimed that Eshkol, Dayan and
Golda Meir had all entertained the idea of transfer: 'I am no more a
racist than my mentor, Ben-Gurion'.

In one sense, Gandhi was not untruthful, since both Jewish and
Palestinian leaderships had considered the idea of population exchange
or expulsion during a period of conflict. Yet all these ideas had been
propagated within a certain political context which related to specific
historical developments.

The idea of separation was inherent in Labour Zionism, since Ben-
Gurion and other leaders laid great emphasis on Avoda Ivrit (Hebrew

labour) to cement the foundations of an independent socialist economy. The Zionist leadership had opposed any proposal to expel the Arabs. In 1931 Weizmann had opposed the slogan of a 'Jewish majority' in Palestine fearing that it would be interpreted as a call to drive out the Arab population. Although the idea had occasionally been mooted, it was the British who formally proposed it in the report of the Peel Commission in 1937. The plan called for the partition of Eretz Israel into two states, one Jewish, the other Arab. It called for a population exchange. Some 225,000 Arabs would move to the proposed Arab state while 1250 Jews would move in the opposite direction. The Peel Commission called for the removal of 100,000 Arabs from their homes in the valleys of Galilee. Whilst there was vigorous opposition to the idea of partition from the Revisionists and from within the Labour Movement, the leadership accepted the plan. The Palestinian Arabs totally rejected partition and continued to press for a Greater Palestine. The impasse persuaded the British eventually to withdraw the plan, but Ben Gurion was clearly troubled by the implications of the proposed population exchange. On the one hand, he understood the moral injustice of such an eviction; he often stated that the Jews did not come to Palestine to dispossess the Arabs of their land. On the other hand, he realized that a separation of populations would solve many problems for the Zionist enterprise, including obvious strategic considerations:

> The clearing of the valleys is an opportunity that we should take now or it may not happen again. The Royal Commission is offering to move the Arabs to an Arab state and it is something which we will be unable to do [if at all] once the state has been established. At that stage, the rights of a minority could not be ignored. . . . Now is the time to do it and the most important step is to prepare ourselves for its implementation. [21]

Even if he were prepared to back the enterprise, Ben-Gurion found it hard to believe that the British would set aside their moral convictions and forcibly evict 100,000 people from their homes: 'I can see only great problems in uprooting 100,000 Arabs from villages where they have dwelt for hundreds of years – would England dare do it?' However, the failure to establish a Jewish State in even a tiny segment of historic Eretz Israel at this time, coupled with British capitulation at Munich, induced a change in Ben-Gurion's outlook. As his biographer has commented, 'Ben-Gurion now saw a world in which force prevailed. His vision of Zionism too underwent a transformation. He had once viewed Zionism as absolutely just; now necessity demanded that he lower his moral sights'. [22]

Such a changed outlook was clear during Israel's War of Independence. In 1948, Ben-Gurion's campaign to safeguard the survival of the Jewish State in time of war sometimes led to selective expulsions, such as the case of the Arabs of Lydda, where Yigal Allon and Yitzhak Rabin supervised the exodus of thousands of unwilling inhabitants.[23] Whether Ben-Gurion agreed with the move or regarded this action as a violation of his orders to Allon is open to conjecture.[24]

Whatever his feelings about the expulsion, he was well aware that the result of such actions, premeditated or self-induced, would ultimately enhance both the security and the cohesiveness of the State. Indeed, although he publicly bemoaned the psychological trauma of the Palestinians during the conflict and their mass flight to their Arab brothers as a means of escape, it was also clear that he did not envisage any mass return on the part of the inhabitants of Jaffa and Haifa once they realized that the Jews would not murder them in their beds. The leadership of the State, whilst aware of the immorality of a situation essentially not of their making, understood its benefit too. Moshe Sharett, in a letter to Nahum Goldman a few weeks after independence, reiterated the unofficial hardline position of both leadership and army: 'The opportunities which the present position opens up for a lasting and radical solution of the most vexing problem of the Jewish State [i.e. the Arab minority] are so far-reaching as to take one's breath away. Even if a certain backwash is unavoidable, we must make the most of this momentous chance with which history has presented us so swiftly and so unexpectedly'.[25]

Gandhi's opponents argued that during a time of war, when the very existence of the State of Israel was in jeopardy, such attitudes were understandable. It was something else to extrapolate this viewpoint to the present as if the state of non-peace with the Palestinians was actually a state of physical war and a question of survival.

However, for the majority of those Israelis who warmed to the idea of transfer, it was the total lack of resolution of the Palestinian problem that guided them towards this solution. It was the growing realization of the demographic problem within Israel that permitted the acceptance of transfer as an easy answer. The high birthrate of the Palestinian Arabs compared to that of the Israeli Jews suggested an Arab majority in the foreseeable future and thus an end to a Jewish State. In 1988 Professor Arnon Sofer, a geographer at Haifa University, pointed out that there were 5.9 million people in Israel and the Territories.[26]

Israeli Jews	3,500,000
Israeli Arabs	810,000
West Bank Jews	70,000
West Bank Arabs	880,000
Gaza Arabs	600,000

Effectively: 3.6 million or 61% of the total population = Jews
               2.3 million or 39% of the total population = Arabs

By the year 2000, Sofer pointed out, this would have narrowed to 55
per cent Jews and 45 per cent Arabs.

   Likud and the Far Right placed great hope in the arrival of Jewish
immigrants from abroad and a voluntary departure of West Bank Arabs
for other countries. In fact, nearly 100,000 Jews came to Israel in the
1980s. Yet virtually the same number left. A third of the emigrants
were aged between twenty and thirty, and were essentially of the
professional class. In addition, the emigration of West Bank Arabs
was an erratic phenomenon depending on the economic climate at
home and abroad. Between 1968 and 1983 147,000 left. Moreover,
the true size of the Palestinian population of the Territories was
unknown, as no census has been carried out since 1967. While
ignorance of growth and the low 1967 figures benefited those who
dismissed the demographic argument, it was also in the interests of
the Land of Israel advocates that Arabs should depart the West Bank
and seek new homes elsewhere. In addition, the American restrictions
on Jewish emigration from the USSR to the United States in October
1989, and the subsequent projection of a mass influx of Soviet Jews,
created hope on the Right that the relatively static Jewish population
of the Territories would increase dramatically. When international
pressure curtailed this option, the Shamir government continued a
policy of expanding existing settlements.

Year	Jewish population in Judea, Samaria and Gaza	Increase over previous year[27]
1987	70000	15.00%
1988	75000	7.14%
1989	81200	8.27%
1990	94650	16.57%

   Since the mid-1980s the Labour Party had promoted a demographic
picture of doom and gloom to convince the Israeli public that only a
small Israel – essentially within the 1967 borders – could counteract
this prognosis. Only a small Israel could preserve both the Jewish
and the democratic character of the country. However, in raising
the problem and pushing it, Shimon Peres had opened a Pandora's
box. Inadvertently, it permitted another solution to the demographic
problem to be voiced – that of transfer. In the context of the
Intifada, this became popular and was an issue in the 1988 election.
It introduced arguments for voluntary and involuntary transfer, with

or without compensation, including and excluding Israeli Arabs with the West Bank Palestinians. For example, in an address to the Tel Aviv Commercial and Industrial Club a few months before the election, Gandhi told his audience that the higher birthrate of Israeli Arabs was causing problems in Israel's seats of higher learning: 'they are clogging up the Universities, witness the example of Haifa University'. [28]

Since 1985, opinion polls have indicated that a hard core – 35–40 per cent – of Israelis favour the emigration of Palestinians from the Territories. Although the questions have been all too vague in meaning and consequences, the general idea of ridding themselves of the Palestinian problem in this manner appealed to a considerable minority of Israelis. When Gandhi first put forward his views in the summer of 1987, an opinion poll showed that 50.4 per cent agreed with him. Yet when they were asked to think about it in reality and to consider whether it was feasible, only some 14.4 per cent believed that it could actually be carried out. [29]

When the Israel Institute of Applied Social Research asked nearly 1200 Israeli Jews in June 1989 to consider nine different plans for the Territories, 51 per cent selected 'transfer' as their first choice. The same survey asked, 'If a Palestinian State were established [in the Territories], would most Israeli Arabs be interested in joining?' Some 71 per cent of the Jewish respondents answered 'Yes', but virtually the same proportion of Israeli Arabs replied 'No'. The wishful thinking of Jewish public opinion was all too clear. It also belied a total lack of understanding of Israeli Arab perceptions. Like many American or British Zionists, Israeli Arabs expressed no real wish to uproot themselves and return to the homeland. Although other surveys suggested that support for transfer had marginally decreased and that this was evidence of a pervading reality about the Intifada within Israeli society, radical right-wing politicians seeking election to the twelfth Knesset in November 1988 made use of the issue to the hilt.

Transfer and the 1988 election

When Gandhi formally entered the electoral race in the summer of 1988, 4000 Israelis responded to his advertisements. Unlike Kahane's followers, they were a respectable cross-section of Israeli society, including many who had served in the Defence Forces and the Intelligence Services. Gandhi's attempt to translate this groundswell for the idea of transfer into support for his party, however, was a failure. He secured only two seats in the election. But in the negotiations that followed, when there was a real possibility of a narrow Likud–right-wing coalition, Gandhi offered his two mandates to a Likud government on condition that they held a national referendum on the desirability of transferring the Palestinians from the Territories. Campaigning under the slogan 'Them Or Us!', he canvassed the traditional vote for the radical Right in impoverished areas of the country where many of Afro-Asian origin had settled. Thus, in September 1988, he addressed the crowd in Tel Aviv's Hatikvah quarter market. Standing beside traditional Jewish symbols – a Torah scroll, a *shofar*, two *challot* (Sabbath bread), salt and flowers – the secular Gandhi asked the crowd, 'Who does Eretz Israel belong to?' and 'Where should all the Arabs go?' The crowd replied accordingly. Yet when Techiya's Geula Cohen, one of the progenitors of the radical Right, paid a similar visit to Jerusalem's Machane Yehuda market to gather her traditional support, she was pressed on the sensitive question of transfer. She replied that Techiya really supported the emigration of Arabs, 'without spelling it out in so many words'.[30] Such an equivocal statement disappointed the crowd, who condemned her: 'Not even you will kick the Arabs out of here.' Cohen, the darling of right-wing causes, left with shouts of 'Arabs out!' ringing in her ears.

Techiya's formal stand in 1988 had been to reject the mass expulsion of Arabs. Yet at the 1986 party conference, Yuval Ne'eman, its Chairman, had commented that a transfer of 500,000 Palestinians should be a precondition for peace negotiations.

Tsomet's Raful Eitan was also not slow to jump on this electoral bandwagon. A few weeks before the outbreak of the Intifada, he said that 'the Arabs of Judea and Samaria have every right to remain where they are'.[31] By April 1988 he was advocating a population exchange between West Bank Arabs and Jews from Arab countries. This had been part of the Tsomet–Techiya platform for the 1984 elections. Even though the number of Palestinians in the Territories far outnumbered the remnants of Jewish communities who continued to live in Arab states, the implication in 1984 was that it would be a voluntary exchange of populations. In 1988, under pressure from his rivals on the Far Right, Raful omitted any mention of the voluntary nature of his party's stand. He told the media that, in the event of war, he would be willing to deport a million people if there was trouble on the West Bank: 'You don't need a large force for that; we had a far smaller army in 1948 and it was done wherever it was needed. All you need are the orders and the soldiers to carry them out'.[32]

The 1988 elections returned Techiya, Tsomet and Moledet to the Knesset. They collected only 6 per cent of the vote between them, which permitted them to send seven representatives to the Knesset. Yet this was but the tip of the iceberg. Even before the Intifada, it had been estimated that at least thirteen members of the Knesset supported transfer or had made racist remarks.[33] Over the years there had been comments that official plans existed to exploit any future war by expelling large numbers of Arabs.[34] The leading Israeli daily, *Ha'aretz*, devoted an editorial to this aspect of transfer. It claimed that Gandhi's campaign was no more than a bid to start the next war and that international efforts would be directed at a ceasefire and would overlook the expulsion of Palestinians.

During the Intifada and subsequent government attempts to quell the disturbances, President Herzog and Ministers Rabin and Navon had all invoked the Palestinian fear of expulsion by referring to the 'tragedy of 1948' – thus paradoxically accepting the PLO version of the events of the War of Independence.

The appeal of transfer divided Likud. As far back as 1983, Meir Cohen-Avidor, then Deputy Speaker of the Knesset, bemoaned the fact that Israel had not expelled 2–300,000 Palestinians from the West Bank immediately after the Six Day War. More recently, Gideon Patt, then Minister of Science, threatened in an outburst to put Israeli Arabs in trucks and taxis and to dump them at the border. At a local branch meeting of Herut, Michael Dekel, the Deputy Minister of Defence, who had formerly been in charge of West Bank settlements, argued for a transfer of Palestinians to Jordan. Such comments by official figures were not publicly condemned by Likud, but individuals within the party, such as Foreign Minister Moshe Arens, publicly stated their opposition. Shamir himself sidestepped the issue by belittling the demographic question. Officially, Likud believed that emigration was a voluntary option that the Palestinian inhabitants of the West Bank should consider seriously if they did not like the idea of being a minority in a Jewish State. The hawkish wing of Likud was significantly silent on the matter. Ariel Sharon, for example, did not offer any opinion on the matter, even though he himself had prepared plans for the evacuation of Arabs from Galilee in 1964.

It was not surprising that the question of transfer caused a lack of uniform response within Likud, for Moledet owed a certain ideological allegiance to Lehi philosophy. Moledet had originally offered a Knesset seat to Israel Eldad, the Lehi ideologue, who decided to turn them down. When Eldad had run on a Land of Israel platform in the 1969 elections, he too had called for Arab emigration. Moreover, Zvi Shiloah was reputed to be the prime mover behind Moledet – he had resigned from Techiya in 1983 because of their willingness to join the second Begin government despite their perceived ideological betrayal at Camp David.

The National Religious Party opposed transfer because it conflicted with 'the movement's moral ideology'. This attitude was acceptable to all factions of the party, yet it did not stop the NRP's Minister without Portfolio, Yosef Shapira, from commenting that each potential Arab emigrant should be offered an inducement of $20,000 to ensure that he

packed his bags. Others advocated that emigration of Arabs should be
encouraged through a ban on investment in the agricultural and health
infrastructure of the region.[35]

Those Jews who lived in the settlements in the Territories were
naturally most enthusiastic about the emigration of their Palestinian
neighbours. Not only did it increase security for them, but it was one
step closer to a totally Jewish Land of Israel. A survey of seventy
rabbis in West Bank settlements in the winter of 1987 showed that
two-thirds of them believed that the Palestinians should be encouraged
to emigrate voluntarily.[36] A further 15 per cent believed in forced
emigration. Only 10 per cent rejected the idea of transfer. One
of the founders of Gush Emunim, Hanan Porat, believed that the
Israeli settlers on the West Bank could happily coexist with their
Palestinian neighbours; but if there was all-out rebellion, then many
settlers would advocate transfer: 'either we or they will be expelled'.[37]
Unlike Kahane, Porat and others from Gush Emunim, whilst accepting
the literal interpretation of the biblical injunction to 'dispossess all the
inhabitants of the Land' (Numbers 33:52), did not concur with Rashi's
advice to drive them out as well. Yet a rationalization of transfer as a
possible option proceeded in settler circles as the psychological effects
of the Intifada began to make themselves felt:

> First I have to determine whether I can take each one of the
> million and a half Arabs surrounding me, living in the territory of
> Eretz Israel, and look at them as law-abiding individuals who are
> prepared to live with me. Or does the historical nexus force us to
> look upon the individual Arab as part of the Arab nation, however
> it's defined, who can never be trusted because tomorrow he is
> going to become part of that larger Arab enemy? Now should that
> second perspective be adopted, and if that's the truth confronting
> us, then I don't think that transfer is something that needs to be
> ruled out, certainly not on moral or religious grounds.[38]

The final application of 'transfer' was inevitably to those Jews in
the peace movement who continually voiced their opposition. Meir
Kahane's Kach movement threatened to expel all those Israelis with
whom they disagreed. The idea of ridding the country of internal
critics became a feature at counterdemonstrations. For example,
members of the 'Women in Black' peace movement, who silently
demonstrated every Friday in a Jerusalem square, were greeted by
counterdemonstrators who held a placard reading 'Transfer Arabs
and these Black Traitors'. One correspondent wrote to the press
that Israel should consider transferring activists of Peace Now –
'Tragedy Now' – and dovish members of the Knesset before moving
the Palestinians.[39]

3

Inheriting the Land

From time immemorial

Jewish settlers in the Territories are often depicted in a one-dimensional fashion in the Western media. Their religious 'otherness' is viewed solely as a mixture of incomprehensible obscurantism and political extremism, a pariah group denied international acceptability. Their fundamentalism is smoothly equated with that of Christianity and Islam and they are thus easily characterized as latter-day Shylocks living out their fantasies in a sort of Jewish Bible-belt at the expense of the local Palestinians. Such reductionism in the West simplifies a complex reality.

Many of the Jewish settlers do not fit this picture. Although the religious settlers are deeply literate in Judaism and live their lives according to the tenets of the *Halacha* (Jewish law), a good number are highly qualified professionally in the secular world. Whilst many secular settlers take the opportunity to obtain the cheap mortgages available in new towns close to the Green Line which marks Israel's pre-1967 boundaries, many religious pioneers establish their new homes in farflung places with names evoking biblical splendour. Many believe that they are on the threshold of the messianic era and that they therefore stand outside history. There is a mystical notion of time and space. They are actors in an inner Jewish drama delineated by divine dimensions where the vanquished Palestinians are essentially bystanders. They exhibit an historical determinism – a certainty that they know what God requires of them. Zionism is a *mitzva* (commandment) of cosmic proportions. For them, it is a religious duty to settle the Land and to participate in the Era of Redemption.

There is, of course, another people who live in the same Land, who also advocate national rights. How does the religious Jewish world deal with the problem of the Palestinians, the question of peace and the command to settle the Land? These matters, relating to the meaning of Jewish history, are the essence of a far-ranging debate within the religious Jewish community – a debate which rarely surfaces outside

56

the world of Jewish learning.

In the year AD 70 the Romans destroyed the Second Temple and razed the holy city of Jerusalem to the ground. Jewish captives were sold in the slave market in Rome where the local Jewish community competed in an attempt to buy their freedom. Over sixty years later, Simon Bar-Kosiba once more raised the standard of revolt against the Roman Empire. Known throughout history as Shimon Bar-Kochba (Son of the Star), he was believed by Rabbi Akiva and others to be the Messiah – yet he too failed. The Jewish people paid a terrible price for these courageous yet futile adventures: death, imprisonment and exile, the loss of national independence and the suppression of Judaism. The religious leaders of the time were faced with a devastating problem. They somehow had to relate the richness of the Jewish past to the uncertainty of the present. The importance of Jewish history and the Jewish experience had to have some meaning for the world as well as for themselves if they were to survive as a people.

In response, a unique, indeed portable, vehicle of survivalism was created. The rabbis evolved a distinctive procedure of studying Jewish texts to cope with this crisis. If a base verse from the Pentateuch was juxtaposed with an intersecting verse from another Jewish source, an exegetical interpretation could be formulated:

> We read one thing in terms of something else. To begin with, it is the base verse in terms of something else. But it is also the intersecting verse in other terms as well – a multiple-layered construction of analogy and parable. The intersecting verse's elements always turn out to stand for, to signify, and to speak of, something other than that to which they openly refer. Nothing says what it means. Everything important speaks elliptically, allegorically and symbolically. All statements carry deeper meaning which belong to other statements altogether. The profound sense of the base verse emerges only through restatement within and through the intersecting verse – as if the base verse spoke of things that we do not see on the surface.[1]

The rabbis thus created an inner world – a refuge where Jews could feel secure and thereby confront the cruelty and persecutions of the real world. The development of the Babylonian and Jerusalem Talmuds and their study essentially defined the parameters of 2000 years of Jewish existence in exile. It was a response to the loss of the Land, Jerusalem and the Temple. It was a reaction to the rise of Christianity, which claimed to represent the true Israel. It was the erection of barriers against the violence of the stranger. But it was also intellectual and spiritual creativity and solace in the face of an adverse future. Jews were ostracized as a pariah people and religion, but within this status they also secured their separation to ensure both their survival and their sanity: 'It is a people that dwells alone and shall not be reckoned among the nations' (Numbers 23:9).

The advent of the Enlightenment and the French Revolution in the eighteenth century destroyed both the power and the ability of the rabbis to preserve a hermetically sealed Jewish world based on adherence to the Torah and Talmud. The cracks in the ghetto walls led to involvement in several ideological directions which could be related to the legacy of the Torah. In the nineteenth century many Jews were involved in the revolutionary movements which swept Europe. Others embraced Christianity in an attempt to assimilate themselves and their children into majority cultures. But the rise of nationalism brought in its train political anti-semitism. By the end of the century many Jews began to question their place in the scheme of things. Jewish socialists began to think in national terms. Moses Hess, who unwittingly instructed the young Karl Marx in anti-Jewish stereotypes, later began to formulate his ideas on socialism–Zionism in his book *Rome and Jerusalem*.

The evolution of Zionism was thus essentially a secular development, and religious Jews kept their distance. Although a number of nineteenth-century religious leaders, such as Rabbis Alkalai, Kalisher and Mohilver, advocated a return to Zion, the majority of the faithful ignored them. They preferred to await the arrival of the Messiah who would return them to the Promised Land. Jewish social revolutionaries from Russia and Eastern Europe disagreed and took matters into their own hands. They rejected the passivity of the Diaspora that the rabbis had inspired by their belief that no attempt should be made to precipitate the arrival of the Messiah before the appointed time. These Jewish socialists moved the Jewish people into the flow of historical advance after nearly two millennia as meek observers on the periphery.

In addition, the reticence of the rabbis to endorse the Zionist enterprise may have stemmed from an awareness of the incompatibility of *Halacha* as it had developed over the centuries of exile with a Jewish national entity exercising the power of sovereignty.

As Jewish settlement of the Land of Israel proceeded apace and the Zionist movement became more influential in the Jewish world, an increasing number of younger religious Jews aligned themselves with these developments. By the Second Zionist Congress in Basle in 1898, some religious Zionists asked the movement to define its relationship to Jewish tradition. The unsatisfactory answer of the secular leadership was that religion was the prerogative of the individual and thereby a private matter. The creation of a specifically religious Zionist party, Mizrachi, followed shortly afterwards. Its nationalist slogan advocated 'The Land of Israel for the People of Israel according to the Torah of Israel'. An independent religious Labour movement, Ha'poalei Ha'mizrachi, was established after the First World War and occupied a dominant place in the broad religious Zionist movement. It created a well-organized workers' movement and in the 1920s and 1930s was active in building settlements according to the dictum of '*Torah Va'Avoda* [Torah and Labour]'. Settling the Land, even in those early days, was an important credo. Despite their adherence to basic socialist tenets, these religious Zionists also exhibited considerable sympathy for Jabotinsky and the Revisionist movement because of this attachment to the Land. When they eventually joined with Mizrachi to form the National Religious Party, they brought a pioneering tradition to a party of rabbis, intellectuals and businessmen.

The first Chief Rabbi of Israel, Avraham Yitzhak Kook, viewed the atheist pioneers as unknowing spiritual instruments of the divine will to settle the Land and to return it once more to the Jewish people. He believed that 'the brotherly love of Esau and Jacob, of Isaac and Ishmael' would eventually assert itself and that the conflict between Arab and Jew would finally be resolved.

The political agenda of religious Zionists from 1948 until 1967 was essentially an apolitical pragmatic one in that they concerned themselves with Jewish education and Judaism *per se*. Matters of state were left in the hands of the Labour politicians, with whom they had a good relationship. Little was mentioned about retrieving and settling the biblical Land of Israel, even though it was so commanded. Judea and Samaria lay in Jordan whilst the biblical lands given to the tribes of Asher and Naphtali were situated in southern Lebanon. The approach of the NRP politicians was a gradualist one – a step-by-step application of *Halacha*.

The influence of Zvi Yehuda Kook

Israel's victory in the Six Day War literally stunned religious Jews. They saw the Hand of God at work in delivering the whole of the Land to His people. There was widespread agreement amongst orthodox Jews that the victory had been divinely inspired and that this newly acquired part of the Land – Judea and Samaria, or the West Bank – should not be relinquished. For religious Jews, 'In principle, there is no difference between Judea, Samaria and Gaza – and Jaffa, Ramla, Lod and Ashkelon'.[2] Populous Palestinian cities on the West Bank, such as Hebron and Nablus (Shechem), had the same status in Jewish law as did cities in Israel within the pre-1967 borders. The Jews had inherited the Land. It was a promised Land – and those who had controlled it in their absence were temporary participants in the continuum of Jewish history.

The son of Chief Rabbi Kook, Zvi Yehuda Kook, as head of the Merkaz Ha'Rav Yeshiva (religious seminary) was highly influential in mobilizing support for settling and retaining the Territories. In a legendary address on Israel's Independence Day in 1967, shortly before the outbreak of the Six Day War, he strongly admonished his students for their spiritual amnesia in connection with the Land. In a statement on the eve of the 1973 elections, he told the voters that 'all this Land is ours, absolutely, belonging to all of us; it is non-transferable to others even in part'. He pointed out that there were no 'Arab territories', only the Land of Israel. Kook simply regarded the conquests of 1967 as a continuation of 1948. The Arabs who lived in the Land had built without the permission of the absent Jews. In his statement, he berated the Arabs for creating 'refugee camps' which played on the sympathy of the world. He concluded:

> We have continued and are continuing to build and to be built through the awesome wonders of the Lord, Who from His Temple gives strength and fortitude to His people, blessed by the Lord, in the holy labour of reconstructing our nation and our homeland, our Torah and our moral culture, in righteousness and justice, for the restoration of the eternal values implicit in our national identity, and for the reestablishment of the Presence of God and of Israel in Zion. 'The Lord of Heaven and Earth is with us; the God of Jacob is our stronghold' [Psalms 46:12]. 'We shall not retreat from thee. Thou shalt bestow upon us a rebirth of life and we shall proclaim Thy will. Lord of Heaven and Earth, cause Thy face to shine, and we shall be saved' [Psalms 80:19, 20].

The idea of 'chosenness', in the sense that the Jewish people had been selected to take on a divinely ordained destiny, now began to assume a militant and indeed an aggressive character through a fusion of nationalism and religion. Unlike his father, Zvi Yehuda Kook was a product of the generation that bore witness to the enormity of the Shoah. The trauma of the catastrophe particularly conditioned the behaviour of the ultra-orthodox who lost 90 per cent of their adherents. The Shoah distanced Kook from the non-Jewish world because of this. Indeed, the borderline between 'chosenness' and 'exclusivity' is very narrow. His attitude to Jewish–Gentile relations reflected his perception of the Shoah as 'the expression of the evil of the gentiles and their deep hatred of the Jews'.[3]

Rabbi Kook, the son, regarded the establishment of the State in 1948 as the beginning of the messianic era. The Zionist movement itself was catalytic in ushering in this new epoch. Therefore it was not suprising that after 1967 Zvi Yehuda Kook urged orthodox Jews to play an active role in the movement towards redemption. Although Rabbi Kook, the father, had regarded secular Jews as the spiritual instruments of the divine will, there was little actual co-operation between the proponents of religious and secular Zionists. Rabbi Kook, the son, advocated that this approach should be a public reality in the name of Jewish solidarity. Thus settlements of strictly observant and secular Jews were established in the Territories. Techiya was, similarly, a 'mixed' political party.

Whilst there was an undercurrent of 'missionary' activity – however unintentional – in reclaiming secular Jews and returning them to the faith, there was also a very clear reductionist belief that secular Jews were unable to understand the importance of living in the Land – in Judea and Samaria – because of the shallowness of their Jewish identity. Labour–Zionism, it was argued, had secularized the Jewish pioneers and made them Jewishly illiterate. It had separated the Jew and the Israeli:

> The occupation of the Territories could be justified morally only if these areas were seen as part of the Holy Land, Eretz Israel . . . but Israeli self-identification did not include Jewishness, nor the Jewish heritage since Israelis rejected their link with Diaspora Jewry. Thus the occupation of territories in the historical Land of Israel created a serious dilemma and a crisis of identity. The prevalent ideology, based as it was on patriotism alone, could not justify the occupation of foreign land; only Jewishness could do that and the ideology had rejected Jewishness in favour of Israeliness. [4]

Yet many secular Israelis who had settled down to comfortable lives looked upon the religious settlers with a certain benevolence. They overlooked their religious fundamentalism and regarded them as almost their surrogates, since they themselves had renounced the pioneering spirit of their fathers for conventional lives in modern cities such as Tel Aviv.

The Age of Redemption was not simply about territory but also about how it should be used. It was about the meaning of a Jewish State and the character of the Jewish society that dwelt within its borders. This mystical sense of destiny greatly appealed to the younger generation of religious Zionists who had been born in Israel. They were the first products of both the Israeli religious school system and the *yeshivot* since the establishment of the State. As the first nationally 'free' Jews in 2000 years, they reacted against the inherited attitudes of the religious gradualism of their fathers and advocated a policy of applying *Halacha* to all sectors of Israeli life, including foreign policy. On the one hand, they resented the attitude of the secularists, who regarded them as second-class Zionists who had contributed little to the establishment of the State. On the other, they suffered the taunts of the non-Zionist ultra-orthodox who chided them that they were simply a religious appendage to the forces of secularism and assimilation. The desire to settle the conquered territories of Judea and Samaria created a widespread discussion within religious circles on the meaning of it all and how one should tackle each problem as it arose according to *Halacha*. If before 1967 Jewish law and civil law co-existed somewhat uneasily, the religious passions released after 1967 often placed them in conflict.

The importance of the Land

God's promise to the Jewish people is rooted in His promise to Abraham. At the very beginning of the portion, Lech Lecha (Genesis 12:17), God tells Abraham to leave his father's house, his birthplace, his country, and go to 'the land that I will show thee. And I will make of thee a great nation, and I will bless thee, and make thy name great, and thou shalt be a blessing. And I will bless them that bless thee, and him that curseth thee will I curse; and in thee shall be blessed all the families of the earth' (Genesis 12:1–3). These verses characterize the particularism and universalism of Jewish behaviour in Judea and Samaria.

When Abraham came to the land of Canaan, God told him to 'lift up now thine eyes and look from the place where thou art, northward and southward and eastward and westward; for all the land which thou seest, to thee will I give it, and to thy seed forever. And I will make thy seed as the dust of the earth; so that if a man can number the dust of the earth, then shall thy seed also be numbered. Arise, walk through the land in the length of it and in the breadth of it; for unto thee will I give it' (Genesis 13:14–17).

Finally, when God makes His Covenant with Abraham – no longer Abram and now a believer – he tells him, 'And I will establish My covenant between Me and thee and thy seed after thee throughout their generations for an everlasting covenant, to be a God unto thee and to thy seed after thee. And I will give unto thee, and to thy seed after thee, the land of Canaan, for an everlasting possession' (Genesis 15:7–8).

These powerful statements form the backbone of the triangular and metaphysical relationship of God, the Jewish people and the Land of Israel. Indeed, according to the former Ashkenazi Chief Rabbi of Israel, Shlomo Goren, 'the Land of Israel is not a combination of geographical areas, but is one entity, just like Israel and its Torah. It is the underlying principle of the Jewish faith and first among the commandments of the Torah, the purpose and condition of our national, religious and spiritual existence'.[5]

For the late Rabbi Zvi Yehuda Kook, the spiritual mentor of those who implemented the commandment of *yishuv Ha'aretz* (settling the Land), surrendering even a part of the Land possessed the symbolism of conversion. He encouraged his followers to fight for the Land and, if necessary, to die for it. *Ye'Hareg ve'al ya'avor* – one should rather be killed than transgress. For some of his students – at least in principle – the sanctity of the Land was of greater consideration than the value of human life. Analogies from Jewish history assisted in their sense that they were on the threshold of redemption – and opponents and doubters must be swept aside: 'The Land comes to symbolize the entire conflict between Jew and non-Jew and between faithful Jews and those whose loyalties waver. Towards the external enemy, the answer is the triumph of David over Goliath. Towards the internal, it is the victory of the Maccabees over the Hellenizers'.[6] Many subscribed to the rabbinic dictum that the commandment to settle the Land was equal to all the other 612 commandments in Jewish law. Indeed, the *Shechina* (the Divine Presence) had gone into exile with the Jews following the destruction of the Second Temple. According to the second-century sage Rabbi Akiva, 'wherever Israel wandered, the Divine Presence wandered with them'. In settling the Land, the *Shechinah* thereby re-entered the Land and surrendering it was tantamount to a capitulation to the forces of evil, *sitra achra* – the camp of the other side.

Kabbala, Jewish mysticism, often regarded the Land as a motif of *malchut*, the female aspect. During the early years of the twentieth century, the secular pioneer, A.D. Gordon developed mystical concepts about the bond to the Land. Today this is sometimes alluded to by the religious settlers: 'The relationship of the Jew to Israel [is] analogous to that of man and woman', and of Jerusalem as a 'maiden whose time is ripe but whose husband has not come'. The coming of the husband alludes to the redemption of the Jews from exile, God from exile and eventually of the world from alienation'.[7] Martin Buber also spoke about the uniqueness of a chosen people and a chosen Land and the mystery of that relationship. The holy society of the future would be brought forth by the interaction of the people and the Land as active partners. The Land was neither passive nor inert but interventionist:

> Just as nature and history were united in the creation of man, so these two spheres which have become separated in the human mind were to unite in the task in which the chosen land and the chosen people were called upon to co-operate. The holy matrimony of land and people was intended to bring about the matrimony of the two separated spheres of Being.[8]

The works of the thirteenth-century Halachist, Nachmanides (Moses ben Nachman – the Ramban), were frequently called upon to support the argument of the importance of settling the Land. Nachmanides was probably the greatest Jewish scholar in Spain at that time.[9] He was particularly well known for his participation in the public disputation with the convert Pablo Christiani in 1263 which was staged before the court of James I of Aragon as a confrontationist discourse between Church and Synagogue. Although he impressed the King and astounded Catholic zealots by his insightful arguments and eloquent presentation, the anger of Rome forced him to flee from Barcelona to the Holy Land, where he settled in 1267. Nachmanides believed that settling and living in the Land was an overriding religious commandment, obligatory for all generations. In a letter written shortly after his arrival in Jerusalem, he reminded his son that 'you and your brothers and the whole of our family . . . shall all live to see the salvation of Jerusalem and the comfort of Zion'. Unlike previous commentators and scholars, he did not relegate his views to responsa (Rabbinical or scholarly replies or rejoinders) but actually acted on his beliefs and settled in Jerusalem and Acre. Again unlike his predecessors, he related to and wrote about Jerusalem as a geographical entity as well as a spiritual focus.

Nachmanides disagreed with perhaps the greatest scholar of the medieval era, Maimonides (Moses ben Maimon – the Rambam), who formulated the *taryag mitzvot*, the 613 commandments which characterize Jewish practice. Maimonides in his *Sefer Ha'mitzvot* (*The Book of Commandments*) enumerated 248 positive commandments and 365 negative ones. Two generations later, Nachmanides formulated another seventeen positive commandments, which he argued should have been included. One referred pointedly to settling the Land: 'That we are to conquer the Land of Israel; that we are not to leave it in the hands of other nations; that we are not to leave it waste, and that we are to dwell in it – this being a commandment binding for all time' (Numbers 33:53).[10] Nachmanides looked upon the Diaspora with some disdain, and approvingly noted that 'whoever lives abroad should be regarded as an idolator' (Ketubot 110).

Nachmanides was also specific in his understanding of the borders of the Land: 'make your way to the hill country of the Amorites and all their neighbours in the Arava, the mountains, the lowland, the southern desert and the sea coast' (Deuteronomy 1:7).

He lived at a time of conflict between Christianity and Islam over control of the Holy Land. The capture of Jerusalem by Saladin in 1187 heightened Jewish sensitivities to their ancient homeland. Those who came before and did not experience these sentiments were less than interested in the Holy Land in a geographical sense. Thus Maimonides emigrated from Cordova in 1165 to the Holy Land but soon left it for Egypt. The sense of messianic anticipation was common to all three major religions that looked to Jerusalem. In fact, Nachmanides was one of a number of Jewish commentators who were imbued by the sense of living in the Land and who subsequently made their way to Jerusalem during the thirteenth century. Their image of Jerusalem was rooted in the spiritual and geographical reality around them:

> There were no new songs to be sung about Zion. No visions of Heavenly Jerusalem, no royal palace descending from heaven and no expectation of the day of Judgement when God would rebuild the Temple; instead, images of the land's fertility, its wholesomeness, farming, building, and security. These were new realities appearing, rather unexpectedly in biblical exegeses.[11]

Like today's settlers, Nachmanides' world-view was formulated in part as a reaction to an older generation. An older colleague, the kabbalist Ezra ben Solomon, believed that only God's will would eventually return the Jews to Jerusalem: 'Nowadays the Jews are already released from an obligation [to dwell in] the Land of Israel. Their suffering – out of the love of God – the [vicissitudes of] the dispersion, and their afflictions and subjugation are like an atoning altar for them, as it is written 'Yea, for Thy sake are we killed all the day long' [Psalms 44:23].[12] Nachmanides clearly rebelled against this self-imposed passivity, literally in the spirit of the age. For him, an authentic Jewish life could be lived only in the Land of Israel, and Jews were commanded to settle there. Even so, Nachmanides fled to the Holy Land before impending danger and not totally of his own volition. Ironically, in Jerusalem, he made a virtue out of necessity.

The struggle for a Jewish approach

The religious approach to the problem of the Territories and their inhabitants is certainly not characterized by a single conformist outlook. In reality, there are many very different views – based on traditional Jewish sources – on how to interpret this phase of Jewish history and thereby deal with the problem of the Palestinians and their rights. The question of definition is all-important – for only then can the correct Jewish laws be applied. Is the intention of the Palestinians in waging the Intifada in the Territories a demand for national independence and the liberation of their homeland, or the desire to liquidate the State of Israel and destroy the Jewish people? Is the insurrection a war by an entire nation or co-ordinated acts by groups of individual criminals? Such questions could not be answered by religious texts, only by modern military experts. But different opinions would be given by different military experts. Which Jewish values were deemed most

important – the dignity of all human beings created in the image of God
or Jewish national rights to the Land? Was it simply a question of justice
where Palestinian rights were concerned? If unjust acts ensured Jewish
national survival, wasn't it better to be right than just? If the demolition
of the homes of families of Palestinian offenders worked as a deterrent
despite the injustice of the act against innocent, unknowing relatives,
wasn't it right? If the ill-treatment of twenty suspects uncovered the
genuine terrorist about to carry out an atrocity, didn't this outweigh
the injustice done to the other nineteen? For example, the former
Ashkenazi Chief Rabbi of Israel, Shlomo Goren, is a strong advocate of
territorial settlement and an opponent of any territorial concession. He
often draws upon the writings of Nachmanides to fortify his arguments.
The former Sephardi Chief Rabbi of Israel, Ovadia Yosef, however,
believes that peace is more important than land and would be willing
to compromise, given acceptable security precautions. Ovadia Yosef
often quotes Maimonides to support his point of view.

From the four religious parties elected to the Knesset in 1988, two –
Shas and Degel Ha'Torah – placed greater stress on peace and security
than on retaining the Territories.

In addition, religious intellectuals and academics, as well as Western
immigrants, have opposed the fundamentalism and anti-rationalism of
the settlers. 'Eretz Israel is more important to me than anything
. . . but the integrity of Am Israel, the Jewish People, is an even
higher value than this sacred Land'.[13] Shortly after the massacre in
the Sabra and Shatilla camps in 1982, a religious peace movement,
Netivot Shalom (Paths to Peace) was formed. In their platform, they
stated that

> 'the laws of the Torah were not meant to wreak vengeance upon
> the world, but to spread goodness, mercy and peace' – we call
> upon religious Zionism to return the sanctity of life, peace and
> respect for others – Jew and non-Jew alike – to the top of its
> scale of values. It is our religious duty to seek peace. We must
> not let an exclusive commitment to keeping all of the Land
> of Israel under our control stop us from pursuing it – even
> though this may demand that we accept the idea of territorial
> compromise.

All agreed that the Land was holy and that Jews were commanded to
live in it. But what price was to be paid for living in Judea and Samaria?
Would it be contrary to other Jewish traditions to exact that price? Or did
the commandment to settle the Land override all other considerations?
Was it right to argue that this commandment was equivalent to all the
other commandments put together?

On the Palestinians

The Land was not empty but inhabited by another people, the Palestinians. For religious Jews – and indeed for many secular Jews – the Land of Israel had always rightly belonged to the Jews. It was given as an inheritance. Those who lived in it in their absence were there only in a temporary capacity and had no inherent claim to sovereignty.

The status of these temporary inhabitants is the subject of dispute. According to Maimonides, idolators are forbidden to live in the Land on even a temporary basis, yet this does not apply to Muslims, since they are monotheists. Significantly, Maimonides had lived in Egypt and therefore had a positive opinion of Muslims but not of Christians, from whom he had fled and whom he regarded as idolators. Avraham Yitzhak Kook regarded the Arab inhabitants of the Land as *ger toshav* (resident aliens). Kook believed that the Arabs had indeed observed the seven Noahide laws on basic human behaviour applicable to non-Jews. They had refrained from idolatry, murder and sexual perversion, and had thereby earned the status of *ger toshav* in Jewish law.

Shlomo Goren does not accept that the Palestinians have earned this status. Moreover, he observes that a non-Jew can become a *ger toshav* only when the Jubilee laws are in effect. These laws called for the return of property to its original owners every fifty years and were a significant restriction on the accumulation of wealth. Such laws lapsed with the fall of the Second Temple and the dissolution of the Sanhedrin, the supreme political, religious and judicial body in Palestine during the Roman period. In Jewish law the Palestinians are therefore in a legal no-man's land, and even their civil rights cannot be recognized in a halachic sense. Goren has also argued that 'those Muslims among us who do not engage in terror, nor act against the State of Israel' may enjoy the privileges rather than the status of *ger toshav*.[14]

If a *ger toshav* accepts the Noahide laws, carries them out and even converts, then he would be elevated to a still loftier status in Jewish law: *ger tsedek* – the righteous alien. Yet even here, maximalists such as Shlomo Goren argue that 'this is only true . . . if he [the Palestinian] keeps the laws because God commanded them in the Torah, but not if he observes the laws because of his own logic. This proviso, noted by Maimonides, excludes Muslims from gaining this special status'.[15] This suggests that the Palestinians must read Rashi, Maimonides and Tosafot and be conversant with the arguments therein.

Religious minimalists imply that there is a political motive behind the reticence to grant status in Jewish law to Palestinians, since this would lead to equal rights and equality under the law. Instead of analysing the fundamental basis of a problem, minimalists argue that many religious inhabitants of the Territories begin with their general perception of a solution and then locate sources to justify it halachically. They also point out that the status of *ger toshav* is applicable only on an individual basis. It does not refer to the Palestinians in the sense of their existence as an ethnic community.

Maimonides argued in his *Mishna Torah* that once someone is accepted as a *ger toshav*, then 'we are duty bound to avoid judicial discrimination against him' (Hilchot Melachim 10:12). Thus the deportation of Palestinians accused of incitement could not proceed unless this form of punishment were also implemented against Meir Kahane and his followers. Similarly, while the homes of the families of suspected terrorists are demolished without due judicial procedure, no such discrimination was practised against Jewish terrorists convicted of both murder and terror.[16]

Some religious thinkers have found justification for both transfer and expulsion of the Palestinian Arabs: 'When you pass over the Jordan into the land of Canaan, then you shall drive out all the inhabitants of the land before you, and destroy all their figured stones, and destroy all their molten images, and destroy all their high places. And you shall drive out all the inhabitants of the land and dwell therein; for unto you have I given the land to possess it' (Numbers 33:52–3). Rabbi Eliezer Waldenberg, for example, the winner of the Israel Prize in 1976, has argued in favour of banning gentiles from Jerusalem.[17]

Some have justified methods to ensure the creeping emigration of the Palestinian, for God told Moses that 'I will not drive them out from before thee in one year, lest the land become desolate, and the beasts of the field multiply against thee. By little and little, I will drive them out from before thee, until thou be increased and inherit the land' (Exodus 23:29–30). Minimalists have pointed out that this applies only to the seven Canaanite nations and has no contemporary relevance, since the Arabs are not considered to be their descendants. Maximalists have quoted Nachmanides' dictum to drive foreign inhabitants out of the Land. In particular, Moses' address to the people of Israel, telling them that 'when the Lord your God shall deliver them [the Canaanite nations] up before you, and you shall smite them; then you shall utterly destroy them; you shall make no covenant with them, nor show mercy unto them' (Deuteronomy 7:2). The last phrase 'nor show mercy to them', in the sense of showing no grace to them, has often been understood by maximalists as a refusal to permit them to make a camp – *lo techanem*. This, however, is not a direct translation but essentially a Midrashic alteration of the basic Hebrew grammar. In turn, *lo techanem* is interpreted as not allowing the Palestinians to maintain a presence in the Land today.[18]

Many Jewish settlers in the Territories have not so far followed this course of events. Instead, they stress the benefits to the Palestinians of a better life as a result of an Israeli presence. During a march through Jericho on Israel's Independence Day in 1987, Gush Emunim supporters distributed leaflets condemning both the PLO and Peace Now for stirring up nationalist passions. They exhorted the inhabitants to 'go out and see how settlement and Jewish neighbours have brought you livelihood, homes, television sets, cars and a standard of living you and you forefathers never dreamed of . . . when we settle in Jericho, you will also enjoy blessing and prosperity. Jews living in your city is the safest assurance that you and your children will continue living in this country.' Palestinian nationalism in control would lead only to bloodshed and a new Israeli invasion, 'therefore it is in your interest to prevent an Israeli withdrawal to prevent the next war. Under our rule your future is assured'.

Whilst the Palestinians have undoubtedly prospered under Israeli rule – they now have a longer life expectancy and a considerable decrease in infant mortality – their fundamental aspirations to national self-expression still conflict with non-negotiable Jewish inheritance to the Land and the right of the religious settlers to exert Jewish sovereignty over it.

Interpretation of wars and borders

The use of military power to maintain Jewish sovereignty in the Territories is often invoked as a religious principle. According to Maimonides, 'when Israel has the upper hand over them, we are forbidden to permit idolators in our midst even when they live there temporarily' (Yad Ha'Hazaka Hilchot Avodat Kochavim 10:6). Others have pointed out that 'an act of power does not create a right; it is, at best, evidence for the existence of a right'.[19] Whilst power is, of course, an unavoidable factor in possessing and retaining the Land, it cannot resolve a conflict of rights. The army, however, is perceived by the religious settlers as a source of righteousness, in that its power can repel not only any physical threat but also any ideological challenge to the Jewish right to the Land. Any reluctance to use the army to quell disturbances is viewed as a sign of political and moral weakness on the part of the authorities.

The Intifada is perceived as the latest method of waging war – albeit by different means – against the State of Israel. *'im ba l'horgach hashkem l'horgo'* (Sanhedrin 72a); (If someone comes to kill you, rise up so as to kill him'). Yet such an interpretation, resting on a military basis, can only be made by someone with expertise in that area. Many religious Jews, however, take the view that the Palestinian Arabs as a whole are to blame for the Intifada. Even if the technique involves rocks thrown by children, religious settlers believe that they are essentially aimed at eliminating the State and are evidence of Palestinian determination to wage war. Today's uprising may become tomorrow's *jihad* (holy war). This characterization of the conflict lends itself to a definition and to the subsequent question of whether it is an elective war (*milchemet reshut*) or an obligatory war (*milchemet mitzva*) and a war of duty (*milchemet hova*) within Jewish law. Given the hostility of its neighbours, there is a deep belief that all wars are obligatory in order to ensure the survival of the nation. The humanity of Judaism lies in its lack of rigidity: 'you shall live by them [the commandments]' (Leviticus 18:5) and 'you shall not die by them [the Talmud]'. The exception to the rule is when defence is necessary and the life of the nation is at stake. Thus, if all wars including the Intifada, are interpreted as obligatory, then any sacrifice in Jewish lives is justified since there is no violation of the rule 'you shall live by them'. Unlike an elective war, where up to a sixth of the population may perish before action can be taken against the decision-makers, there is no limitation on the number of casualties in an obligatory war. Therefore Shlomo Goren is specific about his attitude towards the Intifada:

> today the Arabs have launched a rebellion against us, with injuries and fatalities to Jewish soldiers and civilians. Their aim is to uproot us not only from parts of Eretz Israel: their ultimate goal is to destroy the entire State of Israel. Our struggle against the Intifada is in the category of an obligatory war which according to the *poskim*, is a super-*milchemet mitzva* [obligatory war] calling for *mesirut nefesh* – the utmost devotion. [20]

There is also an underlying feeling that the Intifada is a symbolic war – a challenge to the Jewish right to the Land. To ignore this challenge would be a sign of weakness and compromise and, in religious terms, tantamount to a *hillul ha'Shem* (the profanation of God's name).

Indeed, in contrast to this approach, some religious thinkers have argued that the war in Lebanon in 1982 was elective, or that the Intifada did not directly threaten the life of the nation. There are also many religious Jews who do not interpret the events since 1967 in terms of a metahistorical situation evoking mystical wonder, but make a critical analysis on the basis of historical development. For example, whilst there is agreement that the Land is sacred and that Jews are commanded to live in it, it is the Land that is holy and not its borders, which, according to a wide range of Jewish sources, are continually changing:

> The boundaries of Canaan at the time of the sons of Noah and their generations are not those promised to Abraham and his descendants in the 'Covenant between the Pieces' [Genesis 10:19, 15:18–21] and both of these differ on the boundaries

promised to the children of Israel in the desert [Exodus 23:31];
or prior to entering the Land [Deuteronomy 1:7, 33:2–4]. There
is a further discrepancy between the various promises in the
Pentateuch and those for the End of Days provided in Ezekiel
[47:13]. None of these boundaries coincides with those the tribes
were to inherit by lot according to Numbers [34:2–12]; nor are
they the same as those of the inheritance and settlement found in
Joshua [12] and Judges [3, 4]. And none of these boundaries even
compares with those of the second inheritance at the time of Ezra
and Nehemiah or in the days of King Yannai and Agrippa I. [21]

Clearly, the lack of definition regarding the exact boundaries of
Eretz Israel gives rise to problems of *Halacha*, since a number of
commandments pertain only to the Land.

In addition, King Solomon is cited as surrendering part of the Land.
He offered twenty Galilean cities to Hiram, King of Tyre, for his
help in constructing the First Temple. This precedent has remained
unexplained and is a source of puzzlement for those who advocate
retaining the Land.

Giving up the Land

By the 1990s, a quarter of a century after the Israeli conquest of the
Territories, settling the Land for many religious Jews was not only a
question of fulfilling the commandment and an exercise of pioneering
enterprise, but also a way of living a religious life within a community
in which they felt comfortable. For example, the new dormitory
settlement of Efrat drew many apolitical religious Jews from Europe
and the United States through the quality of its life. The charismatic
leadership of Rabbi Shlomo Riskin, a mild nationalist who exhibited
American liberal ideals, attracted many. It was not so much a question
of ideology, more one of Jewish identification and religious affiliation.

Efrat was exceptional amongst the settlements. A high proportion of
its inhabitants came from North America and Europe. They were very
highly educated, with a disproportionate number of professionals from
a variety of disciplines, and thereby replicated the liberal attitudes of
Jews in similar socio-economic positions in the West. Paradoxically,
although they lived in the Territories, many voted for political parties
such as Meimad and Ratz which advocated the return of territory for
peace in the 1988 elections. They felt secure that Efrat would not be
returned in the event of a peace settlement, since they were part of
the Gush Etzion bloc which was in Jewish hands until 1948. Moreover,
its inhabitants understood that because of its proximity to the Green
Line, it was highly likely that, if peace were established, Efrat would

be included within the contours of Israel in any border adjustments.

Religious moderates were derided for their faintheartedness and weakness in not living in Judea and Samaria. Those who raised questions of ethical conduct were often labelled *yefei nefesh* (do-gooders). They were accused of not facing up to the real problems of the area and of avoiding tough decisions. Giving back the Territories was the easy way out – it was a way of lifting a personal burden, but it was not a fundamental political and religious answer. Gush Emunim promoted themselves as 'builders of the Land' through settlement, whilst their quibbling opponents could not point to any such achievements. Even pleas for peace with the Palestinians in terms of mutual vested interests were ridiculed as unworthy. The Jewish idea of peace was a total perfection as prophesied by Isaiah and Micah for the End of Days. A liberal disposition, when it came to the Palestinians, was often attributed to growing up in a Christian society. The history of the twentieth century was often invoked to condemn the outsider and the conciliator. Shlomo Goren told Israeli television viewers at the end of 1988 that Hitler and Stalin had bankrupted 'humanism'. The idea of 'a people that dwells alone' justified their approach to the Territories and to their self-imposed isolation from international criticism.

Shlomo Goren's colleague, the former Sephardi Chief Rabbi of Israel Ovadia Yosef, often advocated a more liberal course of action which would involve territorial compromise. He argued that the continued retention of the Territories endangered Jewish life. The saving of Jewish lives, *pikuach nefesh*, superseded every other commandment in the Torah, with the exception of idol-worship, sexual promiscuity and bloodshed. Indeed, as long ago as 1979, he said that Israel could negotiate with the PLO if it renounced its Charter and accepted United Nations Resolutions 242 and 338.[22] Resolution 242 had been passed by the Security Council of the United Nations in November 1967. It called for an end to the state of war, recognition of all countries in the region, Israel's withdrawal to the pre-1967 borders and a just settlement and lasting peace. Resolution 338 which initiated the ceasefire in the Yom Kippur War called for the instant implementation of Resolution 242. In view of the trauma of Jewish history, *pikuach nefesh* has been of more than purely academic value. Indeed, it has achieved a supreme status in Jewish tradition. For example, Rabbi Soloveitchik of Brisk was once asked whether the murder of millions of Jews during the Second World War would have been worthwhile if it had brought forth the Age of Redemption. He replied that it was preferable for salvation to be deferred and that the Messiah should not come rather than sacrifice even one Jewish life. *Pikuach nefesh* was also invoked by a number of outraged religious moderates when the news of the massacre of Palestinians in the Sabra and Shatilla camps reached them. One commented, 'If I could have saved some children's lives in Sabra and Shatilla by desecrating all the Sabbaths in the world, I would have done so'. [23]

Yet Rabbi Shlomo Goren continued to argue that the holiness of the Land superseded the saving of life. One rabbinical response was that this assertion was rooted in paganism:

> Of the 743 mentions of holiness in the Tanach [the Bible], only two are associated with land. All mentions of Holiness refer to God personally and to objects belonging to His Sanctuary, or to man in his attachment or to reflection of God. There is no intrinsic holiness in earth or sticks or stones – such a belief is sheer paganism from which the prophets sought to redeem Israel. [24]

Another argument put forward against the Jewish settlers in the Territories was that the Land in itself was not holy, but that its holiness stemmed from the approach of its inhabitants: 'The sanctity of the Land lies in the significance of the obligation to observe codes of behaviour and commandments which are dependent on the Land. The sanctity is expressed in the way of life and does not constitute an imminent holiness carved in the ground, on a tree, or in a stone'. The suggestion that the Land was imbued with an imminent characteristic of holiness 'leads to the adoption of an extreme stance concerning territory and the resulting policies'. [25]

In an address to the Rav Kook Institute in August 1989, Ovadia Yosef interpreted the biblical injunction to drive out the inhabitants of the Land and to settle it as a promise to be fulfilled when the Jewish people merited it and not as a definitive commandment. Neither did he believe that there was a commandment to conquer the Land at present. This would be active only when the Messiah came.

Whilst accepting the commandment to live in the Land, Ovadia Yosef's approach rested on whether remaining in the Land or relinquishing it would cause the greater Jewish bloodshed. Lacking the military and political experience to make a qualified decision, he consulted four military men, Raful Eitan, Ezer Weizmann, Rehavam Ze'evi and Yitzhak Rabin – and, not surprisingly, received divided opinions. Ovadia Yosef concluded that a decision to leave the Territories could not be made at present while there was substantial opposition to a Palestinian State. His interpretation of Nachmanides also differed from that of Shlomo Goren, for in his view the medieval scholar believed that the Land should be regarded as one's own property. Ovadia Yosef asked how anyone today could relate the dangers of the West Bank with the tranquillity of one's own property.

The PLO's declaration of a State of Palestine and its public intention to engage in a dialogue with Israel did not – at least initially – make any impression on Ovadia Yosef; he maintained that there was still no one to talk to and thus the use of *pikuach nefesh* to give up territory was hypothetical.

The shedding of blood – *shefichut damim* – was an argument increasingly used by religious moderates: 'Who so sheds the blood of man, by man shall his blood be shed; for in the image of God made He man' (Genesis 9:6). Thus King David was not permitted to build the Temple because, as a man of war, he had spilt too much blood. Even the person who had perpetrated an intentional killing was not permitted to return from a city of refuge before the death of the High Priest.

The Mishna deals clearly and heavily with responsibility for the shedding of blood. If through erroneous testimony a witness causes a person to be condemned to death for a capital offence, then the witness is answerable for his blood and the blood of his posterity. When Cain killed Abel, God noted that Cain's potential descendants had also been slain: 'the voice of your brother's bloods cries out to me from the ground' (Genesis 4:10).

The popular saying from Sanhedrin, 'he who saves one life, it is as if he has saved the whole world', was widely quoted in the rescue of Jews in times of adversity. However, it is complemented by its corollary: 'but a single man was created in the world to teach that if any man has caused a single soul to perish from Israel, Scripture imputes it to him as though he had caused a whole world to perish'.[26] Moreover, this Mishnaic emphasis against the shedding of blood was particularized by the addition of 'from Israel' by presumably nationalist commentators in the past. The addition does not occur in the Jerusalem Talmud, only in the Babylonian Talmud.[27]

The new religious political parties

One factor in Ovadia Yosef's clear opposition to the retention of the Territories was the increased economic burden on Israel's Sephardim. The resentment against the Ashkenazi élite, and particularly the Labour Party, was very deep. In an address in 1984, Ovadia Yosef said that 93 per cent of the prison population were Sephardim: 'Whoever heard of Jews committing murder and rape and robbery in the countries from which they had come? They took away our traditions and tried to force European culture on us.'[28] Ovadia Yosef's views tended to be less dogmatic and more open than his Ashkenazi counterparts. This was in line with traditional Sephardi thinking. Paradoxically, many Sephardi parents, rejecting secular Labour education, had instead sent their sons and daughters to ultra-orthodox Ashkenazi schools and seminaries, thus inculcating in them an unfamiliar narrowness and intolerance. Whilst this may have had political ramifications in the

ascendancy of Revisionism, there was a growing antagonism within
the religious world:

> Many Sephardim felt humiliated because they were usually
> considered second-rate students, less sharp-witted than the
> Lithuanians; but they had developed virtually unbounded admi-
> ration for the great masters of *Halacha* who headed the *yeshivas*.
> The insults by Ashkenazis were particularly resented when it
> came to politics. Sephardis felt ignored by the Ashkenazi leaders
> in the strongest *haredi* political party, the Aguda, which was then
> controlled by a combination of chassidic and Lithuanian leaders
> who allowed them no representation. [29]

In the early 1980s Ovadia Yosef decided to break with the Aguda in an
attempt to divert funds from primarily Ashkenazi institutions of religious
learning, thus helping to eradicate the social deprivations which afflicted
the Sephardim. A political party, Shas (Sephardi Torah Guardians) was
formed to fight the 1984 elections. The efforts of many newly religious
young Sephardim in the neighbourhoods sent four representatives to
the Knesset. In addition, Ovadia Yosef found an unlikely partner
in his struggle: the octogenarian and revered former head of the
Agudat Yisrael Council of Sages, Rabbi Eliezer Menachem Schach.
The alliance between the Ashkenazi non-Zionist Schach and Ovadia
Yosef had come about though the former's growing awareness of
the plight of the Sephardim and his emphasis on peace rather than
Territories. He condemned Gush Emunim as a 'false messiah' and
also decried the stand on the Territories of the National Religious
Party, for whom 'blood is not important'. During the war in Lebanon,
Schach had labelled Sharon as a *rodef* (assailant), and during the
post-electoral coalition discussions in 1988 he had refused to receive
him at home because of his stated preoccupation with his studies.

Schach, however, was no Western liberal. He had another motive for
effectively splitting the ultra-orthodox political camp, or at least bringing
divisions into public view by resigning from the Aguda Council of Sages
in 1983. The growing influence of neo-Zionism within ultra-orthodoxy
concerned him theologically – and the influence of the Lubavitcher
Rebbe, Menachem Schneerson, in particular. Schach adhered to a
more fundamentalist school of thought when it came to an appraisal
of Zionism. Even in the Land of Israel, the Jewish people were still in
exile. Only the coming of the Messiah and the Age of Redemption could
usher in the true Israel and the ingathering of the exiles. A secular State
of Jews was not a Jewish State. When the State threatened to conscript
his *yeshiva* students into the Defence Forces, he declared that he would
close down his institutes of Jewish learning and move them with their
inhabitants to another country.

Unlike other sectors of ultra-orthodoxy, members of Schach's Lithuanian school had not softened their approach to Zionism and Israeli society. Despite the earlier antagonism of many ultra-orthodox circles, the impact of the establishment of the State and their participation in its national life had essentially changed their hostile attitudes to the Zionist experiment – although few would embrace the label 'Zionist'. Although the Lubavitcher Rebbe lived in the United States, many of his followers lived in Israel. He had established Kfar Chabad as a Lubavitch village. This had been done because the non-Zionist Lubavitch movement saw modern Israel as yet another repository for the *nitzotzot* (divine sparks) scattered to the four corners of the world. The premise for Lubavitch activity in Israel was not a Zionist one, but one which prepared the way for the restoration of a true Jewish State in a Messianic age. In the non-Zionist Aguda, the Gur Hassidim had played an important role in the establishment of the settlement of Immanuel in the Territories. The Aguda was 'a-Zionist, but not anti-Zionist'.[30] Schach's response was to declare a *herem* (prohibition) on the new settlement.

Schach and the Lithuanian school stood firm against this perceived 'creeping Zionism' and an acceptance of the Jewish State despite all the contradictions which arose from living in it and participating in its affairs. All opponents were termed 'Zionists' even though they may have been far from fitting that definition in a classical sense. Schach regarded Schneerson as a 'pseudo-Messiah' and viewed the Lubavitch movement's worldwide activities with considerable suspicion. Moreover, Lubavitch espoused a maximalist position on the Territories, which he strongly opposed because he believed that the nations of the world should not be provoked on the issue. Thus he condemned Israel's attack on the Iraqi nuclear reactor in 1981. Schach's world-view was traditionally that of a pre-Zionist Diaspora religious leader. Ironically, his position on the Territories as a non-Zionist thus coincided with that of the most dovish secular Zionists.

The 1988 election in Israel provided the public platform for a religious confrontation. The Lubavitcher Rebbe from Crown Heights in Brooklyn entered the political arena for the first time and urged his followers to vote for Aguda. Many thousands who possessed Israeli passports returned from the United States and Europe to cast their vote. Ovadia Yosef also appealed to the faithful, offering to redeem vows they may have made to commit themselves to the Aguda. On television, Ovadia Yosef told viewers to vote for Shas and receive God's blessing. He even ruled that it was a *mitzva* (commandment) to distribute Shas's posters on the Jewish Sabbath. Indeed, Ovadia Yosef's election addresses were received with all the adulation given to a film star. In Ashkelon, a crowd waited until midnight – an extra four hours – to hear him. In Kiryat Shemona, his helicopter was unable to land because a huge crowd blocked the runway.

Rabbi Schach inspired the formation of a new party, Degel Ha'Torah (the Flag of the Torah) to attract the non-Hassidic vote from the Ashkenazi ultra-orthodox. The result was a big increase in the vote for the religious parties. Degel Ha'torah received two seats and Shas six:

Percentage of National Vote

Religious Party	1984	1988
Agudat Israel	1.7	4.5
Degel Ha'Torah	–	1.5
Shas	3.1	4.7
Ultra-Orthodox vote	4.8	10.7

With the inclusion of the vote for the National Religious Party and Meimad, the vote of the religious camp jumped from 11.4 per cent in 1984 to over 15 per cent in 1988.[31]

Aryeh Deri of Shas assumed the position of Minister of the Interior. He inherited and developed a system of political patronage by earmarking increasing sums to go to religious institutions. In 1987, there was a budget allocation of 15 million shekels to religious institutions without providing criteria. Three years later, the Knesset passed the 1990–1 budget law which allocated 230 million shekels to religious institutions. Over 90 million shekels went without any explanation to 223 institutions listed by name. In part, this was due to Shas's use of the balance of power between the two major political blocs. Deri's carrot-and-stick relationship with many municipalities, and his disproportionate distribution of funds to Shas- and Degel Ha'Torah-sponsored institutions, prompted the State Comptroller to initiate an investigation into special funding to religious institutions on the municipal level.

Shas was divided politically, even though Ovadia Yosef had expounded pronounced dovish views during the 1988 campaign. The entry of the religious parties, the minimalist Shas and Degel Ha'Torah and the maximalist National Religious Party and Agudat Yisrael into the coalition government was symptomatic of the political division of religious Israel as well as of its secular majority. It also offered the distinct possibility of switching to a narrow Labour-led coalition in the future.

This possibility manifested itself in March 1990 when the dovish members of Shas brought about the downfall of the Likud government when five out of its six Knesset members absented themselves during a vote of no confidence. This move was masterminded by Rabbi Aryeh Deri and Ovadia Yosef. Both felt that Likud's procrastination on progress in the peace process, its inability to give a coherent answer to the US administration on an acceptance or rejection of the Baker Plan, and the infighting in the party between the hardline 'Constraints Ministers' – Sharon, Levy and Modai'i – would lead the country towards another war rather than towards dialogue with the Palestinians. But they did not bargain for the backlash from grassroots Shas voters, many of whom were former Likud enthusiasts. Deri in particular became a target for opprobrium and was compared to militant left-wing secularists such as Yossi Sarid. Even more important was the reaction to such a move by Rabbi Schach, who emerged as the real spiritual leader of both Shas and Degel Ha'Torah. He called Deri to his home in ultra-orthodox B'nei Brak and gave him a dressing down. Shortly afterwards, the youthful Deri was at pains to forget his hitherto dovish statements and to endorse the Likud enthusiastically. Thus, in a volte-face *extraordinaire*, Shas, having brought down the Likud-led government, proceeded to announce that it still favoured a Likud-led over a Labour government.

This left Ovadia Yosef somewhat in limbo. He supported the Baker Plan as a central path to peace. He warned that a narrow right-wing government would isolate Israel amongst the nations of the world and that only Labour could avert further bloodshed and war. Ovadia Yosef's exhortations were ignored and he soon lapsed into silence. Rabbi Schach effectively held the balance of power between the two major blocs. It was not a position that he relished, since it involved him even more deeply in the heretic 'Zionist' state. Yet his rivals in Agudat Yisrael had agreed to serve in a Labour-led coalition and had extracted lucrative concessions from Labour in return for its support. Thus when Rabbi Schach appeared at the first national convention of Degel Ha'Torah, he attacked the kibbutzim and their 'new Torah' and questioned their Jewishness. Thereby, he indicated his dislike for a Labour-led coalition of left-wingers and secularists and so did not even have to endorse Likud formally. Rabbi Schach put his abhorrence of secularism and his fear of the influence of Agudat Yisrael above his 'liberal' views on the peace process and the future of the Territories. Ironically, in the summer of 1990 both Rabbi Schach and his theological arch-rival, the Lubavitcher Rebbe, endorsed the formation of a narrow right-wing government led by Yitzhak Shamir.

Even so, Israelis from many political viewpoints were furious at Schach's remarks at the Degel Ha'torah convention, where a nonagenarian cleric with exceedingly few votes at the last election could exert considerable influence on the future political direction of the State. The fact that he and his adherents derided the Zionist creed – there was no Israeli flag, no singing of the national anthem and no presence of an Israeli President at their conference – rankled deeply. All this led to a public demand for a new electoral system which would make the country governable and which would not place its destiny in the hands of peripheral groups.

Religion and morality

One interesting development of the 1988 election was the emergence of the religious party Meimad, which campaigned on a platform of religious moderation. It attracted primarily religious intellectuals, Western immigrants and disillusioned adherents of the National Religious Party. Yet it failed to win even one seat. Its appearance, however, indicated a concern in religious intellectual circles with Israeli action in suppressing the Intifada.

The question of morality was at the core of their discomfort. The Torah taught that the Arabs too were created in God's image and possessed a right to national self-expression and to basic human freedoms. For the religious doves it was a question of which religious values would shape their Jewish existence. The emphasis on peace achieved a supreme priority in their religious vocabulary: 'Seek peace and pursue it' (Psalms 34:15).

There was also a sense that the special moral status of the Jew in tradition and in history was gradually being abandoned. If a religious Jew prays that he has been chosen 'from amongst the nations' to fulfil divinely alloted tasks, how can Israel be urged to act like all the other nations – act in a way which may involve violations of human rights, domination over other peoples and acts of violence? The retreat from chosenness and the universalism within Jewish tradition towards a narrow nationalism were the essential factors which motivated the creation of a religious peace movement. Despite their small number, it was a feeling of general indifference amongst the religious public in Israel that catalysed their activities. The war in Lebanon proved to be a watershed. Although Israel did not commit the massacre of Palestinians at Sabra and Shatilla, it also failed to prevent it. As the leading scholar and supporter of the Lubavitch movement, Rabbi Adin Steinsaltz, commented shortly afterwards, 'the State is down to an unadmired natural size'.[32] The danger that 'indifference to evil is more insidious than evil itself' deeply affected religious moderates. Moreover, they viewed the moral dilemmas created by settling the Land as a challenge to democracy and the authority of the State.

In contrast, Jewish inhabitants of the Territories increasingly disregarded the importance of democratic institutions: 'Certain principles cannot be subject to democracy . . . [the Arabs] must accept settlement in Judea and Samaria as a basic principle of Jewish existence and a moral foundation of this State'.[33] Morality in a conventional understanding could thus be construed differently – or not considered at all. Even the fundamental understanding of chosenness could be looked upon in a completely different light: 'The people of Israel are commanded to be holy – but not necessarily to be moral or human according to ordinary criteria. The moral teachings which have been accepted by mankind, in principle at least, do not commit the Jew who was chosen to be beyond them'.[34] The Intifada crystallized moral dilemmas which many Israelis – perhaps the majority – were unable to confront.

There were many alternative and indeed contrasting views of these all-important questions. For example, would the acceptance of Palestinian nationalism eventually undermine the physical security of the Jewish people in Israel? Whilst the right to Palestinian national self-expression could not be denied in view of the Jewish experience, could a Palestinian State prevent even the occasional terrorist attack on the Jewish State? Moreover, if the occupation and its reflection, the Intifada, undermined the moral *raison d'être* for the State, then wouldn't this also be a spiritual threat to the State in that many troubled people would simply leave? If the Intifada was an act of civil disobedience rather than one of all-out war, then how should a Jew respond? How should one respond to personal physical attacks even if the weapons used were primitive? What constitutes a life-threatening situation? What methods should be used to extract information from Palestinians suspected of planning to murder family or friends? How does one determine which Palestinians should be interrogated?

These dilemmas were of deep concern to many religious Jews – and especially to religious moderates who served in the Territories during the Intifada. At a public meeting of Netivot Shalom (Paths to Peace), the religious peace movement, early in 1988, Rabbi Aaron Lichtenstein tried to elucidate the religious problems:

> I was asked a series of questions regarding the circumstances in which it is possible for a soldier to disobey an order. I responded in the only way I could, halachically and morally. In principle it is clear that sometimes one may – in fact, must – disobey an order, as Maimonides emphatically ruled: 'Whoever disobeys a royal decree because he is engaged in the performance of a religious command, even if it be a light command, is not liable, because [when there is a conflict] between the edict of the Master [God] and the edict of the servant [the king], the former takes precedence over the latter. It goes without saying that if the king issues an order annulling a religious precept, no heed is paid to it (Hilchot Melachim U Milchamotahem, 3:9).

Lichtenstein then went on to say that the violence of the throwers of Molotov cocktails and stones should not be allowed to continue

unchecked: 'Terrifying and sickening as it is, there may be no alternative
to much of what is going on presently. But if that is the case, then
what we have before us – at least in part – is what the halachic
vocabulary refers to as "criminal action leading one into a situation of
compulsion".'

A number of Jewish inhabitants of the Territories gradually began
to give some thought to how they could co-exist with Palestinians and
with Palestinian nationalism. The Rabbi of the settlement of Tekoa,
Menachem Froman, enunciated the idea of *ha' medina ha' enoshit* (the
humane state) to replace the conventional idea of the nation-state.
He promulgated the idea of two states on the same territory – 'an
international entity in the Land of Israel'. However, individuals such
as Froman were in a distinct minority and their ideas dismissed as
utopian and unworkable.

The religious problem of how to confront the Intifada was perhaps
symbolic of a fundamental question of Jewish existence: 'What
relationship should the Jews have with people who are the "other",
– given that the "other" in Jewish history has been a frightening, hostile
and problematic proposition. What accommodation should we make to
that history and at the same time live with the moral standards that we
feel is an expression of our best selves?'[35]

A survey conducted amongst the settlers in the early 1980s showed
that only 45 per cent believed that attempts should be made to
cultivate good relations with Arabs.[36] Even before the Palestinian
uprising of 1987, the settlers regarded those who opposed them
more as an issue of social deviance than of moral conviction. Their
fear of the 'other' was deep and often disproportionate to the threat.
Their increasing lack of confidence in both government and military
institutions led to a dependence on vigilantism which was perceived
as a justifiable means of social control. Some 70 per cent of settlers
agreed that a quick and independent response was required to deter
Arab harassment of settlers and settlements. Many religious settlers
came to see themselves as agents of legal control and found it difficult
to distinguish between actions that they had been ordered to perform
as reservists in uniform and those that they performed as settlers out
of uniform defending themselves. It was also in the tradition of the
self-reliance of the early Zionists. Moreover, the religious settlers
believed that their vigilante activities were within the law, for they
regarded themselves and their land as part of 'Israel' and lived in
the expectation that Judea and Samaria would really be annexed at
some point in the near future. The confusion between legal and
vigilante controls exhibited itself during the trial and conviction of
members of the Jewish terrorist underground, which had close links
with Gush Emunim. Whilst some religious settlers were astounded

at their actions, others sought to justify them because they could identify with their motives. Their crimes were for the good of the cause and they were, in the words of Prime Minister Shamir, 'basically good boys gone astray'. Vigilantism as a means to protect family and property could often have the opposite result. The action of a known Jewish extremist who had been banned by the IDF (Israel Defence Forces) from entering Nablus resulted in the accidental killing of one of his charges, a fifteen-year-old girl from the settlement of Elon Moreh. A fracas with stone-throwers from the village of Beita thus indicated the dangers of the law of the gun.

The onset of the Intifada and the official policy to carry out beatings rather than kill people fortified and exhalted vigilantism. The sense that vigilantism was merely a form of legal control in different circumstances deepened.

Part II

Israel and the Diaspora

4

Israeli–Diaspora Relations

A Diaspora with a view

Should Diaspora Jews criticize the policy of a government of Israel? This question has been the subject of an intense debate within the Jewish world since the ascendancy of Likud to power in 1977. The war in Lebanon and the Intifada itself propelled the controversy to the forefront of communal concerns in the Diaspora. No longer could the subject be ignored or its proponents marginalized by a reticent leadership.

The problem of Diaspora criticism of official Israeli policies is not a new one; it has its roots in the origins of Zionism. Although Western detractors of Zionism have attempted to transform it into a monolithic entity, Zionist ideology, in reality, embraces a wide spectrum of diverse thought. However, there have always been considerable differences of opinion which led to repeated schisms and unbridgeable bitterness. Moreover, it was always an open question whether Zionism should be absolutist in its demand that every Jew should move to a future Jewish State. Herzl, Ben-Gurion and Jabotinsky believed that the Diaspora should be rapidly emptied and its inhabitants emigrate to Israel forthwith. Ahad Ha'am, Moshe Sharret and Nahum Goldman took a different view, believing that, like it or not, the reality was simply that all Jews would not uproot themselves. Whilst many were passionate 'lovers of Zion', they were not Zionists. Ahad Ha'am and those who followed him conceived of a Jewish State at the centre of an invigorated Jewish world, supplying spiritual and cultural succour to those brothers and sisters who chose to remain in *galut* (self-imposed exile).

Even so, no one could have foreseen the Shoah and the destruction of the very people for whom the State was being created. This was the cruel irony of the final establishment of the State of Israel after two millennia of powerlessness. Zionism was aimed primarily at the Jewish masses of Eastern and Central Europe, even though Jewish diplomacy acted through the capitals of Western Europe. With the destruction of the Jewish centres of Poland and Lithuania during the Holocaust, the Zionist experiment in Palestine lost a vast number of its potential inhabitants and arguably the source of a deep spiritual commitment and cultural enrichment.

In the stark bleakness of the post-war Jewish world, even Ben-Gurion had to revise his attitude to the Diaspora. Whereas the classical Zionist solution of rescue and redemption might apply both to the pitiful remnant who had survived the concentration camps and to oppressed Jewry in unfree countries, it was clear that, despite the outpouring of emotion and support, the vast majority of Jews in the advanced countries of the West had no intention of leaving them for the Jewish State. In the United States in particular, the Jews did not perceive themselves as a minority in a majority culture: they too participated in its establishment and development as one ethnic group in a society of immigrants. Unlike European Jews, they truly felt at home and were only too willing to offer to each and every US government their opinions – as Jews – on a whole range of subjects. Moreover, anti-semitism and discrimination, although ever present, were certainly on the wane. Jews could live well materially, and also live a rich Jewish life if they so wished. Truly, the 'Goldene Medina' offered an attractive alternative to a Jewish nation-state.

The declaration of the State in 1948 brought to the fore the vexed question of Israeli–Diaspora relations. Although Ben-Gurion still publicly implored the Diaspora to emigrate to Israel, he knew that only a minute fraction of America's Jews would opt for the Zionist solution. The disappearance of the Diaspora, as Theodor Herzl had conceived of it, therefore seemed an unlikely event, at least in the immediate future. How then should the innovators of the Zionist experiment deal with 'lovers of Zion' who preferred to remain outside? Whilst they partially distinguished between the dream and the reality, the founding generation essentially coped with it by weakening the link between Israel and the Diaspora, by eliminating any real substance in that relationship. The downgrading and effective negation of the Diaspora by Ben-Gurion and his followers was a reaction, psychological and political, to the tragic events of the twentieth century and to the fact that, under the weight of those events, classical Herzlian theory had been shown to be incorrect.

Despite all the propaganda that Israel was the state of the Jewish people, by 1948 the question had clearly presented itself: does Israel belong to its citizens or to the entire Jewish people? As a self-defined movement of national liberation, Zionism had not finished its task with the achievement of independence. A central function, *kibbutz ha'galuyot* (the ingathering of the exiles), had been only partially accomplished and was thus a continuing process. So, unlike other movements that achieve independence and then settle down to a certain normality in the conduct of their affairs, Zionist ideology was still being preached in the Diaspora in order to secure more immigrants, whilst at home that ideology came to be seen as redundant, having achieved its central goal of statehood. While developing the normality of the structure of a nation-state, at the same time they were still involved in the abnormality of a dispersion.

The negation of Zionism

Whilst Israel, as a source of political power, was recognized as the senior partner, the Diaspora continued to exude a conviction that it should participate in the destiny of the State. How that participation should be delineated was a subject of controversy in the early years of the State of Israel. Ben-Gurion had no intention of sharing power with the Diaspora. Israel as an independent nation did not wish overseas Jews to speak on its behalf, to act as *shtadlanim* (court Jews) in the time-honoured sense. Yet after 1948 reality intervened: Israel was in bad economic shape and desperately needed Diaspora support. For this reason, Ben-Gurion often modified his fundamental objection to the mere existence of the Diaspora, confining himself to an occasional rebuke to a Diaspora audience that their place should be in Israel. Moreover, his outlook was bolstered by the 1948 generation, who felt that they had made real sacrifices in building up the Land and in the struggle against hostile neighbours. There was an attitude of disdain for those Diaspora Jews who did not avail themselves of the opportunity to live 'a full Jewish life in the Land of their ancestors' after two millennia of dispersion. This sense of rejection was passed on to the succeeding generations. In 1986 Shimon Peres, then Foreign Minister, circulated a list of Israel's priorities to its embassies around the world. Despite all the talk about partnership, interest in the Diaspora ranked a lowly fifth. By the spring of 1988, an academic writer on Diasporas could comment that 'there has been an unusual amount of hypocrisy, duplicity, unclarity and disregard in the attitudes of various Israeli governments towards Diaspora Jews'.[1]

The question of 'Who is a Zionist?' was clear and simple: it was someone who immigrated and participated in the building up of the country. Yet many lifelong Zionists did not make *aliya* (immigration to Israel) and for many different reasons preferred to remain in the Diaspora, while paradoxically still extolling the virtues of the return to Zion. For the 1948 generation in Israel itself, the term 'Zionism' became a term of ridicule, its exponents ageing Diaspora windbags muttering outdated and irrelevant slogans, powerless Galut Jews exhibiting the mentality derived from 2000 years of subjugation.

Yet there were many Diaspora Jews who did not fit this spitting imagery. The mere existence of a 6-million strong American Jewish community with an abundance of intellectuals, writers, academics and a highly professional leadership did not coincide with the caricature of second-rate Diaspora wheeler-dealers. Nahum Goldman, then the most prominent Diaspora leader and President of the World Zionist Organization, not only opposed Ben-Gurion's nihilistic approach but also offered an ideological justification. In his autobiography Goldman comments that

> the alternation between dispersion and homeland, often co-existence of Diaspora and statehood, is unique in the history of mankind. The somewhat naive Zionist idea that a normal life is possible only in a homeland and that Diaspora life is in some way abnormal is understandable in the light of the historical evolution of other peoples, but it does not hold true for us. We have probably spent far more years of our historical lifetime in the Diaspora than in our own country and it makes no sense to characterize as abnormal a way of life that accounts for more than half of a people's historical existence. Diaspora is simply a characteristic condition of our history; paradoxically it might even be said to be more characteristic than statehood, which we share with hundreds of other peoples. Because of this historical background, Zionism never proclaimed the complete ending of the Diaspora as one of its goals.[2]

Goldman, however, was in a minority. Within a few weeks of the Declaration of Independence in 1948, the Zionist Council decided to transfer all the areas pertaining to Israel's sovereignty from the Jewish Agency to the jurisdiction of the government of Israel. The Jewish Agency itself became a separate body. In 1952 the Knesset passed a law on the status of the World Zionist Organization (WZO), and two years later a covenant was signed between the WZO and the Israeli government. The government recognized that the WZO had been highly instrumental in establishing the State, and in effect assigned to it the Diaspora portfolio. The WZO would be responsible for immigration, absorption and settlement. It would be an educational and information service for the Diaspora, and would encourage the centrality of Israel in Diaspora thinking. As a non-governmental organization dedicated to providing a better life for its fellow Jews in Israel, it could now also qualify for tax-exempt status in the United States and elsewhere. The acceptance of a Diaspora portfolio by the government of Israel, although ideologically impure, could now also be justified as a catalyst for fundraising.

Even so, Ben-Gurion regarded this as no more than a short-term measure, and never accepted it as an ideological reality. He never employed the services of the WZO or made use of its leadership.

Time and again he bypassed the organization and downplayed it, often raising funds independently. Clearly he wished the WZO to diminish in status and finally to wither away. But this development also restricted the accessibility of Diaspora Jews to the centres of decision-making in Israel. A moribund WZO effectively closed off channels which Diaspora Jews could have used to make critical and democratic representation to the Israeli government.

As late as 1966, in an interview published in *Moznayim*, the journal of the Hebrew Writers' Union, Ben-Gurion still referred to the abnormality of the status of the Diaspora Jew, who possessed a 'split personality, part Jew and part citizen of the society in which he lived.' He also interpreted Zionism, commenting that there was no real difference between a Zionist and a non-Zionist in the United States: 'The title of Zionist now embraces entirely different things among which there is no connection, and to speak of Zionism *per se* has no real meaning'.[3]

Over the years, Ben-Gurion's determination to erect Israel's sovereignty as a supreme and decisive precept in all issues concerning the Jewish State became a source of division between Israel and the Diaspora. As early as 1949, both the President of the Zionist Organization of America and the Chairman of the US section of the Jewish Agency resigned their positions in protest at Ben-Gurion's evolving policies. The Diaspora was perceived as having no sovereignty, or at best a distorted one emanating from its abnormal situation. Within the Israeli understanding of 'Diaspora' were grouped both non-Zionists, who never had any ideological commitment to the cause, and lifelong Zionists, who did not intend to emigrate. In addition, no differentiation was made between those Zionists who did intend to emigrate at some point in the future and those who intended to remain in the Diaspora. All were granted the same right of non-interference in Israel's internal affairs, regardless of their past commitment and future intention.

There was, however, a difference in approach by these different interest groups. Many Diaspora Zionists committed themselves to an educational programme, and in particular to the reclamation of the Hebrew language. Historically, however, fundraising tended to be the prerogative of non-Zionists. In 1929 the Jewish Agency was enlarged through the participation of non-Zionists – essentially philanthropists and industrialists – to halt a rapidly deteriorating economic situation. Although essentially a pragmatic measure, it was resented in many Zionist circles. Rabbi Stephen Wise, a leading figure in American Zionism, commented at the time that 'a philanthropic, economic, cultural or spiritual interest in Palestine was laudable and helpful, but it was not Zionism'.[4] There was also a class difference. Affiliation to the Zionist movement – from different ideological quarters – was commonly based on the working and lower-middle classes. Philanthropy represented not simply another class but also another philosophy which was essentially non-ideological.

The loss of Zionist vision

This diffuse approach from non-Zionist philanthropists was, ironically, warmly welcomed by Ben-Gurion after 1948. It provided an access to funds and thereby to political muscle, especially in the United States. The accruing of political capital in the United States by supporters of Israel was deemed far more important than discussion and contribution by Diaspora scholars and educationalists labelling themselves Zionists and recognizing the centrality of Israel. The latter posed an ideological vision and wished to engage in a continuing debate. The non-Zionists, however, were in general all too willing to defer to the 'good sense' of the Israeli leadership. Many willingly accepted the view that they were uninformed about Israel since they did not live there and thereby had nothing to contribute except their money. In political terms, their endeavours on behalf of Israel were confined to support for the country in the broadest sense – and in reality this meant support for the Israeli government. Emphasis was placed on unity. 'We Are One', 'Solidarity with Israel', 'Stand by Israel' were all slogans predicated on this approach. Whatever intellectual subtlety may have been contemplated at the time, the noble concept of unity gradually deteriorated into a grey uniformity. Diaspora opinions contrary to official government policy were unwelcome.

The French non-Zionist writer Richard Marienstras described this process as indicative of the Zionization of Jewish culture in the Diaspora.[5] In fact, just the opposite happened. Zionist ideology was relegated to a low rung on the ladder of priorities, a non-ideological pro-Israelization of the Diaspora instead became the dominant tendency. Charles Liebman incisively described this impoverishment of the Diaspora's understanding of Israel:

> The truth is that whereas Diaspora Jews now share the classic Zionist dream of a Jewish homeland, they have no Zionist vision. Israel, perhaps, has a particularist Jewish meaning for Diaspora Jewry: it is important to the Diaspora for its Jewish survival. But Israel has no universal meaning for most Diaspora Jews. It is not integrally related to the variety of visions Diaspora Jews may have of a different kind of world, a different kind of society, a different kind of social order. Hence, the Diaspora is not driven to press Israel into doing anything different from that which it is doing today.[6]

The development of the de-ideologization of the Diaspora, and thus the loss of Zionist vision, fitted the pragmatic needs of successive Israeli governments. They endorsed it and it was symbiotically embraced by non-Zionist fundraisers, who, almost by definition, were always content to accept what is rather than to perceive what could be.

It would, however, be churlish to represent this scenario as a conspiracy. It was rather framed within the tragic events of the twentieth century. The trauma of the Shoah sensitized millions of Jews who had hitherto felt little towards Zionism. The rise of the State of Israel was seen in almost messianic terms, coming as it did so soon after the greatest tragedy ever to have befallen the Jewish people. Diaspora Jews were traumatized by their inability to prevent the Shoah. After 1948, they could at least assist an embattled restored Israel. Thus, although they had no intention of emigrating, they felt a duty to participate in Jewish destiny even on the minimal level of making a donation to a worthy cause in Israel.

The huge increase of funds channelled by the American Jewish Community to *Keren Kayemet* (the Jewish National Fund) and *Keren Hayesod* (the Palestine Foundation Fund) show a parallelism with the awareness of the Shoah and the expectancy of a Jewish State. All figures quoted are in millions of dollars:[7]

Year	Jewish National Fund	Palestine Foundation Fund
1939	1.745	1.745
1940	1.801	1.940
1941	1.713	1.870
1942	1.919	2.270
1943	2.947	3.185
1944	4.689	5.680
1945	6.996	7.810
1946	13.067	13.800
1947	17.737	41.460
1948	39.006	35.841

Thus, after 1948 the definition of who was a Zionist blurred, even within philanthropic parameters. Pre-war non-Zionists and post-1948 reborn Zionists coalesced in their task to bolster the shaky economy of the new State and to engage in the traditional tasks of the ingathering of the exiles and the building up of the Land.

Israeli official policy granted philanthropists a superior status simply because the power and influence that their wealth generated in their host society could be put to good use in support of the

Israeli government policy of the day. Moreover, as the post-war *embourgeoisement* of Western Jewry proceded, the community of Jewish philanthropists increased greatly. Because of their generosity and their munificence, they were regarded as communal representatives. While this function should not be belittled, the role of Diaspora intellectuals and academics, by comparison, diminished. They could argue and were, by definition, people who asked questions. This was not what was required, for it also called into question the acceptance of the demand that the Diaspora should be silent on Israeli government policy. This attitude consequently set in motion a schism between the Jewish intelligentsia and communal representation, including philanthopists, who were content to repeat and justify current Israeli government policy. Literary figures or university professors were often called upon only where their presence constituted a public-relations function within a political campaign, such as that of Soviet Jewry. Thus, their intellectual input was often ignored.

In particular, the political influence of US Jewry became an increasingly important consideration for Israeli foreign policy. Indeed, there was a certain love–hate relationship. Whilst longing for total freedom of manoeuvre, all Israeli governments were dependent on the political and financial efforts of the Jews of the United States. It formed the third side of the political triangle of the US and Israeli governments. Each participant possessed a link with the other and could thus be used to generate pressure on the third party where direct contact or confrontation was inadvisable.

American Jews had been highly instrumental in the creation of the State. Israeli Prime Ministers from Ben-Gurion to Shamir were thus sensitive to the need both for US Jewry's total support and for its adherence to the official policy of an Israeli government. For example, the crucial position of US Jewry in the decision-making process in the United States, and its access to the White House and Congress, was certainly a factor in Ben-Gurion's decision effectively to ally Israel with the West during the Cold War rather than to remain neutral.

However, the decision to honour philanthropists and industrialists, and by extension their political influence, also had ideological effects within Israel itself: 'The government itself, in its search for foreign investment, softened its own socialist policies. Within the government, those more favourable to a free-enterprise system argued against socialist policies, socialist phraseology and sloganeering as injurious to the nation by discouraging investment of foreign capital and the *aliyah* [emigration to Israel] of businessmen and industrialists'.[8]

Ben-Gurion's philosophy ensured the demise of the Diaspora Zionist as ideologue and agent of change. Instead, it encouraged the rise and rise of the Diaspora Zionist as philanthropist and seeker after influence in support of Israeli government policy. For those Diaspora Jews who regarded Zionism as the central solution to the Jewish problem, their increasing irrelevance left them ideologically immobile:

Diaspora Zionists were far from accepting the idea of total Jewish ingathering to Israel either as a personal obligation or as a mythic foundation for their movement – and they had no alternative myth from which to draw any assurance of an historic mission. If the State of Israel did not enact a representative status for them, they no longer had the assurance to act as the legitimate agent of a sovereign Jewish will. They were reduced to spokesmen of established organizational interests and vested rights, seeking to reach a new arrangement with the Jewish State that would meet new needs while causing the least possible disturbance to existing institutions.[9]

In the Diaspora, Zionism thus lost its revolutionary edge and was integrated into the amorphous pro-Israel approach of the community. A Diaspora Zionist became someone who would articulate support for Israel in its broadest sense. Understanding Israel and comprehending Zionism were perceived in terms of the lowest common denominator, since in a Diaspora community there was no real discussion about events in Israel with a view to stating publicly an opinion on an issue. For some, it was easier to switch from Zionist education of a Jewish community and concentrate on public relations on behalf of Israeli government policy. This was facilitated by the nationalist euphoria generated by the Six Day War. The revulsion towards Palestinian terrorism and the advent of the anti-Zionism of the New Left provided a *raison d'être* for total involvement in defending Israel in the non-Jewish world after 1967.

Israeli attitudes towards the Diaspora

'The People of Israel is a tree whose roots are in Israel and whose branches are in the Diaspora. A tree cannot flourish without roots. But how can it bear fruit without branches? Be careful with the branches.'[10]

The presence of 6 million Jews in the United States has always been a source of ambivalence for Israelis. The existence of a self-sufficient, powerful and active community overtly suggests that 50 per cent of the world's Jewish population, whilst using Israel as a central component in their self-identification as Jews, do not accept the Zionist solution. The viability of an alternative, culturally rich and financially well-to-do entity, in a land of the Diaspora, goes against the fundamental tenets of Zionist ideology dedicated to the principle of *kibbutz ha'galuyot*. After all, it was said that Jews came on *aliya*, literally 'a going up', whilst those

Israelis who left were termed *yordim* – those who went down. Despite this ambivalence, there has always been a feeling of considerable closeness, a real partnership, between the two most important centres of contemporary Jewry.

The US Jewish community has always been vociferous in its support for the Jewish State. The rise of the America–Israel Public Affairs Committee (AIPAC) as a professional and powerful lobby, and the emphasis on public relations in the aftermath of the Six Day War, underlined the centrality of Israel for US Jews and symbolized the advent of a unique American 'Jewishness' – an identification substantially different from that of their immigrant fathers and one rooted in Holocaust Remembrance and Zionist Redemption. For Israelis, the new activism confirmed their concept of US Jewry not so much as a symbiotic focus of Jewish endeavour but as a crucial outpost in the survival and development of Israel. A nascent pro-Israelism was encouraged, not just to solidify Jewish identity but also to ensure the cohesion and efficacy of its advocates in Washington. This is not to say that issues such as Jewish education or the struggle against assimilation are of no concern, but clearly the desire to maintain and indeed increase the political influence of US Jewry has achieved primacy in Israeli attitudes.

When the Smith Research Center conducted a poll amongst Israelis in June 1983, 70 per cent agreed that 'most American Jews do not think of their country as *galut* [exile].'[11] Answers to other questions indicated the exalted position in which Israelis held American Jews in the struggle against external enemies and opponents:

	Agree	Disagree
'The focus uniting US Jews is support for Israel'	67	21
'US Jews will always support Israel'	66	14
'When Israel's name is smeared, US Jews are also hurt'	71	19
'The US Jewish lobby is a very powerful force in influencing US foreign policy'	57	17

Ironically, an almost mythical sense of the power of US Jewry was prevalent within Israeli society. When Hanoch Smith asked his Israeli respondents whether the Jews of America have control of important branches of the American economy, 73 per cent replied in the affirmative. Smith comments that this was in fact 'closer to the way numbers of American non-Jews view Jewish power in America'. Paradoxically, Jewish success in America has created a typically non-Jewish stereotype of the Jew in the perception of the average Israeli. In a non-Jewish society, this would have aroused suspicion of anti-semitism, but emanating from a Jewish society it seemed both a matter of pride and of bewilderment.

Israelis were still perplexed over why, after two millennia of persecution and exile, the Diaspora simply did not dissolve and its multitudes flood into Israel. Although Israel respected Jewish influence in the outside world as an adjunct of its foreign policy, it respected neither the basic idea of a still extant Diaspora nor any attempt privately or publicly to offer advice. Even though it was conducted shortly after the débâcle of the war in Lebanon, Hanoch Smith's poll showed that a slender majority of Israelis, some 51 per cent, believed that 'American Jews should not criticize the government of Israel's policy publicly'.

The government of Israel, however, in limiting criticism, also had a vested political interest. From the government's point of view, Diaspora Jews should heed only official Israeli advice and should act upon it. Therefore, during the 1972 American Presidential Elections, for example, there were semi-official hints from the Israeli Embassy in Washington that Ambassador Yitzhak Rabin preferred Richard Nixon over the Democrat candidate, George McGovern, who had commented on the Palestinian problem. These leaks, which were clearly directed at the Jewish electorate, suggested an Israeli belief that US Jewry's support for Israel would supersede its inherent liberalism and usually solid support for the Democratic Party.

The leading Israeli daily, *Ha'aretz*, commented in 1973 that

> for Israel, interested primarily in mobilizing contributions and political pressure, it is more comfortable to make arrangements with the Montors, Schwartzes and Friedmans [past professional leaders of the campaigns to mobilize funds for Israel in the United States] than with the Silvers, Klutznicks or Soloveitchiks [American Jewish leaders with significant constituencies who have been critical of Israel despite their basic sympathy towards the State.] For twenty years, the blessings of Ben-Gurion, Eshkol or Sapir became the certificate of legitimacy to communal leadership.[12]

It was far easier to work with those Jewish leaders who agreed with official policy than with those who asked questions or openly stated their disagreement. It was far easier on both sides to solicit donations than to enter into a genuine discussion over direction. To accept official policy suited Israeli diplomats in pursuit of a trouble-free career as well as Diaspora Jews in search of a utopian Jewish motif with which to identify.

The task of Israeli diplomats and communal leaders was probably made easier because Jewish intellectuals in Europe and the United States may have marginalized themselves as a result of the growing distance in time from the establishment of the State and from the Shoah. The diluted identification with post-1967 Israel was also a reaction to a perceived inadequate approach to the Palestinian problem, as well as the indirect influence of the New Left. Those who perceived an intellectual and creative role for Diaspora Jews, as opposed to fulfilling a primarily propaganda or fundraising function, did not receive a sympathetic response.

Yet even before the breakdown of consensus politics within Israel, there were a number of Diaspora leaders who politely voiced their fears. At the Second Seminar on World Jewry, which took place under the aegis of the President of Israel in Jerusalem in December 1973, the Chief Rabbi of Great Britain, Immanuel Jakobovits, told his audience that 'Diaspora Jews are expected to sign blank cheques to underwrite policies over which they have no control or influence'.[13] Another participant, Gershon D. Cohen, Chancellor of the Jewish Theological Seminary of America, said that 'even within the ranks of the committed, there is an increasingly audible murmur of doubt about the soundness of Israel's policies in the arena of international politics. I am not happy about these rumblings . . . but it is sheer folly to ignore them. Moreover, they will not be silenced by appeals or leadership tours'.[14]

Public relations and public reality

The emergence of unquestioning 'solidarity with Israel' by Diaspora Jewish organizations, or rather of a blind acceptance of government policy, also had a number of side-effects. It provided a method of identifying with Israel without making *aliya*. Standing up for Israel in the face of intransigent foes not only permitted Diaspora Jews to identify deeply with the victory of 1967, it also in some way redressed the failure to save those who had perished during the Shoah. The international campaign for Soviet Jewry was the supreme example of 'Never Again'. While all this was understandable, and indeed praiseworthy, it nevertheless deflected examination of events within Israel, substituting a struggle with an external enemy. The idea of *heshbon ha'nefesh* (self-examination) disappeared.

The 'Israel' that was promoted tended to be one of unreal, utopian dimensions, where public relations had replaced public reality. This natural tendency of Diaspora Jewry to view the Jewish State from afar in emotional and idealistic terms facilitated the growth of the Hasbara industry after 1967. *Hasbara*, which is Hebrew for 'explanation', was the means to convey the objective reality of Israel's situation to an increasingly questioning world where there was a growing awareness of the Palestinian question. The pressure to confront the ever more sophisticated PLO public-relations campaign in the 1970s led to a huge expansion in Hasbara work. Communal funds were diverted for this purpose. Obsession with the media spawned new organizations, expensive consultants and vigilante journalists to cope with real and imaginary anti–Israeli bias in the press. There evolved a belief that public relations were the panacea for all manner of ills, regardless of the reality in Israel itself. All could be explained away by better public relations.

Fact sheets and pamphlets from both Israeli and Palestinian camps were aimed at convincing influential people – parliamentarians and congressmen, writers and academics, human-rights activists and journalists – of the justice of their cause. This material was often highly coloured in its descriptions and deeply selective in its facts. For example, Yasser Arafat cabled the Chinese leadership to congratulate them on brutally suppressing the democracy movement in the summer of 1989. Arafat expressed 'extreme gratification that you were able to restore normal order after the recent incidents in People's China.'[15] Simultaneously, his chief aide, Bassam Abu Sharif, was explaining the peace process to BBC television viewers in Britain, saying that Israel should understand the motivation for the Intifada because all over the world people were struggling for human rights and democracy – 'as in China'.

Arafat's repeated exhortations of 'human rights for Palestinians' did not prevent his paying homage to Iraq's Saddam Hussein, whose respect for human rights in his own country was exceedingly minimal. Indeed, Arafat's words of praise for the Iraqi President came shortly after the execution in March 1990 of the British journalist Farzad Bazoft on unsubstantiated charges of spying. Clearly, Saddam Hussein's support for the Palestinian cause superseded all other considerations.

Public relations, by definition, highlighted the idea that one side was totally right and the other side totally wrong. It did not admit the complexity of history, of good policies and bad policies of different Israeli and Palestinian leaderships. Public relations could speak only in terms of absolutes. My country right or right. Current official policy was always correct, the leadership always infallible in judgement. In the 1980s this tended to be more true of Palestinian double-speak than of its Israeli counterpart, because of the lack of consensus in the Jewish State. Public relations essentially placed obstacles in the path of reconciliation and dialogue, emphasizing differences and glossing over similarities and common interest. Israeli public relations rightly drew attention to the negative in the Palestinian position, but also omitted any mention of positive change. In one sense, public relations had no vested interest in achieving peace, since that would make its own operation redundant. Public relations unintentionally became an instrument for encouraging mutual hostility and distrust. It erected psychological barriers on each side to ensure that current positions were equivalent to religious truths and thus unassailable.

The Hasbara industry

Hasbarah (explanation) sits somewhere between *informatzia* (information) and *ta'amula* (propaganda). Yet *hasbara* is not a neutral concept such as 'reporting information'. 'Explanation' inherently means constructing an image – an image which reflects reality. The problem with Israeli and Palestinian public relations was that they did not always reflect reality:

> The whole image process is its responsibility; when it sets information out on its journey, it is not enough that 'some' of it arrives 'somehow' and does 'something'. It must wholeheartedly investigate what its images turn into; evaluate far more effectively the service its images perform for the whole truth; and above all, it must learn to understate the information it projects.[16]

When Likud came to power in 1977, greater emphasis was placed on the public-relations war. On the one hand, it justifiably reacted to an enhanced Palestinian campaign, fuelled by petro-dollars, to put over its case. On the other, Likud had to persuade foreign governments as well as large sections of the Diaspora that its policies were the right ones. Unlike previous Labour governments, and following the visit of President Sadat in particular, it did not operate within the stability of a national consensus. Herut's 'fighting family' mentality and its traditional distrust of the outside world were the psychological impetus for the Likud government's intensive concentration on better *hasbara*.

Moreover, as Palestinian public relations became more sophisticated, the Israeli operation was perceived as open to question. Until the Six Day War, most Western reporters implicitly accepted the Israeli version of events. Arab attempts, by contrast, were crude and inaccurate. The post-1967 situation, and the Yom Kippur War in particular, induced an unease in the reliability of Israeli spokesmen. It was not so much that their Palestinian counterparts always told the truth, but that the selectivity of the Israelis became more pronounced. The use of language was increasingly susceptible to manipulation. For example, in the summer of 1989, Sheik Obeid, who was believed to be an instigator of the attacks by the pro-Iranian Hezbollah on Israeli patrols near the Lebanese border, was 'arrested' outside Israel's borders – and not abducted. Moreover, such an 'arrest' was not followed by a trial.

The official Israeli response over the years was to regard unpalatable and biased reporting from Western journalists as one and the same. This lack of differentiation stemmed from a belief that Israel was fighting a propaganda war in the media which could easily be translated into political capital on Capitol Hill. Modern technology had advanced political reporting to a hitherto previously unknown level. The advent of the electronic media brought with it competition between rival networks to achieve primacy in instant coverage of events. The tendency to verify events in such circumstances was thus almost certainly weakened.

An IDF spokesman reported that $100 million had been funnelled into the Territories to support the Palestinian information effort during the first twenty months of the Intifada.[17] The confrontation of such a propaganda offensive, as well as the necessity of ignoring continuing dissent within Israel about IDF actions, brought about a general attitude that all journalists who reported on the Territories were 'anti-Israel'. Colonel Ra'anan Gissin, the IDF deputy spokesman, commented at a symposium on terrorism in Jerusalem in 1989 that 'this form of news coverage conditions audiences; instantaneous news coverage, not by its nature, not [by being] deliberate, becomes a form of terrorism by itself . . . there are now some twenty crews operating in the Territories, assimilating pictures, some of them staged, some of them real. Nevertheless, this is a form of war.'[18]

There was considerable frustration that official IDF sources had to react – and often slowly – to an event about which they may have known little at the time. Thus, the right to construct an alternative image of an event was often eliminated.

Reporters, however, faced criticism from both Palestinians and Israelis – if not from one side, then most certainly from the other. It was extremely difficult always to make an independent judgement about a specific incident, since it was often claimed that central contacts on both sides were 'biased people', determined to prove the justice of their cause rather than to provide essentially neutral information.

In 1969 a commission of inquiry on Hasbara submitted similar conclusions to Prime Minister Golda Meir. Its chairman later commented that 'the main problem was that we are in a real conflict between two groups fighting for the same piece of land. Each party is convinced of the justness of its claim. We think we are more just, more right. The Arabs probably think the same thing. This creates a basic problem for Hasbara, a problem which I do not believe an advertising gimmick can easily solve'.[19]

Yet the ability of the media to inform was clearly discerned in the Bus 300 incident in 1984 when Palestinian terrorists murdered Israeli passengers on the Ashkelon–Tel Aviv highway. The bus was finally stopped by Israeli commandos and the news given out that all the Palestinians who had participated in this atrocity had been killed in the shoot-out. A couple of days afterwards, the daily newspaper *Hadashot* published a photograph on its front page which clearly showed that two of the terrorists had been captured alive. The lies told to the Israeli public by the military spokesmen, and the ensuing scandal surrounding the intelligence services, indicated the important role that the media could play in a democratic society.

Successive Likud governments believed that dissent or Diaspora criticism was bad for Hasbara, and thereby contrary to government and national interests. The other side of the coin was that this argument also silenced meddlesome critics and confirmed the Israeli government's refusal to permit Diaspora comment on foreign-policy issues.

The annual America–Israel dialogue in 1984, under the aegis of the American Jewish Congress, was devoted to Hasbara – 'Israel's Public Image: Problems and Remedies'. During the deliberations, a leading Israeli diplomat attacked a highly critical statement issued by the Congress following the Phalangist massacre at Sabra and Shatilla during the Lebanon war:

> I ask you, how can a Jewish organization issue such a statement when, at the same time, Israel is attacked vehemently by a hostile front in the United Nations, smeared publicly and indiscriminately by the majority of the American media and besieged by an aggressive unholy alliance of the Arab–Communist bloc at a crucial moment? Aren't Jewish leaders accountable for what, where and when they say about Israel at a time of crisis? And furthermore: Do they want (as I believe they basically do) to help Israel with its Hasbara challenge or do they aspire to dictate to a democracy a course of action? The delicate yet important line and distinction between helping in Hasbara in the United States and interfering in the policy-making in Israel should be clearly set – and this will help to achieve better cooperation and work for our common goals in this vital sphere'.[20]

Henry Siegman, Executive Director of the American Jewish Congress, felt constrained to reply:

Mr Gilboa would have the Hasbara role of American Jewry be that of a loudspeaker, an inanimate object that does no more than amplify whatever is said in Israel. In his view this role exhausts the justification for Diaspora existence. American Jewry by definition opposes it. . . . Many of the most committed Jews and Israelis understood that it was more important to respond to the tragedy of Sabra and Shatilla as Jews than to distort that response by Hasbara considerations. Cabinet ministers resigned. Important army officers said they could no longer serve; 400,000 Israelis took to the streets of Tel Aviv and expressed their outrage. The significant thing was not only that these protesters ignored Hasbara, but, that by doing what they did, by acting on their instincts as Jews, they unwittingly fashioned a Hasbara victory that I suspect many Government officials, including Moshe Gilboa, do not understand to this day.[21]

This exchange exemplified the parameters of relations in 1984 between the Likud government and a major American Jewish organization. The differing perceptions of Diaspora responsibilities were very clear. Moreover, even if American Jews refused to condemn specific Israeli actions publicly, this did not mean that they would wax lyrical about policies which they felt were fundamentally wrong in the cause of Hasbara.

The Likud government also distanced itself from anyone who could contribute fresh ideas to the Hasbara policy. Leon Wieseltier, the literary editor of the *New Republic*, observed that

the introduction of new ideas into the bloodstream of a culture is powerful and lasting. After all, the basic orthodoxy concerning Israel's right to exist was built after Israel's founding largely by intellectuals, writers, editorialists and scholars. One of the real deficiencies of Hasbara in the United States has been its own indifference to its own intellectual quality.[22]

Furthermore, there was no recognition that criticism of Israeli government policy could actually be an asset in portraying a realistic Israel. Instead, it projected a consensus in Israel where none existed. Thus, when hundreds of thousands of Israelis demonstrated in Tel Aviv after the Phalangist massacre at the Sabra and Shatilla camps, pro-Israel public-relations organizations in the Diaspora were embarrassingly silent. Despite the fact that international opinion perceived this as a redeeming factor following the débâcle of the Lebanon war – and thus a point in Israel's favour as a vibrant democracy – not a word was written.

Although it was clear to many Diaspora workers that a consensus within Israel was necessary in order to fashion and project a 'real' image, the Likud governments of Begin and Shamir refused to differentiate between pro-Israel and pro-Israeli government Hasbara. Even when forty-one prominent American Jews sent to Shamir during his US visit in November 1989 a letter which differentiated between Shamir as a national symbol of Israel greeting fellow Jews and as a Likud politician seeking their support for his policies, the reaction of his spokesman was to ignore the distinction in an attempt to marginalize the significance of the letter.

This pinpointed a greater internal need of governments in general: the desire to control the flow of information and thereby to fashion public opinion in accordance with the government's own perspectives. In Israel, in particular, the establishment of a Ministry of Information had floundered because it could forge different images – and indeed counter-images – to those demanded by other government ministers or factions within the ruling élite. Thus Shimon Peres under Golda Meir, and Aharon Yariv under Yitzhak Rabin, had limited tenure of office as Labour Ministers of Information during the 1970s. Moreover, the advent of coalition governments in the 1980s has made the re-establishment of such a ministry virtually unachievable, for it is essentially impossible to define the parameters of Hasbara which would please both Likud and Labour. This has led to the decentralization of Hasbara in real terms with many *ad hoc* groups and individuals filling the vacuum.

Whilst all this could be interpreted in terms of the *Realpolitik* of the public-relations war, the Hasbara industry also became, albeit initially unintentionally, a method of educating the Diaspora in Israeli affairs. Many ordinary Jews who wished to be active on Israel's behalf used this same material as a source of information about the Middle East conflict. The irony was that what was *ta'amula* (propaganda) aimed at non-Jews was simultaneously regarded as *informatzia* (information) by many Diaspora Jews. For example, as a result of the dictum that the PLO was responsible for all Palestinian terrorist attacks on Jews and Israelis, in 1982 British Jews were repeatedly informed that the Israeli Ambassador in London, Shlomo Argov, had been shot by PLO terrorists. [23] For many Diaspora Jews, this unwitting belief in one's own propaganda was harshly dispelled by the shock of the Lebanon war.

Ironically, such selective public relations forced many Jews to think through the situation. The inadequacy of Hasbara induced a genuine educational process about the reality of the Israel–Palestine conflict. In turn, it allowed some Jews to deflate such selective Hasbara and to understand that the *golem* could easily be turned on its head. For example, during the 1980s, 'Jordan is Palestine' groups were formed in many parts of the Diaspora. The official view reasoned that 'Jordan is

Palestine' because the Palestinians formed a majority of the population in the Hashemite kingdom. Conversely, it could also be argued that the 'West Bank is Palestine' because the Palestinians outnumbered the Jewish settlers. Since the 'Jordan is Palestine' argument became a necessary plank in Likud attempts to divert attention away from negotiating directly with the Palestinians in 1989, such counter-Hasbara was unwelcome.

The increasing logic of talking to the Palestinians began to influence many Diaspora Jews after Arafat's press conference in Geneva in 1988, at which he appeared to recognize Israel and to call for a cessation of cross-border attacks. Yet this desire to participate in a real political process seemingly conflicted with the public-relations role of the Diaspora.

The British Labour Friends of Israel had for a long time defended the cause of Israel within the party. Yet it played a limited part in the debate within the Jewish community and left the field to other organizations, such as the British Friends of Peace Now, to advocate the dovish case. At the Labour Party Conference in the autumn of 1990, the Labour Friends of Israel and the pro-Palestinian Labour Middle East Council held an unprecedented joint meeting. Israeli Labour figures and PLO representatives were in the audience and the usual acrimonious conference resolutions were avoided. However, the Labour Friends of Israel was funded largely by philanthropists who disagreed ideologically with them – one was a leading supporter of the Far Right Techiya – but viewed them as an important tool in the public-relations arena. The moment they declared themselves to be more than a projection of public relations through participating in a dialogue with their opponents, their funding was cut.[24]

5

Diaspora Dissent and Jewish Intervention

Crossing the threshold

The increasing ranks of Diaspora dissent from Israeli government policies in the 1980s and the large numbers of disaffected Jewish intellectuals among the post-war generation who felt disenchanted with single-minded Israeli attitudes, were easily able to locate a movement with which they could identify.

Yet Diaspora dissent did not mean Diaspora intervention. It could mean criticism, both public and private. It could mean passive protest in a refusal to propagate an area of official Israeli policy, or professing an inability to meet a public figure or a government minister in a host country. It could mean an overt display of opposition, such as sharing a public platform – as a self-proclaimed Zionist – with a PLO representative. Diaspora leaders had moved some considerable distance since 1970 when Nahum Goldman attempted to meet President Nasser in Cairo but was vetoed by Premier Golda Meir. At that time, not even the harshest Diaspora critic considered an active alternative policy. Instead, a purely reactive approach to official Israeli government policy was determined to be the correct – and loyal – approach.

The election of Menachem Begin changed everything. Government policy in the 1980s and the development of a widespread peace movement in Israel which encouraged Diaspora criticism pushed many committed Jews into an interventionist mode.

Likud governments also encouraged the official promotion of the Conference of Presidents of Major Jewish Organizations as a representative body of American Jewry. This *ad hoc* group originally came into existence through a request to Nahum Goldman from the White House that a US Administration needed only one address from the Jewish community instead of the dozens of organizations which regularly met officials. This administrative formality evolved into a

104

political instrument for successive Israeli governments, which wanted to present their position to the White House through an apparently independent, indigenous body. The Presidents' Conference wished to be seen as representative of all American Jews, even though there was much duplication of membership amongst its constituent parts. Unlike other Jewish lobby organizations, it did not register its essential 'agent' status and was perceived by the media, both in Israel and in the United States, as a democratically elected body. Israeli leaders ensured that they spoke to the Presidents' Conference whenever they visited Washington and that their words were relayed to the press – even if such meetings were deemed to be behind 'closed doors'. The exceedingly close contact with official Jerusalem ensured that it presented only Israeli government positions and not independent American Jewish ones. Although the Presidents' Conference elected rotating chairmen, the outspoken liberal Arthur Hertzberg of the American Jewish Congress failed to become its head, reputedly because of a veto by Menachem Begin. By contrast, in 1989 its director, Malcolm Hoenlein, was master of ceremonies at a dinner for the Ateret Ha'Cohanim Yeshiva which later attempted to purchase the St John's Hospice in the Christian quarter of Jerusalem. Ariel Sharon was its guest speaker.

In September 1987, the American Jewish Congress broke the tradition of silence on the part of official Jewish organizations. Using the demographic argument, they insisted that the continued occupation of the Territories would lead 'inexorably to a cycle of violence and necessary repression'. They seemingly urged Israelis to support Shimon Peres's call for an international peace conference. A few weeks later, the American Jewish Committee and the Reform Movement issued similar statements.

When the Intifada commenced, some Jewish leaders felt vindicated in their earlier dissent and then began to pursue a clearly interventionist approach. For example, in January 1988 a group of leaders from the American Jewish Congress visited King Hussein of Jordan at his palace in Amman to discuss the Middle East situation. In addition, they also conversed with King Hassan of Morocco and President Mubarak of Egypt, as well as Prime Minister Yitzhak Shamir in Israel.[1] The concept of the Diaspora Jew as 'honest broker' between the two sides in the conflict became more pointed when Jerome M. Segal, a Jewish academic at the University of Maryland, challenged the accepted idea that a Palestinian State could only emerge through negotiations and when prior Israeli approval had been given. Segal drew upon the analogy of Israel itself, in that the Israelis simply proclaimed the existence of their State without prior approval from any Arab nation. In an article in the *Washington Post*,[2] and in Arabic in the Jerusalem daily *Al Quds*,

Segal proposed that the PLO issue a 'Declaration of Independence and Statehood'. The new State of Palestine, situated in the West Bank and Gaza, would issue two laws:

> Law 1: The State of Palestine declares itself at peace with the State of Israel; the State of Palestine will not maintain an army.

In addition, the new government would offer Israel mutual recognition and an exchange of ambassadors.

> Law 2: All acts of terrorism are forbidden. Severe penalties will be invoked if this law is violated.

Furthermore Segal proposed that the provisional Palestinian government ban all lethally violent attacks on Israeli soldiers and that West Bank settlers should only be attacked in self-defence.

In order to secure Israeli withdrawal, Segal proposed that 'at the same time, the Palestinian people are called to enter into only symbolic activity directed against Israeli soldiers in the Territories'. Segal's new approach coincided with that of several east Jerusalem intellectuals, such as Faisal Husseini, head of the Arab Studies Society, who personified the pragmatic pro-PLO tendency within the Territories.

In the upper echelons of the PLO itself, there was a clear tendency to break the impasse. Within weeks of the appearance of Segal's article, Bassam Abu Sharif sent up a trial balloon, calling for a two-states solution, a repudiation of terrorism and a recognition of UN Resolutions 242 and 338 – the very points which the United States and Israel had indicated for over a decade were the minimum basis for discussion. Segal's association with Faisal Husseini was the catalyst for Arafat's declarations at Algiers and Geneva at the end of the year, where many of the proposals were accepted by the PLO, including the proclamation of a State of Palestine. Segal ended his *Washington Post* article with a justification of his approach:

> If it seems odd that a Jew should offer his thoughts on how Palestinians can be successful in their struggle for statehood, I should state my conviction that the struggle for an independent Palestinian state is also the struggle for a humane and safe Israel, and that there can be no Judaism without a committment to justice.

During the first half of 1988, there appeared to be a convergence of approaches between the Palestinian leadership and liberal Jews in Israel and the Diaspora. In March 1988 the Swedish Foreign Minister, Sten Andersson, visited Israel and came away with a feeling of deep despondency and foreboding for the future. His Under-Secretary

of State, Pierre Schori, was authorized to contact an old friend
and peace activist, the Los Angeles lawyer Stanley Sheinbaum, in
an attempt to translate the ongoing Intifada into something more
politically meaningful. The Swedes deliberately did not contact leaders
of official Jewish organizations, since they understood that 'they would
immediately consult with Shamir and Peres, who would quash the
initiative'.[3] Through Sheinbaum, a small group of concerned Jews,
prominent for their activities in espousing dialogue, coalesced. Soon
a Swedish envoy was delivering a statement to the PLO concerning
the crucial arguments of recognition of Israel, no terrorism and
acceptance of Resolutions 242 and 338. The PLO accepted the
basis for discussion and a meeting was arranged for November,
under the auspices of the Swedish Foreign Ministry. Ironically, the
date set was a few days after the Algiers meeting of the Palestine
National Council. Arafat's tendency towards ambiguity permeated
his pronouncements and did not satisfy the US Secretary of State,
George Schultz, to the extent that he later denied Arafat a visa
to attend the UN General Assembly in New York. The lack of
clarification in Algiers thereby provided the occasion for a high-level
meeting between American Jewish doves and PLO representatives.
At a meeting in December 1988 in Stockholm, Arafat worked with
the Jewish delegation and Foreign Minister Andersson to produce a
statement which was acceptable to Schultz and the State Department.
Following Arafat's announcements at a Geneva press conference a
week later, President Ronald Reagan and President-elect George
Bush then announced that the PLO chairman's pronouncements
were a satisfactory basis for an American–Palestinian dialogue. No
doubt the US government was informed throughout and the incoming
Bush Administration was very much in favour of the initiative, but the
significance of Diaspora intervention was all too clear. Although the
members of the Jewish delegation were often submitted to concerted
criticism and insult on their return, it showed that a coherent liberal
pro-Israeli group which was not pro-Israeli government was able and
willing to create a diplomatic initiative – and outside the traditional
organizational framework.

What do Jews think?

The interventionist strategy of dovish Jewish leaders raised the
question of who represents Diaspora thinking on the Israel–Palestine
conflict. Did traditional organizations speak for the Jew in the street?
Outside the United States of America it is very difficult to know the
opinion of a Jewish community on a specific matter. The opinion
of a Jewish organization or synagogue may be understood through

resolutions or statements, but this does not necessarily mean that it is a representative view of the community as a whole. Most Diaspora communities exist as minorities within majority cultures and they have traditionally presented their views to the indigenous powers-that-be through an alliance of wealthy *shtadlanim* and organizational bodies. History, however, has transformed Jewish identity into a plethora of paradigms. Since the Enlightenment caused a fragmentation in the self-evidence of Judaism, European Jews have defined their 'Jewishness' in a wide variety of ways. Whilst maintaining a religious lifestyle, some imbibed the waters of the French Revolution and adopted the language, clothes and customs of their host country. Others saw their Judaism in predominantly secular terms, embracing socialism, liberalism and Zionism, and their hybrids. Still others refused to acknowledge the arrival of modernity and quickly rebuilt the ghetto walls.

By the bicentenary of the French Revolution in 1989, it was possible to discern a general distinction between Jews who defined their 'Jewishness' through membership of a synagogue or Jewish organization and those who remained unaffiliated though not alienated. The former defined their Jewish particularism through communal involvement, whether organizational or synagogal – however peripheral – whilst the latter's Jewish particularism was paradoxically defined by an intense commitment to a universalism emanating from Judaism. Organized Jewish bodies thus represented organized Jewry. The views of the unaffiliated, by definition, were not represented. Thus, the Board of Deputies of British Jews repeatedly stated that they were 'the representative body of British Jewry', despite the fact that a high percentage of British Jewry was not affiliated to their constituent organizations.[4] Whereas the Board of Deputies of British Jews had indeed been just what its name implied at the time of its founding in 1760, it had become the Board of Deputies of British Jewish Synagogues and Organizations over 200 years later.

The meaning of 'Jewishness' is an ongoing and unresolved question in the Jewish world, yet the Jewish motif which these two broad divisions within the Jewish community in Britain shared was a common support for and identification with the State of Israel. The events of the 1980s, the Lebanon war and the Intifada, were thus traumatic ones for the unaffiliated. Their universalistic symbol, Israel, which represented their Jewishness, had turned into an illiberal *golem*. They therefore had to develop rational arguments which they could use in conflicts with non-Jews which would encompass both their liberalism and their pro-Israelism. They also discovered that they were struggling on two fronts, for they found that Jewish organizations and leaders, speaking in their name, always justified Israeli government policy. Ironically, their lack of communal involvement allowed communal bodies falsely to represent them. Although they often made common cause with concerned affiliated Jews within umbrella organizations such as the British Friends of Peace Now, there was considerable anger that only Jewish organizations formally represented Jewish opinion on the Israel–Palestinian question. If 'Israel' defined a central component of 'Jewishness' for Diaspora Jews, then exclusion from participation in the debate was tantamount to an exclusion from 'Jewishness' for the unaffiliated. Statements by Jewish leadership in Britain tended to represent essentially themselves and their organizations. No genuine mechanism existed to determine what Jews in Britain really thought about events in Israel.[5] Moreover, although Jewish organizations in the United States had pioneered such techniques to provide genuine indicators, Jewish communal organizations in Europe and elsewhere were in no hurry to adopt them. Clearly, they did not want to have policies imposed upon them by public opinion polls of Diaspora Jews. In the United States, however, it was a different story. Demographic analysis was considered an important tool in policymaking. This was a reflection not simply of the sophistication of the American Jewish community, but also of how its outlook differed from that of Diaspora communities. The contrast can be traced back to two different but similar influences in recent history. The French Revolution of 1789 liberated Jews as a minority with equal rights. The American Revolution of 1776, however, established a state where all minorities are created equal. American Jews never suffered from the classical European minority complex, since all were immigrants. American Jews never felt that they had to be overtly circumspect about their utterances. They were foremost among the originators of the American Dream and the builders of a new society. Unlike English Jews, with whom they shared a common language, they were not a tolerated minority. As good American citizens, they espoused the openness of that society. In recent times, the US Jewish community has strongly supported solid research to determine trends and patterns which other Diaspora communities have been reticent to conduct, often in the belief that the less a host country knows factually about its Jewish community, the less the possibility of persecution. Hence, the Board of Deputies of British Jews opposed any mention of Jewish origin in successive censuses in the United Kingdom. Since 1981, Professor Steven M. Cohen, under the auspices of the American Jewish Committee, however, has conducted surveys based on detailed questionnaires.[6] The valuable information which Cohen has extracted from the replies has provided, for the first time, real answers to serious questions facing the Jewish world. Not what Jewish leaders think, not what Jewish organizations think, but the opinions and thoughts of a wide and representative cross-section of American Jewry.

In his 1989 survey of American Jewish attitudes towards Israel and Israelis, Cohen postulated that US Jews could be divided into three categories. One third were totally indifferent to Israel; a second third were sentimentally pro-Israel but totally inactive; whilst the last third were committed workers for Israel. Cohen also showed that Jewish support for Israel was rooted in pro-Israelism rather than in an identification with classical Zionist philosophy.

Have you ever seriously considered living in Israel?

	Yes	No	Not sure
1989	14	82	5
1986	14	79	7
1983	15	85	–

Do you consider yourself a Zionist?

	Yes	No	Not sure
1989	25	61	15
1988	24	64	13
1986	27	57	16
1983	36	64	–

I feel I can live a fuller Jewish life in Israel than in the United States:

	Agree	Disagree	Not sure
1989	10	74	16
1986	10	73	17

In addition, Cohen devised a set of questions which measured 'attachment to Israel'. Of the respondents, 73 per cent agreed that 'caring about Israel is a very important part of my being a Jew'; 65 per cent agreed that 'if Israel were destroyed I would feel as if I had suffered one of the personal tragedies in my life'. He also showed how different sectors of American Jewish life felt about Israel in terms of an 'Israel-Attachment Index':

1989 Israel-Attachment Index
(mean scores)

Total	65
Under 35	55
35–44	59

45–54	63
55–64	70
65+	74
Orthodox	86
Conservative	78
Reform	57
Just Jewish	52
Unaffiliated	46
Affiliated	65
Activist	86
High School	69
Some College	66
College Degree	61
Graduate School	65
Liberal	68
Middle Road	65
Conservative	62

From these statistics, Cohen showed that both traditional religious affiliation and Jewish communal affiliation are closely associated with higher levels of pro-Israelism.

Significantly, more Jewish liberals than Jewish conservatives identify with Israel – the exact opposite of the non-Jewish ideological spectrum. The problematic events of the 1980s should therefore have caused a significant decrease amongst Jewish liberals. Despite the hawkish policies of successive Israeli governments, support for Israel from Jewish liberals was not diluted, whereas non-Jewish liberal support certainly wavered. Moreover, in the 1988 US Presidential Elections, once again American Jews voted for the liberal candidate. Nearly 70 per cent of American Jews came out for the Democratic candidate, Michael Dukakis – a figure only exceeded by the vote of American Blacks. Thus, although Israel and the United States both possessed overtly right-wing administrations, US Jews could distinguish between identification with government policy and support for the state.

In the 1988 survey conducted by Professor Cohen, 45 per cent agreed that they were often troubled by the policies of the Israeli government, but 82 per cent answered that it didn't change 'how close I feel to Israel'. Another 72 per cent disagreed with the statement that 'because of the recent violence, I feel less warmly about Israel than I used to'.

Cohen asked a number of questions about Israel's approach to the Intifada. His conclusion was that

a third are genuinely untroubled by Israel's actions; they feel that
Israel is doing the right thing yet getting a 'raw deal' from the
press. At the other end of the spectrum is a third with severe
moral objections to Israel's actions; they cannot say that Israel
is acting reasonably and appropriately, they are embarrassed by
Israel, and they are not sure that Israel is being mistreated by
the press. In the middle is the third who voice public support
for Israel's actions, who feel that Israelis are victims of slanted
reporting, but who also feel privately some misgivings about
Israeli behaviour.

Cohen also compiled an index to show how different sectors of US
Jews viewed Israeli policy towards the Intifada:

1989 Index of Negative Attitudes Towards Israeli Policy on the Intifada

	(mean scores)
Total	34
Under 35	40
35–44	34
45–54	36
55–64	32
65+	32
Orthodox	23
Conservative	31
Reform	38
Just Jewish	38
Unaffiliated	38
Affiliated	34
Activist	31
High School	29
Some College	33
College Degree	33
Graduate School	39
Liberal	40
Middle Road	33
Conservative	29

Cohen's statistics suggest that those deeply enmeshed in the Jewish
world in a religious sense, and thereby distant from the outside world,
tended to give Israeli policy their wholehearted support. Those who
work hard for Jewish causes similarly found the official interpretation

of events more credible than Jews who were unaffiliated and less active organizationally. There was also a significant generation gap. The older generation who see the State of Israel centrally in terms of the Shoah are also unquestioning supporters of official policy. Finally, the level of education played an important factor, with those who had never attended college revealed as the government of Israel's most loyal adherents.

Cohen analysed his respondents' opinions on Israeli foreign policy for the 1980s and concluded that 'it is fair to characterize American Jewry as tilting in a dovish direction'. Majorities opposed annexation of the West Bank and the expansion of settlements. Yet a sizeable proportion of respondents felt uncomfortable in expressing an opinion. No doubt this unease could be explained by a genuine ignorance about the situation, a confusion about the right course of action and a sense of lack of moral standing in advising Israel. Even so, those who did voice opinions 'rejected hawkish policies and those with a definite stance tended to endorse most [though not all] of the dovish policies offered them'. In the surveys conducted between 1983 and 1989, US Jews agreed by a 2:1 margin that 'Palestinians have a right to a homeland on the West Bank and Gaza, so long as it does not threaten Israel'.

The decision of the US government to open a dialogue with the PLO in December 1988 was welcomed by a small majority of respondents – 38 per cent to 28 per cent – whilst many still remained undecided. A large majority rejected direct Israeli–PLO negotiations without preconditions, but 58 per cent endorsed the view that 'if the PLO recognizes Israel and renounces terrorism, Israel should be willing to talk to the PLO'.

When Cohen framed questions designed to bring forth Jewish perceptions of the Palestinians, he found that a majority were suspicious of Arab intentions. Even after Arafat's declarations in Algiers, US Jews thought that 'the PLO was hostile and threatening', while also viewing 'Israel as vulnerable and insecure'. Some 49 per cent agreed that 'you can never trust the Arabs to make a real peace with Israel'.

On the question of dissent, American Jews came out strongly in support of the right to offer different viewpoints. Some 63 per cent disagreed with the statement that 'American Jews should not publicly criticize the policies of the Government of Israel'. In addition, 72 per cent supported the right of Jewish critics to speak in synagogues and community centres. From other questions posed, Cohen also detected a real reticence about whether criticism served any real purpose: 'The hypothetical respondent in the political centre seems to be saying to Jewish critics of Israel, "I support your right to criticize, especially if you do it in my synagogue or Jewish community centre where gentiles won't hear you, but I am not sure that I want you to exercise that right.'"

For most American Jews, the symbolism of 'Israel' is part of their identity as Jews and to criticize 'Israel' is in reality self-criticism. Although an initial reaction has been to evade the issue, the problems that have arisen, especially since 1977, have forced an internal self-reckoning – a recognition that what one may have believed yesterday may not be true today. Given the traumatic and emotional events of the twentieth century, this was an exceedingly difficult process. Although this has not been easy, a coming-to-terms with the Israel of the 1980s has slowly but surely been taking place. The 'Who is a Jew?' controversy, which was integral to the inter-party negotiations following the 1988 Israeli elections, rattled the vast majority of Diaspora Jews. Unlike the problem of Israel's approach to the Intifada, the issue of 'Who is a Jew?' was targeted at the very core of Diaspora 'Jewishness'. For some, Israeli actions during the Intifada created moral dilemmas in terms of their 'Jewishness'. These internal conflicts could be safely distanced as an indirect threat. The 'Who is a Jew?' issue was altogether different in nature. It was direct, central and immediate. The sense of exclusion from 'Jewishness', simply to meet the demands of political horsetrading in forming a government coalition, created an unprecedented wave of anger from America's Jews. Shamir was astounded at the fury of the response, including that of his own supporters in the United States. His astonishment was so profound that it was undoubtedly a factor in the formation of the coalition with Labour.

Moreover, those who had formerly condemned critics of Israeli government policy were now amongst the loudest protesters. This episode brought to a head the distinct unease with which Diaspora Jews had regarded the approach of successive Israeli governments. The 'Who is a Jew?' issue provided them with a legitimate avenue through which to channel grievances and frustrations without actually transcending the formal barriers of non-criticism which they had erected for themselves. Stepping across one threshold increased the possibility of open opposition in other areas. For a growing number of Diaspora Jews, the 1980s was an epoch of the gradual disintegration of the pre-1967 utopian image of Israel in Diaspora eyes. No longer was Israel infallible. Exalted still, but there had been too many instances where an Israeli government had gone wrong. Leonard Fein pointed to the dilemma emerging for American Jews:

It is not at all clear from the sources – from the Biblical texts, the Talmud, the poems and the folk tales – whether the Jerusalem, the Zion, of our millennial longing is the earthly Jerusalem or the distant and inaccessible heavenly Jerusalem. It is not clear whether our expression of hope for redemption is a ritual hope or a lively anticipation. It is not clear what the relationship is between the two Jerusalems, nor which of them is truly Zion.[7]

Between leadership and constituency

The 1989 National Survey of American Jews showed that Jewish leaders were actually more hawkish than those they purported to represent. Compared to both affiliated and unaffiliated Jews, Jewish leaders believed that a PLO State would threaten Israel. Whilst some 70 per cent of unaffiliated and just under 60 per cent of affiliated Jews agreed with the proposition 'If the PLO recognizes Israel and renounces terrorism, Israel should be willing to talk to the PLO', only 45 per cent of Jewish leaders accepted this.

This could certainly be interpreted as implying that the leaders were more informed about events than the masses and could therefore come to more certain conclusions. Alternatively, the attitudes of Jewish leadership could also be ascribed to the result of social and political conditioning through their intense involvement within the Jewish world. Since 1977, Diaspora leaders have found themselves in an unenviable position. Their traditional role was to represent the views and opinions of their communities – and after 1948 also those of the State of Israel – to host governments and to the non-Jewish world in general. Since the election of Menachem Begin, their task has been made virtually impossible owing to a distinct lack of consensus in Israel and its reflection in the Diaspora. Moreover, this polarization was accentuated with each new crisis: the war in Lebanon, the settlements in the Territories, and, of course, the Intifada itself. For a variety of reasons, a majority of Diaspora leaders pretended that this division did not exist. Moderate voices were ignored and the authoritative policies of the Israeli government adhered to.

The stunning victory of the Six Day War in 1967 right up until the rescue of the hostages at Entebbe in 1976 was a heroic period for Israel and for the whole Jewish people. A real sense of achievement was felt. Jews throughout the world devoted themselves to Jewish causes with genuine pride. The courage of the national movement of Jews in the Soviet Union to obtain the right to leave the USSR enthralled and involved tens of thousands of Diaspora Jews. In addition, the then intransigence of the Palestinian National Movement was also very visible. Their declarations were highly negative and were regarded with a certain degree of despair even by Israeli moderates. Instead of formulating a political strategy, they seemed more interested in righting injustices through reconstructing past history and fighting an ideological war against 'Zionism'. They evinced little interest in a dialogue with leaders of the peace camp and confined themselves to speaking to minuscule peripheral groups on the Israeli Left, such as Matzpen, whose anti-Zionism proved palatable. Whilst the infamous 'Zionism is Racism' resolution at the United Nations proved successful in terms of propaganda for the PLO, it was totally meaningless, and indeed self-defeating, in convincing the Israeli public and the Diaspora that there was a solution to the conflict. Jews were relegated to a theological entity who would live happily in an amorphous 'democratic secular state' which would be Arab in character according to the PLO Covenant.

All this simply irritated Jews and alienated them. The core of their anger, however, resided in their perception of Palestinian terrorism, which had resulted in the deaths of scores of innocents. PLO sources justified atrocities by pointing to Israeli bombing raids on Palestinian camps and a belief that official Palestinian sponsorship of international terrorism would bring the Palestinian problem to the attention of the international community. Even after 1974, when the PLO formally renounced terrorism in the international arena, many Palestinians officially believed that their armed struggle against 'the Zionist entity' would somehow result in victory and a Greater Palestine, from the Jordan to the Mediterranean. Whilst a benevolent interpretation would suggest that this was a historic phase through which the Palestinian National Movement had to pass, what they really achieved was the fortification of the state of siege that had always characterized the Jewish outlook. Psychological barriers against the outside world were strengthened.

In Israel, it assisted the nationalist cause and helped in the demise of the rudderless Labour bureaucracy. In the Diaspora, it revived memories of the Shoah and the inadequacies of Jewish leadership to avert that terrible tragedy. Moreover, those elected to office in Diaspora communities at that time were those who in their youth had witnessed both the murder of 6 million of their brethren and the subsequent redemption of Israel through the establishment of the State in 1948. Clearly, any hint that a government of Israel might be following the wrong policies would not have been welcome at that moment of history, and the very idea of talking to the Palestinians was deemed treasonous. Attempts to create Diaspora organizations which believed in reconciliation with the Palestinians or disapproved of Israeli settlement in the Territories were doomed to failure. *Breira* (Alternative) lasted for a few years in the 1970s before outside pressure forced it to disband. Indeed, the basis of national purpose became a distorted survivalism in a period when Jews were least threatened by physical extermination. Even though Israel had militarily guaranteed its own survival in both 1967 and 1973, paradoxically the possibility of its destruction was felt most keenly in the Diaspora. The fact of Israel's ability to defend itself was virtually disregarded. By the 1970s, the centrality of Israel in Jewish life as a product of Shoah remembrance – in the United States particularly – became a reference point in the contemporary definition of Jewishness. The politics of survivalism were built upon a number of basic premises:

> The survival of Israel is at stake; the meaning of Jewish life everywhere is dependent on Israel; a threat to Israel's survival is a threat to Jews everywhere; Jews must be militant in acting to ensure Israel's survival; in acting to ensure Israel's survival, Jews are thereby acting to ensure their own survival and continuity; the response of non-Jews to Israel's struggle for survival is indicative of their attitude to Jews in general; in the light of history, indifference to these concerns is as dangerous as outright antisemitism.[8]

The rise of the new Jewish politics in the Diaspora dovetailed neatly with the electoral triumph of Likud in Israel in 1977. Moreover, Palestinian terrorism and the growing isolation of Israel internationally further underlined its relevance and importance.

The outlook of the practitioners of the new Jewish politics was a reductionist one. Thus, despite the growing political schism within Israel during the early 1980s, Jewish leaders in the Diaspora found it psychologically difficult to cope with any Israeli viewpoint other than the official one. The advocates of the new Jewish politics could not contemplate sitting down with the Palestinian enemy. This survivalist mentality based on 'oneness' with Israel had the effect of turning the Diaspora – in the eyes of some critics – into 'a rotten borough in the hands of a Prime Minister of Israel – whoever he might be'.[9]

Adapting to Likud

Although the earthquake of Menachem Begin's ascendancy initially sent private tremors throughout the Jewish world, communal leadership convinced themselves within a few weeks that little had really changed. Diaspora Jews fervently embraced Begin when he visited their communities, whereas a few years earlier they had been prepared to relegate him to the scum of the earth. Yet it was not simply coming to terms with a new reality. For Diaspora Jewry, the Prime Minister of Israel was a national symbol, the embodiment of Zionism. Ideology did not enter into the equation.

Whilst the success of the Camp David Accords provided the achievement to unite communities and to quell any visible dissent over Begin's policies in the Territories, it was quite clear even at an early stage that intellectuals and young people in the Diaspora were unhappy at the direction that the official face of Israel had taken. Following the assassination attempt on the Israeli Ambassador in London, Shlomo Argov, in 1982, Jewish leadership strongly supported the response of Prime Minister Begin and Defence Minister Sharon to cross the Lebanese border and attack PLO positions. When the incursion became an invasion, rallies and meetings were organized and attended by large numbers of people to support 'Israel'. Many related to the invasion in a non-ideological sense of solidarity with the State of Israel, and in terms of the survival of the Jewish people, without looking at the reality of the political situation. This war, in their eyes, was like past wars, simply a continuation of Israel's struggle to live in a world dominated by enemies and opponents. Jewish leaders bellowed solidarity and passed resolutions. Financial donors were taken to Lebanon on 'fact-finding tours'. Ordinary members of the community were given 'the facts' – according to the Israeli government – through public-affairs committees. No mention was made of awkward facts such as the long-time cease-fire with the PLO on the Lebanese border or the shooting of Shlomo Argov by the anti-PLO Abu Nidal Group stationed in Iraq and Syria, not Lebanon. No mention was made of Sharon's reckless military behaviour in the past. And, most important of all, nothing was said about the growing roar of protest within Israel itself at the deception that had been practised.

A central focus of Diaspora attention was media bias. Whilst undoubtedly a lot of erroneous reporting did take place, clearly not all of it fell into that category. Although some reporters were unfriendly at the outset, it was unrealistic to pretend that all were anti-semites determined to vent their wrath on the Jewish State. Yet comparisons with the Nazis, exaggerated descriptions and faulty statistics effectively diverted Diaspora attention. Instead of asking whether the policy of the Israeli government was a wise one and confronting the growing division within Israel itself, distortions in the media, by default, provided an escape mechanism for many a troubled Diaspora Jew. In one sense the media helped to create Jewish solidarity with Israel in the Diaspora far more effectively than the Jewish leadership. A few months later, the chairman of the Jewish Agency reported that the war had actually increased donations to Israel. Similarly the United Jewish Appeal in the United States reported that 1988 – the first full year of the Intifada – had been 'the best year yet' for donations, achieving an estimated $735 million.[10]

While liberal Jewish organizations such as the American Jewish Congress and the American Jewish Committee genuinely opposed the war, others backed it fully. Julius Berman, Chairman of the

Conference of Presidents of Major American Jewish Organizations, consistently advised Diaspora Jews not to make suggestions to the Israeli government and 'to support Israel unconditionally'.[11] Other communal leaders attempted to develop a consensus with critics to preserve a modicum of public communal unity. But here, too, it was a consensus of understanding for the war, rather than of overt support of it. The President of the Board of Deputies of British Jews wrote to *The Times* that 'we all well understand the reason for Israel's military action. As in the democracy of Israel, so here there is argument as to the extent of the campaign, but none as to its necessity'.[12] All arguments and justifications dissipated following the Phalangist massacre of Palestinians at Sabra and Shatilla camps – and the terrible implication of Israeli involvement. When Prime Minister Begin refused to establish a commission of inquiry with a characteristic dismissal of all admonitions that such barbarity was the prerogative of non-Jews, outraged Jewish leaders who lived amongst non-Jews virtually unanimously supported the demand of President Navon for an investigation into Israel's role in the atrocity. For many a Diaspora leader, the spectacle of that carnage coming into the living rooms of millions was just too painful. It conflicted with the self-image of the Jew as victim, as survivor and as defender of the downtrodden. It pushed many staunch defenders of the war over the threshold into undisguised criticism.

The aftermath of the war gave rise to sobering reflections. Many realized how unreal their perceptions and beliefs had been at its inception. Others, however, continued to justify the war despite the Kahan Commission and the resignation of Menachem Begin. Some vented their fury on those who had opposed the war in Israel. One irate Diaspora writer to the *Jerusalem Post* attributed Palestinian terrorism to the activities of the Israeli peace camp: 'Their reckless statements (whether pronounced in clipped Oxford English or with a coarse Polish accent) have contributed heavily to the blood libel against Israel in the case of Beirut, and to an orgy of Jew-baiting that goes on in the world's media, with such tragic consequences as the attacks on Jews in Paris, Brussels, Vienna and Rome'.[13]

Within Israel itself, the nationalist camp strongly resented those Diaspora Jews who had chosen to speak out during the course of the war. Their disdain not only reflected a demand that the Diaspora had no right to give public voice to their opinions, but also represented an attempt to limit criticism of their own role in the matter. The peace camp in Israel, on the other hand, welcomed and indeed encouraged such criticism of government policy. Even so, there remained an undercurrent which still questioned the participation of the Diaspora in internal debates, however vital the issue. Professor Shlomo Avneri, who was known for his dovish views, played down Diaspora anxiety: 'Israel is a value; the Diaspora is merely a fact'.

Liberals, leaders and lobbies

The years between the siege of Beirut in the summer of 1982 and the start of the Intifada in December 1987 were relatively tranquil. Shamir's lacklustre style was a welcome change from Begin's penetrating rhetoric. Moreover, many Diaspora Jews clearly felt more comfortable with the urbane Peres as Prime Minister, regardless of his policies. Peres seemed to symbolize a return to the safe days of Ben-Gurion and Golda Meir when issues were clear-cut. The establishment of a National Unity government in which Likud and Labour formed an uneasy coalition was – at least on the surface – a pleasing development for Jewish leaders in the Diaspora. It seemed to suggest that the schism within Israel had been overcome. Unity could once more be promoted within Diaspora communities and dissidents could be depicted as unrepresentative. Moreover, appeals to host governments would carry an authoritative mandate.

The reality, however, was considerably different, since effectively two governments co-existed in an antagonistic symbiosis – a union of irreconcilable opposites. Israeli embassies around the world thus received conflicting instructions and simply passed on the confusion to hapless Jewish leaders. By 1988, both Diaspora communities and the Israeli public itself expressed a strong desire to see the emergence of one party in government after the elections. The outcome of the vote was indecisive. Shamir's determination to create yet another National Unity government with Labour was, in part, provoked by the vociferous reaction of American Jewry to the issue of 'Who is a Jew?'. Diaspora leaders thus paradoxically catalysed a continuation of the unwanted confusion of an unworkable coalition because this was the price that had to be paid to avoid the trauma of 'Who is a Jew?'. Although officials in Israel and the Diaspora continued to promote the idea that the National Unity government represented the majority of Israelis, it did not in reality reflect the wishes of the electorate. People voted for political parties and presumably for their stated policies. It was the parties themselves who constructed yet another unwanted National Unity government – a process which involved considerable political horse-trading and a continual backsliding on principles and policies.

If the years between 1982 and 1987 were not years of violence and war, there were many other problems which troubled Diaspora leaders. Irangate and the Pollard affair highlighted Israeli interference in American affairs, much to the embarrassment of US Jewry. Israel's collusion in facilitating the Reagan Administration's arms trade with

Iran, and the subsequent spin-off for the Nicaraguan Contras, made a mockery of the U.S. leadership's 'no truck with terrorists' stand. But the case of Jonathan Pollard, an American Jew, who with misplaced Zionist zeal had been caught passing defence secrets to the Israelis, was even more damaging. The Pollard affair in particular openly raised the spectre of double loyalties, which had hitherto been a taboo subject. The umbrella Conference of Major American Jewish Organizations continued to oppose any open discussion of such questions and thus was happy to support the policies of whichever Israeli government was in power. Yet its advice was often rejected by some of its liberal constituents. For example, it requested Jewish organizations in the United States not to comment on the General Security Services (GSS) scandal in Israel in which its head was granted immunity to prosecution. This did not deter the American Jewish Congress, which pointed out that 'there were better ways of balancing urgent security considerations and the integrity of a lawful society'. Prominent figures such as Edgar Bronfman of the World Jewish Congress and Rabbi Alexander Schindler of the American Reform Movement continued to project liberal views, whilst the Anti-Defamation League continued to support the official line of no public dissent and an emphasis on Diaspora unity.

Leftist groups such as New Jewish Agenda became more visible and increased their supporters. Others adhered to 'friends' of dovish Israeli organizations such as Peace Now and Yesh Gvul. But perhaps the most important development came from the initiative of some American Jews who were not readily identifiable in an overt political sense. A younger generation of philanthropists, tired of the visits of Israeli public figures and their admonitions 'to support Israel' developed the New Israel Fund and expanded their operations to deal with serious social problems in Israel such as battered wives and AIDS, as well as funding human-rights and peace groups. A Jewish Peace Lobby was established to rival the pro-Israel government AIPAC in vying for the loyalty of congressmen. Serious new magazines such as 'Tikkun' appeared without Jewish organizational support or finance and quickly built up a mass readership of disaffected liberal Jews. Within the intellectual world, there was a deep and bitter conflict between liberals such as Leonard Fein and Arthur Hertzberg and neo-conservatives such as Norman Podhoretz and Cynthia Ozick. Yet quite often the rhetoric was a reaction to their opponents' style rather than to their ideology. While Norman Podhoretz saw the Intifada as 'nothing more and nothing less than the opening of a new front' in the continuing Arab attempt to liquidate Israel, other neo-conservatives, such as Irving Kristol, hinted at adopting the Allon Plan and coming to a settlement with the Palestinians. Indeed, many neo-conservatives were closer to the right wing of the Israeli Labour Party which advocated 'iron-fist' policies whilst proclaiming its willingness to surrender part of the Territories in exchange for peace. But the neo-conservatives were united in condemning what they considered to be the pious breast-beating of the liberals.

> We know well the history of assassinations of Arab moderates, the use against Israel of bloody methods of terror and the continued unwillingness of some Arab elements to contemplate anything other than murderous and unforgiving war against Israel. But we decry strong-arm methods by Israel. What can such methods lead to but a harvest of hate, an intensified and more extremist rebellion by Palestinian Arabs, a brutalizing of Israeli boys drafted into the army?[14]

Such sentiments in a letter from Irving Howe, Arthur Hertzberg, Henry Rosovsky and Michael Walzer to the *New York Times* earned the scorn of the neo-conservatives. But overall, as Professor Cohen concluded in his annual national surveys of American Jewry, there was a 'dovish tilt' throughout the 1980s. Peres tried to encourage this trend when he asked Jewish leaders to take a more active role in an address to the Presidents' Conference in September 1987. Although large sums were raised, Cohen himself remarked that United Jewish Appeal Federation campaigns during the decade were 'sluggish, barely keeping pace with inflation'. Moreover, the allocation of those funds showed a redirection in favour of domestic concerns. In 1976 some 55 per cent of monies raised went overseas. By 1986 that percentage had dropped to 45 per cent.[15] This probably had more to do with the changing complexion of American Jewry than with disaffection with Israel. Even so, the attitude of donors clearly shifted in the aftermath of the 1982 war. The United Jewish Appeal Chairman was able to write in early 1987 that 'Israel, while remaining the central fact of Jewish existence, will attract American Jewish financial support based not only on the positive and even passionate instincts of the contributors but also on the judgement of her merits'.[16]

Yet this did not mean any slackening of political support for Israel on Capitol Hill. The margin of support for granting military and economic aid to Israel in both Congress and the Senate increased during the 1980s despite the invasion of Lebanon and the Intifada. The Israeli lobby organization, AIPAC, expanded its membership fivefold during the decade and tripled its number of staff. By the onset of the Intifada, it boasted an annual budget of $6 million. AIPAC was known for its efficiency and professionalism in rallying political and financial support through its network of pro-Israel Political Action Committees (PACs) for Israeli government policies. While its techniques of persuasion were often controversial and sometimes quite ruthless, AIPAC was also extremely successful and highly respected by political opponents.

As an independent organization, AIPAC occasionally developed policies in opposition to the official Israeli government line. It is believed that in 1988 AIPAC helped the US administration develop the Schultz Plan which Shamir so vehemently rejected – 'only the signature is genuine'. Prior to Shamir's visit to Washington in March 1988, a group of thirty US senators signed an open letter supporting Schultz's peace initiative. It was instigated by two Jewish senators, Carl Levin (Michigan) and Rudy Boschwitz (Minnesota) and attracted the signatures of Edward Kennedy and Daniel Moynihan as well as five out of the seven Jewish senators. Indeed, had the US Senate been sitting at the time, it is quite likely that the letter would have gained another fifty signatories. Many of those who signed received financial backing from pro-Israel PACs in the AIPAC network. Given its close contacts with these senators, it is inconceivable that AIPAC knew nothing about its existence at an early stage. Moreover, it did not try to halt its publication. Indeed, some have even suggested that the letter was conceived by AIPAC itself and written by its staff.

6

The Diaspora and the Intifada

Facing the Intifada

The onset of the Intifada in December 1987 accentuated the divisions which had existed since 1982. Predictable protests came from predictable sources. In Britain, within a few weeks of the commencement of the Intifada, virtually every Anglo-Jewish writer signed an advertisement in the *Jewish Chronicle* under the title of 'Jews for a Just Israel'.[1] Although the text criticized the Israeli government's policy of 'might, force and beatings', it was the very title of the advertisement and its implications which created debate and consternation in the newspaper's letters page. In contrast to 1982, in every major Jewish community considerable numbers of individuals were willing to cross the line dividing silence from speaking out. Whether they represented the majority of the community was unknown, but clearly the liberal opposition was neither marginal nor small. There was a determination that the quiescence and servility of the Diaspora during the Lebanon War should not be repeated. Many who were sympathetic but still uncertain doubted the value of protest – especially if it was conducted in full view of non-Jewish onlookers. Yet those who openly dissented felt that it would be tantamount to a lack of self-respect for themselves as Jews if they sat back in silence and allowed the traditional leadership to repeat the explanations which emanated from Jerusalem. The emergence of a body of liberal but loyal opposition also served as a focus for many young Jews who were disillusioned by the actions of both the Jewish leadership and the Israeli government. Such widespread disaffection from official policies undoubtedly weakened the mandate of traditional leadership in dialogue with national governments. No longer could they speak for the entire community when consensus no longer existed.

The arena where arguments were conducted was also a subject of detailed discussion. For some, it had to be within a specifically Jewish environment. For others, the national media sufficed. This difference stemmed not simply from a fear of the outsider but from a genuine belief by Jewish liberals that it would encourage those who opposed the existence of the State of Israel and not simply those who criticized its government's policies. Distinguishing between critical friends and dedicated opponents was not always easy.

The split in the American Jewish community allowed the US administration to support the UN Security Council Resolution in January 1988 which called upon Israel not to deport any more Palestinians. Moreover, both the American and British governments were willing to show their support for liberal Jews who opposed Israeli government policies. For example, William Waldegrave, then Under-Secretary of State at the British Foreign Office, attended a meeting in December 1989 chaired by Evelyn de Rothschild and Lord Goodman, at which Hani el-Hassan, Arafat's political adviser, spoke. This not only provoked the consternation of the Board of Deputies of British Jews but also pushed the Israeli Foreign Ministry into issuing a directive to all embassies on the problem of PLO–Diaspora Jewish contacts. Shortly after the commencement of the Intifada and prior to Shamir's visit to Washington to discuss the Schultz Plan, a delegation of the Presidents' Conference visited Israel. Morris Abram, its Chairman, came to brief and discuss the situation in the United States with Israeli government representatives, but pointedly not to advise them on what to do. Whilst Abram publicly repeated the official line, he significantly emphasized that there would be a serious slippage of support if the situation continued. Rather than drawing attention to policy itself, he confined himself to observations on its effects in the United States, both within the Jewish Community and on Capitol Hill. Abram reiterated his belief that it was unwise and imprudent for American Jews publicly to disagree with Israeli government policy. Arguments always returned, and indeed were reduced, to a basis of Israel's survival and its security considerations. American Jews were 'limited partners with limited liability' and public criticism would have the effect of 'ungluing American commitment to Israel's security'.[2]

Despite all the manifestations of dissent, Abram told Shamir a few weeks later, on his arrival in the United States, that American Jewry still stood behind the Prime Minister.[3] This seemed to be confirmed when Shamir addressed 3000 members of the young leadership of the United Jewish Appeal at the Washington Hilton. They gave Shamir a standing ovation, repeatedly broke out in prolonged applause during his speech and demanded several curtain-calls at the end. This was presented by many American Jewish leaders as clear evidence that the ordinary Jew in the street was foursquare behind the Prime Minister of Israel. In Israel, too, it appeared that American Jews supported official policies to the hilt and this was underscored by Likud propagandists. Yet, although Shamir had won an unexpected public-relations victory, those who came to the rally were unelected fundraisers, 'young, attractive and out for a good time'.

Before Shamir's appearance, they were warmed up 'by an hour-long professionally staged Zionist tear-jerker' amid three huge maps of Israel and the Territories with the Green Line significantly absent. The audience was treated to a rendition of the youthful diary of the popular sexologist and former Israeli, Dr Ruth. When Shamir appeared, he directed his appeal towards his audience's deep unhappiness with the negative reports appearing on the nightly news. He differentiated between American Jewish involvement in civil rights and the Palestinian uprising: 'Make no mistake about it, what you see are not demonstrations. They are not sit-ins. It is not civil disobedience. It is war – a war against Israelis, against the existence of the State of Israel'.

The appeal to survivalism went down extremely well amongst an audience which a journalist present described as 'woefully ignorant of the Aleph Bet [Hebrew ABC] of Israeli politics'.[4] Finally, Shamir was presented with an award depicting the Knesset and the Capitol by the Chairman of the proceedings, who described the former Lehi leader as a founding father of Israel.

Liberal Jewish intellectuals who were troubled by the Intifada were appalled at this spectacle. Arthur Hertzberg, a leading dove, later remarked on the differing perceptions in the United States and Israel:

> Some were, no doubt, really on his side, inspired by a defiant assertion of 'Jewish power'. Many wanted to imagine that the Israeli leader was acting like an American politician, posturing as intransigent as a way of preparing for an inevitable compromise with the Palestinians. Here the fundamental difference between Israel and American Jewish perspectives was apparent. The same political performance had different meanings for two different audiences. In Washington, younger American Jews were asserting their pride in their homeland. In Tel Aviv and Jerusalem, the standing ovation they gave Shamir was seen as support for the tough ideologue known to the Israelis, not for the 'reasonable' Shamir of the Americans' imagination.[5]

Shamir understood that confusion and ignorance benefited him in that those who were uncertain would naturally gravitate to a focus of authority such as the Prime Minister of Israel. It was in his interest to propagate generalities about the situation and to evoke crude survivalism and expressions of unity because an open debate would probably have resulted in support for the views of his dovish opponent, Shimon Peres – as opinion polls had shown. Moreover, it was important to maintain the support of the traditional Jewish leadership and indeed to manipulate it to ensure that only government policies were advocated in Jewish forums and in discussion with the Reagan administration. Yet, in private, many American Jewish leaders appeared to be increasingly dovish – and this seems to be borne out by opinion polls. For example, the Israel–Diaspora Institute in Tel Aviv reported in 1990 that 76 per cent of the American Jewish leadership favoured territorial compromise, assuming genuine security guarantees were given. In public, however, they tended to don the mantle of survivalism and hawkishness, thereby undermining their own moderate convictions. This may indeed be the psychological legacy of centuries of persecution and a desire not to fritter away hard-won political capital, but there was an element of opportunism as well. To break ranks and to voice different opinions was also to step outside the respectability of elected office. It opened the gate to criticism from rivals for future office. It risked accrued political and financial influence within the power structure of the Jewish community.

Dovish figures such as Arthur Hertzberg were harshly critical of this mentality and viewed Shamir's relationship with Jewish leadership as a supremely, symbiotically opportunist one. Familiarity with a Prime Minister of Israel conferred a certain legitimacy on Jewish leaders in the eyes of the community, even more so when they participated in a 'mission' as part of a visiting Diaspora delegation. As Arthur Hertzberg cynically remarked, 'What the Prime Minister requires in return for listening privately in his Jerusalem office to a polite, perhaps even pained, disagreement with his policies, is the staging in America of political support'.[6]

When Shamir returned from his meeting with Shultz to report to a large gathering of American Jewish leaders in New York, he was greeted 'as a conquering hero, fresh from the wars' and 'not as a failed diplomat who had blundered into saying "No" to an American peace initiative'. Yet Shamir's opposition to the Shultz Plan conflicted with their own moderate views as manifested before the Prime Minister's visit and also with the views of the community as confirmed by opinion polls. When a number of leaders with dovish views rose to present alternative opinions,

> one would have imagined [from the audience's response that] we had presented a brief for Jesse Jackson to the Jewish Defence League. Mr Shamir lowered the boom on us, suggesting that public criticism of Israel by Jews plays into the hands of anti-semites and helps the government of the United States pressure Israel. Thunderous ovation. It was an atmosphere hostile to diversity and more akin to mass hysteria than to pluralism.[7]

Although it was not widely publicized, Shamir took time off from official state duties to raise funds for his Likud Party. Private dinners where the Prime Minister made an appearance would reap thousands of badly needed dollars for party funds. Generous Diaspora Jews would often give willingly to 'Israel' at such dinners, in the ignorant belief that it would benefit the country rather than the party. Often, little distinction was made between the roles of Prime Minister and party leader. The Labour Party was also deeply involved in this use of public office and public funds for private party fundraising. During the 1988 election campaign, observers conservatively estimated that Labour and Likud privately raised $10 million each for the party coffers. Another $7 million was allocated to the two major parties from public funds. Many of the smaller Israeli political parties objected strenuously to these practices. Mapam's Yair Tsaban publicly complained that the greed of the major parties in taking an increasingly greater proportion of state funds was at the expense of the nation's poor. Shinui's Amnon Rubinstein commented that 'in one single fund-drive in London among wealthy Jewish businessmen who have interests in Israel, Likud figures told me they raised over one million English pounds – the big parties sent their ministers abroad at the taxpayers' expense to raise money for their coffers'.[8] Israeli political leaders were clearly adept at circumventing their country's rules on donations from abroad. The State Comptroller showed that during the 1984 elections the National Religious Party spent twice its financial ceiling, the Tami Party three times its limit and Ezer Weizmann's Yahad Party fourteen times its allocation for its three seats in the Knesset. The major parties often employed the services of prominent figures to solicit funds. Ehud Olmert was the co-ordinator of North American fundraising for the Likud. Although Meir Kahane was reputed to raise half a million dollars each year in the United States, the Israeli public has no legal access to a full list of donors to his Kach movement. Although the Israeli State Comptroller is in possession of the facts, she is not empowered to publish them. Unlike in the United States, there is no right to public disclosure.

A large percentage of electoral campaign expenses was paid for by Diaspora sympathizers. During the 1988 electoral campaign, a North American businessman put his public-relations firm at the disposal of the Labour Party and footed the bill for the party's telephone canvassing. While donations and sponsorship are common practice in Europe and the United States, and such Diaspora funds were minuscule in comparison with fundraising for the Palestinian cause in the Arab states, it undoubtedly projected double standards for those who suggested that the Diaspora should maintain a studied silence when it came to government policy. If there should be no intervention in the internal affairs of the State of Israel through public criticism of government policy, then how could donations be given to one party or the other, thereby supporting a particular policy through financial endorsement? Moreover, why did communal leaders attack public critics but remain silent on the practitioners of financial intervention?

The Prime Minister's Solidarity Conference

At the beginning of 1989, Diaspora Jewish leaders were visited by two senior members of the Knesset, Likud's Ehud Olmert and Labour's Motta Gur. They were informed that it had been decided to hold 'The Prime Minister's Conference of Jewish Solidarity with Israel' in Jerusalem within a few weeks.

The idea to stage such a conference had its genesis in the lack of criticism from the Jewish leadership of the US Administration's decision to commence a dialogue with the PLO. Indeed, the 1989 National Survey of American Jewry showed that more were in favour of the dialogue than against it. In addition, quite a few Diaspora figures had only just returned from Israel and were reluctant to become involved in what appeared to be a propaganda exercise in support of Shamir's policies prior to his visit to meet the new President of the United States, George Bush.

In the second National Unity government with Labour, Likud not only had a Prime Minister for a full term of office but also directed the Foreign Ministry through the appointment of Moshe Arens as Foreign Minister and 'Bibi' Netanyahu as his deputy. The new inhabitants of the Foreign Ministry rightly perceived that a divided and thus weakened Diaspora would find it difficult to deliver the political clout required in difficult times. Moreover, the ease with which the US administration proceeded to a dialogue with the PLO was perceived as threatening for Likud policies and particularly for their relationship with George Bush, who was believed to be less sympathetic than his predecessor in the White House. In addition, there was a clear determination to strengthen mainstream government positions in the Diaspora and thereby marginalize the influence of the Israeli peace camp which had made a considerable inroad.

An unspoken assumption was that a conference exuding patriotism and solidarity would not only tie the Diaspora formally to Likud policies but also detach Labour from its association with the peace movement. To the surprise of many in the Labour Party, Shimon Peres agreed to the staging of the conference. Motta Gur – who saw himself as a future candidate for the Labour leadership – was appointed to liaise with Diaspora organizations. Many Jewish leaders thus became less sceptical about the *raison d'être* if a Labour man was involved with a Likud idea. Yet although it was promoted as a Conference of Solidarity with Israel, Gur and Olmert told Diaspora leaders that it was primarily an Israeli government project. This meant that speakers and participants who opposed government policy were not welcome. While Shamir gave interviews – especially to the English-language press – expounding the right of participants to disagree with him, he did not intend them to disagree with the policies of the National Unity government. It was possible to be anti-Shamir at the conference, but not to be anti-government. Opposing Shamir only meant supporting Peres. Differences of opinion could take place only within the context of full support for the National Unity government.

Although the Conference purported to be dedicated to Jewish unity, ironically this could be achieved only at the price of Jewish disunity since known Diaspora opponents of government policy were not invited. In some countries Israeli embassies dispatched invitations themselves rather than asking representative communal bodies. This ensured that only reasonably compliant delegates would go. In Britain, for example, the nominal lay head of the community, the President of the Board of Deputies, could not even locate a list of delegates to convene a meeting before departure. Thus, few writers and academics attended the conference since they – by definition almost – would be those most likely to ask difficult questions. Those who did go were essentially communal leaders and philanthropists whose limited outlook allowed them to accept the agenda of one ministerial speech after another with very little participation by delegates. The conference concluded with a declaration of support for the government of Israel – a clear difference of focus from its emotive and apolitical opening title of 'Jewish Solidarity with Israel'.

At the closing ceremony outside the Western Wall in Jerusalem, Shamir revealed his concern over divided views in the Diaspora: 'When I come to this Old City, I have visions of the flames rising to the sky when the Temple was burnt and the city was razed – because our people was divided. Therefore I believe with every fibre of my being in Jewish unity, in Jewish strength, in Jewish commitment to this city and Eretz Israel'.

Some organizations, in their statements and advertisements, also evoked the spectre of past destruction and disunity as a means of supporting Shamir's policies. One advertisement from the Anti-Defamation League compared the Nazi onslaught on doomed European Jewry with the contemporary diplomatic offensive of the PLO: 'We still talk about what our grandparents, our parents and we did or did not do to help the Jews of Europe during the Holocaust. Our new trial is upon us. How will history judge us? How will we judge ourselves?'9

In addition to organizations which supported Shamir's policies, a number of liberal figures also attended in the hope of softening any overt hawkishness. Many also stayed away. Although no figures were published on the number of invitations issued, official sources in London

admitted that there had been only fifty acceptances in Britain out of
130 invitations issued. In other countries too, only approximately a
third of invitees actually went to the Conference. Thus, although
the figure of 1581 delegates was officially announced, it is likely
that well over 3000 did not go. No doubt some were otherwise
occupied, given the short notice in calling the Conference, but others
clearly did not go because they did not wish to be aligned with the
politics of the Israeli government. In Britain the philosopher Sir Isaiah
Berlin, a former President of the Board of Deputies, Greville Janner
MP and Mrs Vivienne Duffield, daughter of the late philanthropist
Charles Clore, declined to attend because of their unhappiness with
government policy. In addition, many liberal Jews in the Diaspora
announced their criticism through advertisements and by letters in
both the Jewish and national press.

Paradoxically, the necessity to stage such a conference was the
clearest indication yet that Shamir did not have full support for his
policies in the Diaspora and that loyal dissent was an important factor.
Indeed, the international press made much of those who did not attend
the Conference, so that when Shamir finally did meet George Bush
shortly afterwards, he carried with him no visible mandate of support
from the Diaspora.

At this summit, Shamir revealed his plan to hold elections in
the Territories. The development was welcomed by both the US
administration and the American Jewish community – especially those
critics who viewed this as a breakthrough. There was a clear sigh
of relief that the Israeli government had come up with at least the
rudiments of a credible proposition. Jewish leadership welcomed it as a
basis for rebuilding a consensus in support of government policies. The
Anti-Defamation League even rescinded its plan to place 'Israel Wants
Peace!' advertisements in the national press.

Yet some warned even at the outset that the election plan would
simply become bogged down in problems of procedure and, like
the Camp David negotiations on Palestinian autonomy, would lead
nowhere. Six months later, Shamir returned to Washington to discuss
the lack of progress and to receive a very cool reception from the
White House. The euphoria earlier in the year had been replaced by a
perception of Shamir's procrastination in advancing the peace process
and nitpicking over Mubarak's ten-point plan as well as over the Baker
Plan. The differences between Bush and Shamir were now admitted
publicly and this caused great uneasiness amongst Jewish leadership
in the United States. In addition, on the eve of his departure, the
provisional findings of a poll of lay and professional leaders in the
community by Professor Steven Cohen showed that a majority
favoured negotiations with the PLO and in general adopted a dovish

position.[10] Thus a speech to 3000 Jewish leaders in Cincinnati earned Shamir a 'polite but restrained' reception. Pro-Israel congressmen queued up to ask questions about Israeli assistance for South African missile-development programmes, while over 200 rabbis requested the Israeli Prime Minister to accept the principle of land for peace.

On top of all this, forty-one prominent American Jews who had held high office in the community sent a letter to Shamir. Mindful of the misrepresentation enacted the previous year, they told the Israeli Prime Minister, 'Please do not mistake courtesy for consensus or applause for endorsement of all the policies you pursue'. Although both the Prime Minister and the Chairman of the Presidents' Conference dismissed them as 'a few individuals who are out of sync. with the Jewish mainstream',[11] the letter received wide coverage and represented a deepening unhappiness in the Diaspora.

Despite all these setbacks, on his return Shamir reported to the Knesset Foreign Affairs and Defence Committee that US Jewry's overwhelming support for the peace process would avert any collision with the Bush administration. Contrary to Cohen's findings, he told them that American Jews supported him in opposing demands for a Palestinian State.

The metamorphosis of the Jerusalem Post

Shamir also had problems with his own right-wing within the Likud – the Constraints Ministers Sharon, Levy and Modai'i – over the election proposal. In an attempt to neutralize internal criticism, he again pointed to the support of American Jewry by quoting an unidentified Diaspora visitor who advised the Prime Minister 'not to pay attention to what is printed in the *Jerusalem Post*'. Contrary to the *Post*'s coverage of events, 'American Jews fully supported the government's position'. An attack on the English-language *Jerusalem Post* provided a diversion for his critics, since the newspaper's liberal and independent policy was heartily resented by the Israeli Right. Yet this attack ultimately served another purpose. The *Post*'s editor, Erwin Frenkel, decided to respond in an editorial, commenting that 'stigmatizing the press has, therefore, become a favourite political sport, relished by, though not restricted to, the Prime Minister's party. For claiming a monopoly on patriotism, they would dishonour dissent'.[12]

But the *Post*'s liberal tradition was also under fire from its new owners, the Canadian-based conglomerate Hollinger Inc., which already owned the conservative British *Daily Telegraph*. Hollinger's David Radler paid the Histadrut, the Israeli Labour Federation, the huge sum of $17.5 million. Clearly the change of proprietor from a left-wing trade union to a right-wing entrepreneur meant fundamental alterations. In addition, although the *Post* was only a small cog in the Hollinger empire, it seemed bad business practice to pay such a high price for the newspaper. Many believed that the payment expressed more than a commercial desire to make money. The excessive outlay was used to justify a broad plan to develop the *Post* into an international newspaper. This could only succeed, it was argued, if the newspaper reflected 'the Israeli reality'. Only highly committed Jews, interested in Israel, would initially subscribe to the newspaper and they, Hollinger believed, would tend towards a position which supported the status quo and government positions in general. Hollinger installed Yehuda Levy, a military man with virtually no newspaper experience, as the *Post*'s publisher and friction quickly developed.

In December 1989 the publisher informed the editor that his editorial in response to Shamir's castigation of the *Post* would not be published in the weekly overseas issue. In mid-December Levy sent a letter to the Editors' Committee of the *Post* saying that, 'as President and Publisher, I intend to become very involved in the work of the editorial staff, with all that this implies. Nevertheless, I have decided, at this stage, to refrain from appointing myself as responsible editor, in order not to harm the position of the editor, Erwin Frenkel'.[13] Shortly afterwards, Frenkel tendered his resignation, reasoning that he would be displaced and dismissed eventually. What political manoeuvres went on behind the scenes is a matter of conjecture, but clearly a liberal *Jerusalem Post*, which was a source of information and differing viewpoints to an increasingly critical Diaspora, was highly unwelcome in government circles.

Early reservations were realized when the large number of departing *Post* journalists failed in their attempt to raise the funds to establish a rival newspaper in the spring of 1990. While the *Post* rectified faults in presentation and balance of subject matter, its editorials were now written by a former speechwriter for Netanyahu, who also organized his conferences on terrorism. They inevitably took a sharp turn to the Right. As the new owner, Conrad Black, pointed out: 'Let's not play games. It was universally perceived to be a very left-wing paper before. Well, the Far Left isn't the only game in town'.[14] In general, the status quo was quietly supported and any Diaspora criticism of government policies frowned upon. Under its new management, the *Post* lost its investigative bite and an ability to challenge accepted views. It presented to the Diaspora an image of Israel which was both comforting and bland.

The start of the US–PLO dialogue

The suspension of the US–PLO dialogue by President Bush in June 1990 represented an important victory for the Likud government of Yitzhak Shamir and its American Jewish supporters. It was also a personal triumph for the Deputy Foreign Minister, Benjamin 'Bibi' Netanyahu, who had led a collective effort to breach the dialogue since its inception in mid-December 1988. But it was the attempted seaborne attack at the end of May 1990 on a crowded beach near Tel Aviv by armed members of the Palestine Liberation Front, a faction of the PLO, which forced the US Administration's hand.

Netanyahu had made his reputation as an articulate foe of 'international terrorism'. His brother, Yonatan, was the heroic commander of the famous raid on Entebbe, falling in the line of duty at the hands of Palestinian terrorists and Idi Amin's troops. This loss, in such fateful circumstances, provided the moral foundation for Netanyahu's campaign waged against a monolithic terrorist international symbolized by the PLO – 'a struggle between the forces of civilization and the forces of barbarism'.[15] It supplemented an ideological foundation, since the Netanyahus were an old American–Israeli Revisionist family dedicated to the retention of the Territories and to the rejection of any compromise with Palestinian nationalism. Shortly after Yonatan's death, his brother created the Jonathan Institute in his memory. Its *raison d'être* was to awaken the passive nations of the West to the mortal danger of the terrorist menace.

Netanyahu's ability to publicize and indeed to accentuate terrorism was well received by the Likud government in Israel, and by a Reaganite America emerging from the trauma of the war in Vietnam. The preoccupation of the American New Right with terrorism provided Netanyahu with strong allies in the United States. Thus, when the proceedings of the second conference of the Jonathan Institute eventually appeared as a book, *Terrorism: How the West Can Win*, its contributors were, in the main, a roll-call of American neo-conservative intellectuals. Their enemies were the Soviet Empire, Arab nationalism and Islamic fundamentalism – the forces of evil which had to be confronted and defeated. Embattled Israel was in the front line and an important component in the fight against this evil which was threatening to overwhelm the democratic and civilized nations of the world. In Bibi Netanyahu's words, 'We have a protracted struggle on our hands – Israel is not Disneyland'.

Critics scoffed at such a simplistic approach, yet Netanyahu's virtual daily appearances on the American media were highly compelling and persuasive. His smoothness and his barrage of criticism of those perceived to have gone soft on terrorism won friends and understanding for Israel in the public-relations area.

The rising toll of American lives in the first half of the 1980s, as a consequence of Middle East terror, focused public attention

on numerous personal tragedies. Here Netanyahu was assisted by
the public lack of knowledge of the plethora of Palestinian groups,
some of whom were members of the PLO whilst others were totally
opposed to it. Moreover, he did not differentiate between factions of
the PLO, between those moving towards a resolution of the conflict
through political means and those who continued to perpetrate acts of
terrorism in the context of the armed struggle. The delegitimization
of Palestinian nationalist claims to a homeland could thus be achieved
through continual linkage with terrorism.

Yet this approach, while attractive and plausible in the media, did
not coincide with the developing mood of successive Republican
administrations. Bush was concerned about the rise of Muslim
fundamentalism, which he believed could fill the vacuum created
by the deflation of communism. The fury of Islamic revolution
would destabilize the Middle East and was especially threatening
to the oil-rich Gulf States. Whilst Israel was a strategic asset, the
longer the delay in a settlement with Palestinian nationalism, the
more likely that the Palestinians would turn to Islam as a remedy.
The growth of Hamas, the major Islamic group in the Territories, and
the election of fundamentalists in Jordan were cited as evidence of this
trend. From the White House's point of view, the PLO was the most
rational organization with which they could deal.

No doubt Bush realized that the division within American Jewry
would allow him to develop his strategy. In addition, the attraction
of being 'peacemaker' in this seemingly intractable dispute must have
appealed in historical terms. Moreover, the US Secretary of State,
James Baker, probably viewed this rare opportunity for peace as a
means to establish an impressive reputation which could serve as a
stepping stone to the presidency.

Whilst Fatah, the mainstream Palestinian nationalist group, did
carry out terrorist activities during the 1980s, it also represented
a political option which was probably supported by the majority of
Palestinians in the Territories. Thus, although there was a virtual
doubling of incidents of international terrorism by Palestinian groups
in 1985 over the previous year, Fatah carried out just over a fifth
of these attacks. Moreover, Fatah's attacks were directed towards
three types of target: Palestinian rejectionists, Syria and Israel. After
a failed attempt to develop activities in the Territories in the early
part of 1985, Arafat turned to international terrorism for the first
time since 1974.[16] Politically, these acts proved to be extremely
counterproductive. A selective terrorism which somehow avoided
injury to bystanders was just not a reality. Attacks on Israelis in
Barcelona and Larnaca were carried out by Arafat's personal group,
Force 17. But the *Achille Lauro* affair, which was organized by a PLO

faction, 'began to turn sour for the perpetrators, its leader Abul Abbas even ordered the hijackers to apologize to the ship's passengers for victimizing them untentionally'.[17] This led to a reiteration of the PLO's official renunciation of international terrorism by Arafat in Cairo at the end of 1985. Ironically, these acts of terrorism strengthened the hands of the PLO pragmatists, who urged recognition of Israel and an end to the cycle of violence. Arafat clearly could not pursue both international terrorism and a political policy at the same time.

This marked tendency towards a political two-state solution was ideologically unacceptable to the Likud. Netanyahu dismissed this as simply a tactical ploy. The political face of the PLO, in Netanyahu's view, was thus a matter of negative public relations which could be remedied through appropriate techniques.

Netanyahu's facts

During the hijacking of the *Achille Lauro* in 1985, Netanyahu frequently implied that there was a close co-operation between the hijackers and the European neo-Nazi movement. This arose because a notorious neo-Nazi, Odfried Hepp, had met Abul Abbas, the mastermind behind the assault on the *Achille Lauro*, at PLO headquarters in Tunis shortly before the attack. Yet whatever atrocities may have been committed, Fatah terrorists never co-operated with neo-Nazis in attacks against Israel. Middle East terrorists and their Western counterparts had their own political and geographical agenda. Similarly, Netanyahu referred to Ian Davidson, a British member of Arafat's Force 17, picked up for the killing of Israelis in Larnaca, as a 'British neo-Nazi'. Yet Davidson, a loner and politically unaware, had drifted into Palestinian terrorism as a means to solve personal problems. According to his testimony after his arrest, it was the Sabra and Shatilla massacre that changed his life. Davidson joined Fatah in 1983 and later became a member of Force 17.

The PLO had technically given up acts of international terrorism in the 1974 meeting of the Palestine National Council, at which its resolutions led to the supposition that a Palestinian State would be established in any area from which Israel withdrew. But it still resolved to carry out cross-border assaults on Israel and to instigate domestic attacks. This led to a schism with Abu Nidal, the PLO representative in Iraq, who established his own Fatah Revolutionary Council and even sentenced Arafat to death. Abu Nidal was responsible for some of the most terrible acts of international terrorism during the 1970s and 1980s. Yet the similarities of names and general ignorance about the spectrum of Palestinian groups allowed subsequent Likud governments to attribute responsibility for every act of terror to the PLO. The most visible example of this technique was to allocate responsibility for Abu Nidal's attempted assassination of the Israeli Ambassador in London, Shlomo Argov, in 1982. The attempt was used by Sharon to implement his plans to invade Lebanon and destroy the military infrastructure of the PLO, which had been inactive for the best part of the previous year. The tragic outcome of this exercise in subterfuge was the war in Lebanon which claimed countless thousands of lives.

When the Labour government of Shimon Peres came to power in the mid-1980s, Netanyahu, as Israeli Ambassador at the United Nations, often found himself in conflict with his own Foreign Ministry, which attempted to pursue a moderate line and was not given to such a demonization of the PLO. Yet Netanyahu continued to advocate an approach which depicted a monolithic all-powerful enemy:

> How does the Syrian terror machine work? Damascus uses three separate groups to wage its clandestine war. The first is made up of Arab terrorists. Among the most prominent are the groups known as Al Saiqa, the Palestine Liberation Organization faction headed by Abu Musa and the Abu Nidal group which Syria wooed and won from Iraq. Syria also hosts sundry other PLO groups, including those led by George Habash, Nayef Hawatmeh and Ahmed Jabril. All are headquartered in Damascus and carry out terror attacks at Syria's behest. [18]

The anti-PLO Ahmed Jabril and the anti-Arafat Abu Musa would not have agreed with Netanyahu's formulation. Neither would Habash and Hawatmeh have felt comfortable, since they had spent considerable time resisting Syrian ploys to bring them under their control and thereby extinguish their freedom of manoeuvre. Yet the common denominator that they were all domiciled in Damascus allowed Netanyahu to telescope them into a PLO connection for public consumption.

Arafat and terrorism

The mood of Reaganite America in the mid-1980s, fortified by neo-conservative intellectuals and Netanyahu's campaign, was reflected in Section 1302(b) of the International Security and Development Cooperation Act of 1985. This stated that

> no officer or employee of the United States Government and no agent or other individual acting on behalf of the United States Government shall negotiate with the Palestine Liberation Organization or any representatives thereof (except in emergency or humanitarian situations) unless the Palestine Liberation Organization recognizes Israel's right to exist, accepts United

Nations Security Council Resolutions 242 and 338 and renounces the use of terrorism.

The necessity of American Jewish organizations and friendly congressmen to read this into law reflected Likud's desire to propagate the belief that discussion with the PLO as a political option was both unlawful and unthinkable.

Even though the PLO had formally renounced international terrorism, Yasser Arafat did not totally detach his own person from the possibility of such actions. His personal bodyguard answered extension 17 in the PLO headquarters in Beirut. When the PLO was driven from Beirut by the Israelis in 1982, he transformed this unit into a personal force – Force 17 – for his own use in the international arena. Although technically outside Fatah, and therefore not responsive to its strictures on terrorism, it was directly responsible to Arafat and operated on both Lebanese and Israeli fronts as well as in the international arena. It came into existence to decrease Arafat's dependency on Abu Jihad's control of military and terrorist operations. It was established to rival Abu Jihad's Hawari group, which operated on the Syrian front. Moreover, Force 17 personnel were present in PLO legations in many parts of the world and could be activated at a moment's notice. Force 17 was thus deemed responsible for the assassination of a Palestinian cartoonist, in London, for ridiculing Arafat in a sketch implying a liaison with a woman.

In addition, Arafat did not break from PLO Executive member Mohammed Zaidan Abbas, known as Abul Abbas, when he masterminded the *Achille Lauro* hijacking on behalf of the PLO. Abul Abbas had originally been a member of the Ahmed Jabril group, the Popular Front for the Liberation of Palestine – General Command. When the PFLP–GC's Syrian controllers attacked Palestinian camps in Lebanon in 1976, Abul Abbas broke with Ahmed Jabril and established the Palestine Liberation Front under Iraqi patronage. At the same time, he moved closer towards the PLO and was often described as 'loyal to Arafat', even though he propagated more extreme policies. Moreover, Arafat's refusal instantly to jettison Abul Abbas after the abortive attempt at Nitzanim beach in May 1990, which provided the pretext to suspend the US–PLO dialogue, prompted many to ask what hold Abul Abbas – a relatively minor figure in the PLO – had over the new President of the State of Palestine.

By 1988 and the advent of a lame-duck presidency, there was a clear desire in State Department circles to circumvent the ruling which prohibited discussions with the PLO. Trial balloons by senior PLO figures in the summer and autumn of 1988, accepting American stipulations for a dialogue, were welcomed by the Reagan administration and condemned by the Shamir government. There followed the meeting of the Palestine National Council (PNC) in Algiers at which the State of Palestine was declared, followed by Arafat's address to the United Nations in Geneva. Finally, Arafat unequivocally declared at a press conference after the UN address that, 'I renounced [terrorism] yesterday in no uncertain terms and yet I repeat for the record that we totally and absolutely renounce all forms of terrorism including individual, group and State terrorism'.

This declaration was welcomed by large numbers of Diaspora Jews, who felt that this was the breakthrough that many had awaited for so long. The State Department commented enthusiastically that the way was now open for a dialogue with the PLO, since all prior conditions had been met. However, as many parties to this development, the Americans themselves, and also Likud and the Palestinian hardliners realized, there was more to Arafat's proclamation.[19] Despite his statement that his clear declarations at the press conference had simply been a reflection of the PNC resolutions in Algiers and his address to the United Nations in Geneva, there were important and subtle differences. At Algiers, there had not been any straightforward, unambiguous statement that the PLO recognized the right of Israel to exist. Instead, the impression had been projected through indirect language and inferred statements that this was indeed the case. Presumably, Arafat had wanted this formulation in order not to incur the wrath of his hardliners on the Left, Habash's PFLP and Hawatmeh's DFLP who had initially opposed the Algiers declarations. The PNC declarations were also preceded by support for 'the right of peoples to resist foreign occupation, colonialism and racial discrimination and their right to struggle for independence'. Neither had the PLO Covenant been abandoned, with its demands for an Arab Palestine. Yet the entire tenor of the PNC gathering and Arafat's address was to suggest that the PLO had moved some considerable distance towards confronting reality through recognizing Israel and abandoning terrorism. The loose wording thus allowed the PFLP and the DFLP to interpret the PNC resolutions differently.

When Arafat's press conference took place after repeated postponements, his clear-cut renunciation of terrorism clashed with the ambiguity of the PNC declarations. The rejectionists, the PFLP and the DFLP, were not pleased. From their point of view, Arafat's personal declarations contradicted their interpretation of the PNC resolutions. Although he had carried them with him when they agreed to support the PNC resolutions in Algiers, they flatly opposed his abandonment of terrorism at the Geneva press conference. Whilst the Americans were prepared to view the press conference as 'official' and as an extension of the PNC gathering in order to initiate the dialogue, the rejectionists held to the letter of the law and formally condemned Arafat's declarations. On Christmas Day 1988, Habash and Hawatmeh issued a joint statement that Arafat's comments were not PLO policy and did not commit them. For Likud, anxious from the outset to disrupt the dialogue for ideological reasons, the schism in the PLO proved to be the straw that finally broke the camel's back.

Palestinian terrorism could be classified into three general categories: international, cross-border and domestic. The first category had ostensibly been abandoned by the PLO in 1974, and Arafat had reaffirmed this position in the 1985 Cairo Declaration. After Geneva, a fundamental difference between Arafat and his rejectionist wing was that he was now prepared to call a halt to cross-border attacks into Israel while his opponents were not. A month after Arafat's pronouncement, Habash remarked: 'In the PFLP we fight the Zionist enemy militarily inside Palestine and from the borders of Israel. Full stop. Others in the movement think they have the right to fight anywhere'.[20] Both Fatah and their opponents within the PLO agreed that the third category, 'domestic terrorism' as personified through the Intifada, should continue and this was not interpreted as solely in the Territories. Nabil Shaath, Chairman of the Political Committee of the Palestine National Council, commented that 'Palestinians engaged in the military struggle have every right to continue to strike at military targets within the pre-1967 borders of Israel. Otherwise you are giving one party a totally one-sided right to fight its battles and the other side is given no right to fight back'.[21] Thus, within a short time of the commencement of the US–PLO dialogue, the PFLP, the DFLP and Abul Abbas's Palestine Liberation Front all attempted attacks on Israel from the Lebanese border. Arafat's Fatah refrained from carrying out any cross-border assaults. Thus, while the Bush administration monitored Fatah for violations of the conditions for the US–PLO dialogue, the Likud Foreign Ministry and its supporters in American Jewry spread their net wider and monitored the whole of the PLO. This, of course, included the rejectionists, who had opposed Arafat from the outset. Therefore, Moshe Arens and Bibi Netanyahu quickly 'discovered' violations and instantly called for the dialogue to cease.

The campaign against the dialogue

In Israel, the Likud-directed Foreign Ministry resolved to blur the aims and intentions of the wide range of Palestinian groups in the public perception, thereby obscuring the difference between those who were attempting a political solution and those who were still ready to conduct the 'armed struggle' through acts of international terrorism and cross-border raids. For example, when Pan Am 103 blew up over Lockerbie in Scotland in December 1988, killing all its passengers, Netanyahu told the Israeli press that the PLO was behind the bombing.[22] Moshe Arens, the Foreign Minister, made similar utterances on British television and implied that the incident was a consequence of the US–PLO dialogue. Such comments, a few days after the dialogue had commenced, contradicted Israeli experts such as the Jaffe Centre's Ariel Merari, who logically concluded that this was probably the work of anti-PLO elements who also did not wish the dialogue to proceed. Some months later, after British experts had examined the wreckage, their conclusion was that the Syrian-backed Ahmed Jabril group was the most likely culprit. This non-selective use of language and the psychological reductionism of Palestinian terrorism often reached the press, who used it unknowingly. For example, *Time* magazine referred to the chief suspect for the Lockerbie disaster as 'Abu Nidal's PLO faction'.[23] Another technique was to draw attention to the fact that Arafat spoke in one voice to a domestic Arab audience and in another to the West. Whilst this was true of the political practice of a large number of governments as well, many preferred to wait and see what the PLO did rather than believe what it said. Sometimes this search for incriminating material to unhinge the dialogue itself came unstuck. For example, Netanyahu's statement that Abu Iyad, a senior PLO figure, had commented in two interviews after the Algiers Declarations that the PNC's pronouncements were no more than a stage-by-stage approach aimed at dismembering and eventually destroying Israel. Such comments were analysed by the Israeli Arabist Nissim Rejwan. He found that the two interviews in the newspaper *Al Yawm al-Sab'i* in fact took place before and after the Algiers conference. Rejwan concluded that, although there was 'a good deal of convoluted rhetoric . . . however one reads it, I fail to find in these pronouncements any way to justify Netanyahu's interpretation and the theory of stages'.[24]

Both Arens and his deputy, Netanyahu, were unnerved by the virtual silence of the American Jewish leadership on the commencement of the US–PLO talks. At a meeting just a few days after Arafat's press conference in Geneva, even the normally docile Presidents' Conference adopted a 'wait-and-see' attitude. Significantly, they did not condemn the talks with the PLO. The decision of the US administration was a psychological watershed for many American Jewish leaders who had spent years acting out what was expected from them. One participant at the meeting later wrote: 'And after some ten or fifteen minutes of inconclusive discussion, somebody said "We're all saying we have to respond, but what do we believe?" It was a simple question without an immediate answer.'[25]

Yet even at this early stage, some US Jewish organizations were pronouncing on the PLO's intentions and stipulating the parameters of agreement. The role of the US Jewish Community, one Jewish leader commented, 'will be to keep the administration honest and remind it of its commitments. These include direct negotiations as the only way to peace, opposition to any imposed settlement and to an independent Palestinian state, and continued support for Israel's security'. Other requirements followed: the renunciation of the PLO Covenant, the abandonment of Jerusalem as future capital of a Palestinian State, a cessation of violence in Israel and an end to hostile statements to the Arab world. [26]

The Chairman of the Presidents' Conference, Morris Abram, acting within the constraints of no opposition to the dialogue, still felt free to accentuate the negative and eliminate the positive in the situation. Although Professor Cohen's poll later showed that there were more American Jews who supported the start of a dialogue than opposed it, Abram remarked that the process had sent 'shock waves' throughout Israel and the US Jewish community: 'Conceivably, Arafat now accepts Israel's existence. Hitler likewise recognized Poland, France and Czechoslovakia. But that hardly mattered when his troops invaded. . . . Because the US decision was presented as a procedural one based on a thirteen-year-old agreement and because the Secretary [Shultz] enjoyed the confidence and respect of the Jewish community, his action was not met with a great public confrontation'. [27]

By mid-January, the commander of the IDF, Dan Shomron, reported to a Knesset committee that there had been no cross-border attacks by Arafat's Fatah. Ahmed Jabril had even complained that he was unable to reach Israel's northern border to attack Israel because of interference from the PLO. Although Foreign Minister Moshe Arens was enthusiastic about mounting an immediate campaign against the dialogue, there was little reaction from the Jewish leadership. One Shamir aide noted that 'Israeli officials were aghast that our friends in the United States did not rise in unison to criticize this step . . . our friends are either passive or critical or paralysed'. [28] When Arens made an eloquent appeal to the Presidents' Conference meeting in Jerusalem in February 1989, he received a lukewarm reception. Despite Israeli pressure, the Presidents' Conference refused to condemn the US decision to establish the dialogue. Only a watered-down statement from the Chairman of the Conference that President Bush should reassess the situation was issued. Netanyahu was sent to New York to appeal once more to the Presidents' Conference: 'You came to us when you had a problem with "Who is a Jew?" and we heard you and for the good of the Jewish people we shelved this. Now we come to you with a problem. We are under tremendous propaganda and political assaults. And where are you?'

Underlying Netanyahu's scolding was an irritation that the approach of the Jewish leadership did not replicate his understanding of the meaning of Jewish power and how it should be utilized:

> Jews are used to viewing themselves, and to be viewed by others, in a state of powerlessness, with all its attendant effects: for example, the effect of being victims or martyrs, the effect of being pitied or ridiculed. A lot of these millennial conceptions have been jarred over the last forty years, when the Jewish people amassed enough power to begin to control their destinies. [29]

The American Jewish leadership was clearly more discerning about the situation and differed with Netanyahu's narrow understanding of the meaning of Jewish history. They privately differentiated between support for the State and endorsement of government policy. Moreover, they did not take kindly to implied explanations that the reason for their silence was a fear of confronting the US administration – 'aspects of timidity', as one Israeli official commented.

Yet there were those within the Jewish leadership who believed that inaction and an acceptance of the PLO's 'good intentions' would lead to a weakening of Jewish support for Israel and a deterioration in US–Israel relations. Both the Anti-Defamation League and AIPAC commenced an intensive monitoring programme in conjunction with Israeli officials. Yet early attempts to use Congress as an ally faltered badly. In February 1989 Dante Fascell, the Chair of the House Foreign Affairs Committee, refused to sign a critical letter to Secretary of State Baker from a number of traditionally pro-Israel congressmen. Fascell, who was known for his ardent support for Israel and important work for Soviet Jewry, did not agree that contacts with the PLO should be restricted.

Gradually, the more conservative Jewish organizations began to resurrect their positions towards the PLO with greater confidence. In the summer of 1989, US representatives met with Abu Iyad, who was believed to be responsible for acts of terrorism in the early 1970s. The readiness of the Bush administration to meet such a senior PLO figure worried the Shamir government in case Abu Iyad's request for an upgrading of the dialogue was acceded to. Thus, AIPAC supported a congressional effort to push through the Helms Amendment, which was designed to stop a dialogue with any PLO representative who had 'directly participated in the planning or execution of a particular terrorist activity which resulted in the death or kidnapping of an American citizen'. Although the Helms Amendment was supported by some organizations, such as the ADL, it was opposed by liberal

organizations such as the American Jewish Congress and the American
Jewish Committee. The amendment fell, not least because Jesse
Helms had a reputation as a hardline defender of dictatorial regimes
as long as they were anti-communist and for a long period had kept
his distance from Israel. Instead, it was left to President Bush to use
his discretion in such matters.

The continuing American dialogue with the PLO in Tunis seemed
to lead nowhere. Yet a number of the more conservative Jewish
organizations continued to press for an end to it on the basis that
the PLO had violated the conditions for the exchange. Legislation
enacted by Senators Mack and Lieberman early in 1990 obliged the
State Department to report three times a year on PLO involvement
with terrorism. On 19 March 1990 the State Department issued its first
report, in which nine cross-border terrorist acts were examined. They
concluded that none of the attacks was carried out with the knowledge
of Arafat or the PLO Executive Committee. Neither could the State
Department find any evidence to suggest that Force 17 or the Hawari
group had committed any acts of terrorism after December 1988.
Senators Mack and Lieberman had particularly requested that these
two groups be investigated, for they were under the personal control
of Arafat and Abu Jihad respectively.

The Israeli Foreign Ministry also had a list of terrorist offences
which were publicized by supportive Jewish organizations. Thus the
ADL published a twelve-page report detailing how the conditions for
the dialogue had been being violated. The ADL published a list of
fifteen cross-border incidents between December 1988 and January
1990. The State Department covered the period December 1988 until
March 1989, listing nine cross-border attacks whereas the ADL listed
only five for the same period. Both sides had established different sets
of criteria for the examination of PLO involvement. Both sides had
interpreted information and defined events to fit their own political
agendas. The State Department wished to continue the dialogue
with the PLO whilst the Israeli Foreign Ministry and its allies in
the American Jewish leadership wished it to cease. The Americans
effectively monitored the cross-border activities of the mainstream
Fatah, whilst the ADL also monitored the rejectionists who had
declared at the outset that they would continue their activities. The
Americans 'discovered' that Fatah had generally complied with the
conditions laid down, whilst the ADL 'discovered' that the PLO had
violated them. Fourteen out the fifteen cross-border incidents listed
by the ADL were committed by the rejectionists, the PFLP, DFLP,
PLF and the PSF. The fifteenth incident was quoted by the ADL
from the press and held Fatah responsible for an incursion into the
Negev from Egypt on 5 December 1989. However, this cross-border

incident was actually perpetrated by an Islamic Jihad group. They had formerly worked with Abu Ali Shahin, Fatah's contact with the Muslim Fundamentalists in south Lebanon, but had broken with Arafat after Algiers and the Geneva declarations. They too were rejectionists. [30]

The State Department and the ADL also differed over interpretation and definition of the Intifada. Following the Likud line, the ADL characterized it in terms of the third category of terrorism – 'domestic terrorism'. The State Department report noted that it did not believe that 'the PLO was responsible for starting the Intifada. Since its inception, the Intifada has been directed by indigenous elements who look to the PLO for political support and coordination, but who operate, by and large, independently on a day to day basis'. This coincided with the view of Israeli experts on the genesis and management of the Intifada to the extent that 'decisions of a strategic nature are, by and large, controlled from within the Territories, albeit in consultation with the PLO'. For the State Department, acts of terror in Israel and the Territories were construed within the context of the Intifada as a civil insurrection. For the ADL, there were no extenuating circumstances for acts of terror against Jews. The Israeli Prime Minister's office noted that Fatah was believed to have been responsible for at least twelve terrorist attacks within the Green Line since February 1989. The ADL also listed acts of violence against fellow Palestinians and details of hostile statements made by PLO figures. The State Department also condemned 'numerous examples of contradictory and ambiguous statements by leading PLO officials and constituent groups'. Yet the State Department was willing to overlook such misdemeanours as long as Fatah did not violate the conditions for a dialogue. The Israeli Foreign Ministry looked for any instance of PLO deviation to call for the cancellation of the talks. At the end of May 1990 the Palestine Liberation Front failed in its attempt near the popular Nitzanim beach, south of Tel Aviv. It was the Shavuot holiday and the beach was crowded. The Israeli Foreign Ministry immediately accused Arafat of being behind the operation. Within hours, there were demands from Congress and from numerous Jewish organizations to the White House to call off the dialogue. Despite four meetings between PLO representatives and US diplomats, Arafat did not unequivocally and unambiguously condemn the PLF raid or move immediately to expel Abul Abbas. This raised further questions about the relationship between Arafat and Abul Abbas. Some suggested that Arafat did not wish to fragment the fragility of the PLO structure. Others believed that Abul Abbas was a front man for Arafat who had to reply to the increasing frustrations within his organization at the lack of progress. All suppositions were highly speculative in the absence of hard evidence to incriminate Arafat. The head of Israeli

Military Intelligence, Major-General Amnon Shahak, believed that
Arafat probably did not know about the operation in advance and that
the Libyan navy was heavily involved.[31] A few days later 'a military
source'[32] told the Knesset Foreign Affairs and Defence Committee
that Arafat did know what was happening, since such an operation took
some considerable time to plan and would therefore have attracted the
PLO Chairman's attention.

There is good reason to believe that Iraq was behind the attack since
Saddam Hussein – like Likud – wished to see an end to the US–PLO
dialogue. Significantly, the attack from the Iraqi-sponsored PLF came
shortly after an Arab League summit in Baghdad condemning Soviet
Jewish emigration.

All previous cross-border attacks on Israel since Arafat's Geneva
statement had actually been carried out by the pro-Syrian Talat Yakoub
faction of the PLF. Indeed, although Abul Abbas had disagreed with
Arafat's policy of dialogue, he had done little to hinder it. Now suddenly
he became active. Moreover, the type of attack was dramatically
different from previous assaults by Palestinian rejectionists who had
concentrated on the Lebanese border since December 1988. The
PLF group was allegedly going to attack the Sheraton Hotel and the
American Embassy. Moreover, Abul Abbas was still remembered
in the public eye in America for the murder of the crippled Leon
Klinghoffer on the Achille Lauro and for his evasion of justice.

The very nature of the attack indicated a lack of planning and
an amateurism which suggested that it was a sudden decision for
immediate political considerations. One of the captured PLF group
told the Arabic service of Israel Radio that 'they gave us maps, a
picture of Tel Aviv and a piece of paper on which the address of the
Jaffa lighthouse and the electricity company were written, so that we
could find the targets'.[33] It seemed that Abul Abbas had been activated
to cause the maximum embarrassment for Arafat and other Palestinian
advocates of dialogue with the Americans.

Moreover, it was not the first time that Saddam Hussein had
resorted to instigating terrorism to head off Palestinian attempts to find
a political solution to the conflict. Iraqi intelligence strongly facilitated
the actions of the Abu Nidal Group which was responsible for the
worst acts of international terrorism in the late 1970s and early 1980s.
Following the civil war in Lebanon, Iraq had set out to undermine PLO
dependence on Syria through a campaign of assassinations of those
Palestinian pragmatists favouring a dialogue with the Israeli peace
camp. There was also considerable suspicion that Iraqi intelligence
had been behind the attempted assassination of Shlomo Argov, the
Israeli Ambassador in London, by a unit of the Abu Nidal Group, and
that the weapons were brought into Britain with the help of the Iraqi

Embassy. The ensuing mêlée, and inevitably strong Israeli reaction, it was argued, would be an excuse to parade Muslim solidarity over all other issues, thereby allowing Iraq to extricate itself from its disastrous war with Iran.[34]

At the time of the PLF attack on Nitzanim beach, the PLO had just relocated large numbers of its forces to Baghdad, and Arafat had accepted Iraqi influence over the Palestinian cause. It was also a period when it was becoming abundantly clear that Arafat's Geneva policy of recognition of Israel and a cessation of terrorism had produced no tangible political results. Thus, it seemed likely that Arafat was highly reluctant to criticise Abul Abbas not only because the latter was sponsored by the Iraqis, but also because such a move would also emphasise his diplomatic failures in the eyes of other Palestinians.

Three weeks after the attack, when it became absolutely clear that Arafat would not condemn the raid, President Bush suspended the talks but did not cancel them. Ironically, it was not the first Palestine Liberation Front cross-border attack on Israel. Six out of the fifteen cross-border attacks listed by the ADL had PLF participants. The difference between these attacks and the one on the beach at Nitzanim was that previous attempts had been infiltrations from Lebanon. They had not taken place along Israel's coastline; indeed, it was the very drama of the situation, a potential massacre of innocent holidaymakers, that forced Bush's hand. The PLF, which had rejected Arafat's renunciation of cross-border terrorism, had continually violated the terms of the US–PLO dialogue while Fatah seemingly remained faithful to its conditions.

Part III

The Use and Abuse of National Security

7

National Security and the Rule of Law

The meaning of national security

The security of the State of Israel is the central psychological factor which governs the approach of the ordinary citizen to the Palestinian problem. But how is national security interpreted? Does control over the West Bank and its inhabitants increase Israel's national security or does it ultimately endanger the existence of the Jewish State? If a Palestinian State on the West Bank brings an end to the Intifada, will it also bring with it the prospect of Katusha rockets raining down on Jerusalem? These are legitimate questions which all Israelis ask.

In addition to voicing the security concerns of the Jews of Israel, Likud and the parties on the Far Right have ideological reasons for retaining the Territories in accordance with Revisionist doctrine. It is therefore in their political interest not to differentiate between the two issues and to subsume all questions arising from the Israeli presence in the Territories within concerns of national security. Thus, whilst ensuring the security of the State of Israel, a Likud government also conducts an ideological war against all Palestinian nationalists who reject Israeli national sovereignty over the Territories. The reluctance of Likud to countenance negotiations with Palestinians and Shamir's prevarication over the Baker Plan in 1989 and 1990 are a natural result of this ideological preoccupation.

Likud views the PLO – at least publicly – as solely a terrorist organization. To accept the PLO's political dimension and development would mean a recognition of Palestinian nationalism in a real rather than in an existential sense. It would mean the first step in the abandonment of the ideological war. The use of the principle of national security for purposes other than safeguarding the existence of the State has been a political weapon wielded by Israeli politicians of all colours. The ascendancy of Revisionism in 1977 and the rhetoric of the Far Right in the 1980s extended 'national security' into hitherto untouched

151

areas which ultimately impinged upon the rule of law and freedom of expression.

Yet the blame should not be laid solely at Likud's door, since national security is a standard, all-purpose argument in the repertoire of any politician. If such arguments are intended by politicians to mislead the Israeli public, they have also been successful to some extent with the judiciary. Judges are also members of society and thereby reflect a prevailing national mood. A former Attorney-General, Israel's top law officer, remarked: 'Who likes to be regarded as unpatriotic, especially in times of national crises? In Israel, possibly more than in most countries, national security enjoys the status of a sacred cow.'[1] Moreover, Israelis trust their military leaders and give their political leaders the benefit of the doubt on security matters even when they are couched in the vaguest and most general language. On other issues, however, Israelis demand precise and specific facts from the politicians before they are prepared to accept a position. On questions of national security, the indeterminate and often inscrutable are regarded as signals of the confidence which the public assigns to its leaders.

The argument of national security is, of course, invoked in cases which are not a cover for other designs, where it is sincerely felt that a specific action is a genuine threat. Yet here, too, in the public domain there is very little scrutiny of the meaning of the term 'national security'. Is foreign press coverage of events in the Territories a threat to national security as many Likud figures have claimed? Is an atrocity carried out by terrorists on Israeli civilians a threat to the existence of the entire State? What characterizes a threat to the existence of the State of Israel? No distinction is made in law between the general hostility – both internal and external – towards Israel which has been present since 1948 and exceptional situations such as all out war with one of its neighbours. As a result of the usage, and indeed differing interpretations, of 'national security' by political parties and ideological forces, the civil liberties of individuals and organizations are often called into question.

A legal inheritance

The Israeli government and the Knesset have wide-ranging powers in the name of national security. Section 9 of the Law and Administration Ordinance, 1948, enables the establishment of emergency regulations for a period of ninety days, involving a severe curtailment of civil rights such as the ability to search and detain. Government ministers can override all other laws. Yet, ironically, these laws, which have the potential to enact great violations of civil rights, are not of Israel's own making, but are an unwanted inheritance from the days of the British Mandate.

In the pre-State days, the leadership of the Yishuv intended to set forth an Israeli Constitution in the spirit of the UN Declaration of Human Rights. Thus many basic and human rights were enshrined in the Israeli Declaration of Independence in 1948.

The UN Resolution of 29 November 1947 which called for the establishment of two states – one Jewish, the other Arab – in Palestine also stipulated that elections for Constituent Assemblies for both states should take place two months after the termination of the British Mandate. A major task of such Constituent Assemblies would then be to draft a Constitution which would enshrine civil rights for the citizens of both states and safeguard the rights of their minorities. The outbreak of war, the Arab rejection of a Palestinian State and its ultimate incorporation into Jordan delayed such elections. In the interim, a provisional State Council performed the role of the legislature in the new State of Israel. The first elections to the Knesset were eventually held at the beginning of 1949 and the legislative powers thus passed to the Constituent Assembly – the Knesset.

However, the hiatus in legal continuity which was caused by the war forced the provisional government to adopt an interim measure, the Law and Administrative Ordinance, 1948 (Official Journal no. 1). This essentially comprised all laws which were in effect up until the proclamation of the State, but excluded those which opposed the right of Jewish self-determination or discriminated against Jews. The detested Emergency Defence Regulations of 1945, which the British had used with great determination during the pre-State troubles – regulations which Menachem Begin had labelled 'Nazi Laws' – was thus inherited by Israeli law. One week after the Declaration of Independence, the Emergency Detention Law (Section 1) came into force.

The first Knesset decided against a proposal for a separate Bill of Rights which would encapsulate within the law civil rights such as freedom of expression. Instead, it was intended that an all-embracing Constitution comprising separate chapters of Basic Laws would safeguard civil liberties.

This was the task allotted to the Knesset Constitutional, Law and Judicial Committee. However, owing to differing secular and religious interpretations of such issues as the status of religion, the Committee was unable to reach a consensus. Religious members of the Knesset did not wish to create or recognize a secular document which could possibly conflict with their own vision of a Jewish State and thereby with obedience to the tenets of Jewish religious law. In addition, Knesset members who supported the government did not not wish to create any legal restriction on their power. Thus, Ben-Gurion argued in 1950 that Israel, like Great Britain, did not need a Constitution. Significantly, only those members from both Left and Right who opposed the Mapai-led administration argued in favour of a Constitution. The lack of a Constitution suited Ben-Gurion, since it avoided problems of relations between the State and religion as well as the status of the Arabs in Israel. Thus, no Constitution was ever drafted and no Bill of Rights ever enshrined in Israeli law. Attempts were periodically made to repeal the British Emergency Defence Regulations, but with no success. By 1984 only eight basic laws were on the statute book. In late 1989 a Human Rights bill floundered on the rock of religious opposition, even though it had the full endorsement of the Likud Minister of Justice, Dan Meridor, and initially many leading figures in his party.

The Declaration of Independence drew clear lines between the powers of the Legislature and the Constitution. The telescoping of these powers within the authority of the Knesset in the absence of a Constitution meant that the Knesset maintained 'parallel powers – legislative and constituent – and that it may limit its own legislative powers while exercising its constituent powers'.[2] Religious opposition to the introduction of such Bills – the hallmark of many a Western democracy – led to anomalies such as Israel's refusal to sign the International Covenant on the Civil and Political Rights of Man. The presence of the Religious Parties in government produced a situation where the Israeli Minister of Education has neither printed nor distributed the UN Declaration of Human Rights since 1958.[3] The Mandatory Laws have thus remained in force. The Emergency Regulations which provide the legal power to close down newspapers, to enact censorship, to carry out administrative arrests, to ban the formation of political associations, to restrict freedom of movement and to confiscate property, while dormant for Israeli Jews, have effectively been activated to quell all manifestations of Palestinian nationalism in the Territories. The Israeli government promulgated the Order Concerning the Security Enactments (378) to ensure the full implementation of the Emergency Regulations in the Territories to the extent that their inhabitants can be punished for what they think as opposed to what they actually do – for their opinions as opposed to their acts. In Israel itself, although successive governments have refused to do away with such legal instruments of restriction, they have always remained passive precepts, on the statute book only.

Israeli society has always been characterized by its individualism and its frequent invocation of civil rights. This approach has been tempered only when an issue of national security required a higher level of adherence. Up until the Six Day War there was often a consensus on which took a higher priority in a given situation – 'the rule of law' or 'national security'. The post-1967 situation provided differing interpretations. Although it appeared possible to separate these two levels of legal behaviour in Israel and the Territories – in the sense that democratic practice functioned in the former but not in the latter – the reality was that the political situation psychologically affected the general Israeli perception of what it was and what it was not permissible to say and do.

A comparison of surveys carried out in 1975 and 1987 – that is, before the rise of a Likud administration, the Lebanon War and its aftermath – shows a significant increase in those answering 'yes' when asked whether they suspected those who had contrary views on questions which ultimately touched on national security:[4]

	1975	1987
Do you suspect people who say that there is discrimination against Israeli Arabs?	5%	17%
Do you suspect people who say that they favour talks with the PLO?	19%	43%
Do you suspect people who favour the establishment of a [Palestinian] State on the West Bank?	22%	45%

Whilst tolerance of those with a different approach to national security may have decreased, a majority of Israelis in the 1987 survey felt that abiding by the law of the land, no matter how unpalatable that law might be, was still of considerable importance:

It is our duty to obey any law adopted under proper procedure	52%
Where a law goes against a person's conscience, he/she should be required to obey it or else all laws will lose their meaning	68%
Laws considered wrong should be obeyed, but we should work to change them	66%

It would also be incorrect to blame Likud administrations for the feeling that civil rights in Israel has become less important – especially as there have also been trends which suggest that the opposite is true. It could be argued that the Likud Ministers of Defence Moshe Arens and Ezer Weizmann were actually far more liberal than their Labour counterparts. It should be recalled that pre-1967 Mapai, with its nineteenth-century ideological baggage, placed civil rights on a low rung on its ladder of priorities. It was the cause and the party above everything else. Paradoxically, the coming of Likud permitted a lessening of the rigidity of such ideological regimentation.

A new generation of Israeli-born judges came of age. Unlike their predecessors, they did not participate in the building of the Land and did not feel that they should, as a matter of course, always defer to the executive power of the government and the military. The judiciary came to believe that the overriding use of anti-terrorist legislation as a permanent feature by the Executive projected potentially dangerous prospects for the rule of law. In 1948 many justified its original use because there was a genuine danger to Israel's existence. Twenty years later this was no longer the case. After 1967 there was a greater willingness amongst the judiciary to question Executive wisdom, especially when it came to interpretations of national security, which resulted in the subsequent curtailment of civil rights. Such willingness to challenge the Executive also extended to the press. The Yom Kippur War nearly ended in disaster for Israel, despite prior widespread knowledge of a huge build-up of Egyptian forces. Israeli journalists and editors refrained from reporting this news to the public on the advice of the military. They accepted that their adherence to 'national security' on this occasion was on a higher plain than their journalistic duty to inform their readers. They accepted the wishes of the Executive not to publish scare-mongering stories, with the result that the citizens of Israel, the government and the army were caught by the surprise attack of the Egyptians in October 1973. The lack of preparedness brought Israel to the brink of defeat. The upshot of the débâcle gave credence to a new form of adversarial journalism which continually questioned people in positions of authority. This accounts in part for the detailed investigation and exposure in the Israeli press of government policy and actions during the war in Lebanon in 1982. New newspapers and magazines, such as *Hadashot*, *Koteret Rashit* and *Monitin*, did not join the Editors' Committee of Israeli newspapers which occasionally enacted collective self-censorship on the advice of the military or government.

A central consequence of Israeli failures during the Yom Kippur War was the appointment of the Agranat Commission of Inquiry into the failure of the military and the politicians to anticipate the war. It condemned the military but evaded the question of political responsibility. Public protest and criticism forced Golda Meir's resignation as Prime Minister and Moshe Dayan's exit from the political scene until 1977. It marked a turning-point where those who wielded executive authority were held accountable for their decisions instead of being given the benefit of the doubt simply because of their position.

Yet many cases in the 1980s showed the government's reluctance to involve the judiciary unless absolutely necessary. Investigations and inquiries were deemed to be within the orbit of government authority. This was accentuated by a growing Likud antagonism towards the courts and the press.

Following the killing of Palestinians on the Temple Mount in October 1990, the United Nations condemned Israel and held her responsible. A verdict was reached before any formal investigation had taken place. No one knew whether the police had overreacted brutally, or whether they had acted in self-defence in a life-or-death situation before thousands of inflamed demonstrators. Although Shamir denounced the United Nations decision to send an investigative team, he vacillated in ordering an official inquiry. When a three-member team was established, it consisted of non-judicial figures with no power to subpoena. Two were traditional Jews and therefore unable to visit the site of the tragedy, the Temple Mount where the Second Temple had stood. Indeed, Shamir's approach was contrasted to that of Golda Meir, who in 1969 was faced with the attempt by a deranged Australian to set fire to the Al Aqsa Mosque on the Temple Mount. She placed the matter in the hands of the Supreme Court of Justice, which also involved Arabs in an official capacity in the course of the inquiry.

Arabs and Jews

Do legal attitudes differ towards Arabs and Jews, within the Green Line and beyond it? Do Jews receive preferential treatment? The answer is not always clear cut, for the perceived national security of the State often disturbs the legal equilibrium between Arab and Jew enunciated in the Declaration of Independence of Israel.

In the Dahar case in the mid-1980s, an Israeli Arab lawyer was prohibited from travelling abroad for a period of twelve months by the Israeli authorities because his activities abroad were considered to be prejudicial to the security of the State. The petition against the restriction on travel abroad was rejected by the Supreme Court. The defendant's intention was to raise funds for the 'Soil Foundation', which was in all probability a PLO front. The judges weighed considerations of whether there was 'genuine and serious apprehension of prejudice to State Security' against the restriction of the citizen's freedom of movement. Judge Bach commented during the case that 'prohibiting departure from the State is a severe infringement of individual freedoms, a sort of infringement to which the Israeli public should be particularly sensitive'. Bach further noted that the right to leave one's country was enshrined in both the UN Declaration of Human Rights and the 1972 Uppsala Declaration on the Right to Leave and to Return. Even so, the judges applied the 'genuine and sincere apprehension' test to the petition and found it wanting. One judge declared that the petitioner's activities abroad invalidated his travel, whilst the other two judges believed that meeting PLO members abroad or raising money for a legal foundation did not merit such a prohibition. Judge Bach declared that it was the petitioner's activity in arranging the flow of PLO funds into Israel that constituted the 'genuine and sincere apprehension', while Judge Goldberg felt that it was the petitioner's activities *in toto* that must persuade him to concur with the twelve-month ban on travel.[5]

The legal problems arising from Jewish settlement in the Territories, and the Territories' accountability to Israeli law, have by contrast indicated how threats to national security can be used to further political goals. In June 1979, a group of Palestinian inhabitants from the village of Rujeib petitioned the Supreme Court about the confiscation of some 700 *dunams* (almost 200 acres) of arable land by the army, ostensibly on grounds of national security. The land, which was under cultivation, was in reality required by Jewish settlers to establish the township of Elon Moreh. The judges ruled in favour of the villagers and dismissed this version of 'national security' considerations as outside the interpretation according to the Hague Conventions. The Begin government soon developed other channels to cope with such loopholes such as the differentiation between privately owned and state land, yet the Elon Moreh case marked a watershed in indicating that the judiciary was willing to coerce the Executive to justify decisions made on grounds of national security:

Under Israeli law where the authority exercising a statutory power is granted absolute discretion, the authority may refuse to disclose the grounds for its decision. However, if the authority decides to disclose the grounds – even though it is not legally bound to do so, the Court will review the reasons and will, in addition, require the authority to reveal evidence to support its conclusion.'[6]

The first and second Begin administrations, in their enthusiasm for advancing Jewish settlement in the Territories, created specific situations which made large numbers of Israeli lawyers very uneasy, even though the government made strenuous efforts to legitimize their general policies in law. In particular, there was the sense that there was one law for the Jews and another for the Arabs. In 1980 a group of law lecturers from the Hebrew University of Jerusalem and the University of Tel Aviv sent a letter to the Attorney-General. It commented that

> when there is suspicion that an offence has been committed, governmental authorities must investigate the case, take actions to locate the offenders and prosecute them, with complete disregard for their identity, their nationality or the motivation behind their actions . . . there is suspicion that the investigation of the offences committed by settlers in the Territories against Arabs was not conducted properly. There is suspicion of discrimination between one offence and another. This suspicion calls for thorough inquiry.

Deputy Attorney-General Yehudit Karp was appointed to head such an inquiry and investigated seventy cases – some fifteen in detail – between April 1981 and May 1982. It was discovered that fifty-three out of the seventy cases had been closed without any resolution. The fifteen detailed cases were similarly closed. The complaints against the settlers ranged from trespassing to damage of property, as well as armed threats directed at Palestinians. Moreover, these stemmed not so much from the desire of the settlers for self-preservation and security considerations, but rather for reasons of demonstrating Jewish rights to the Land.

Complaints by West Bank Palestinians were often not submitted because they were not followed up by the police. Conversely, complaints were not pursued because they were not submitted. The inquiry noted that 'the rule of law and public order surely do not come out the winners in this matter'. One indicator of the failure to solve cases filed by West Bank Palestinians was the lethargic pace at which the police followed up complaints and the long period before an investigation actually started.

The inquiry team also met with, at best, an ambivalent attitude on the part of the police, who assisted them in a half-hearted manner. Moreover, the team found that the police were reluctant to monitor the Arabic press, in which complainants often reported offences. The inquiry discovered that Jewish suspects were perceived differently if they had committed their alleged offence in the Territories rather than within the Green Line. The inquiry team interviewed the head of the police investigation department in Judea, Superintendent Kalij, who told them that pressure was often brought to bear on the police by the military authorities to release Jewish suspects held for questioning. The team noted that 'when such pressures are applied directly, station chiefs are unable to withstand them, as they hesitate to enter into a confrontation with the Governor and to act contrary to his directives.' They also reported Kalij's beliefs that

. . . Israeli residents of the Territories are given to understand
that they are soldiers to all intents and purposes and are subject
to army investigations. Israeli residents of Judea and Samaria
explicitly refuse to co-operate with the police or to provide
information; they reject any contact with the police, basing
themselves on 'high level policy' and declaring that they are
under no obligation to co-operate in this matter.

The Council of the Jewish settlement of Kiriat Arba at Hebron even
urged residents not to co-operate with 'military investigations' if there
was no assurance that the evidence provided would not be handed over
to the Jerusalem District Attorney's office.

Yehudit Karp and her team completed their highly critical report on
23 May 1982, but clearly the findings proved so politically damaging to
the Likud government that it was not released for public consumption
until 2 February 1984 – and then only after many internal protests.
Thus, although all citizens were supposedly equal before the law,
the reality was somewhat different when it came to Israeli citizens
living in the Territories. Although the Karp Report enraged those
political activists who supported Jewish settlement in the Territories,
it also implied that executive zeal was accountable for this situation
in deeming that the instruments of government policy were beyond
the rule of law. The Karp Report concluded with a warning that this
situation was symptomatic 'of a much deeper problem, containing the
beginning of a dangerous process whose end is difficult to foresee.'[7]

One factor which permitted the public airing of latent feelings of
animosity towards Arabs was undoubtedly the 1981 election campaign.
Menachem Begin was able to exploit the deep resentment of the
Sephardim towards the ruling Labour Party and the Ashkenazi élite
in general. Begin conferred a sense of legitimacy on such behaviour
through his inflammatory rhetoric. It won Likud the election, but it also
encouraged the rule of the mob. Even Likud officials were unable to
control their supporters for some considerable time afterwards.[8] One
symptom of such resentment was a fierce condemnation of anyone
who offered any hint of a conciliatory position towards Arabs. Those
who were willing to uphold the rule of law and who advocated a softer
approach were *Ashafistim* – PLO lovers – even if they opposed the
organization. Clearly, if such a mentality were encouraged by the
Executive it would inevitably clash with the judiciary which interpreted
the rule of law – as transpired in the case of William Nakash.

The long-distance Jewish criminal

In March 1985, William Nakash was arrested on the Jerusalem–Jericho
highway with a number of accomplices. Police found IDF uniforms,

masks, communication equipment and other material that could be used for setting up a roadblock. Police believed that it was all part of a plan to stage a robbery. The victim was probably the Armenian Patriarch, who was returning from Jordan with considerable funds. When the police checked Interpol records they found that Nakash was wanted by the French police for the killing of an Arab in Besançon in 1983. The twenty-year-old Arab had been found with eight bullets in his body and was known to be a gang leader in Besançon. The crime had been committed from a Renault 5 and Nakash had been traced as the person who had hired the vehicle. He had fled to Israel and had been sentenced to life imprisonment *in absentia*.

Once detained for this crime and awaiting possible extradition Nakash claimed that he had committed his crime for national, patriotic reasons. The murdered Arab and his friends had harassed many Jews and was known as someone who publicly paraded his aversion to Jews. Nakash's background helped to give credence to his explanation of events amongst nationalist circles in Israel. His family came from Algeria, where his grandfather had apparently been killed by Arab gangs during the national revolt against the French. His uncle had been handed over to the Nazis during the Second World War. The French authorities, however, viewed the case as little more than a clash between rival gangs in the town.

Nakash's personal history was one of petty crime. His two brothers had been arrested at the tender age of thirteen and had been in and out of prison. Nakash himself had been caught at the age of sixteen for house-breaking. Between 1981 and 1983 he had been part of a Betar group which had specialized in guarding Jewish meetings and homes.

A few months after the intended hold-up, the Jerusalem District Court ruled that he was liable for extradition and that it was the responsibility of the Minister of Justice to carry it through. However, Nakash had the backing of many in the nationalist camp.

On fleeing France, he had lived in Ein Harod and had then attended *yeshiva*. He had apparently become observant and lived a traditional life with his new wife. Nakash claimed that his life would be in danger if he were returned to a French prison. His lifestyle and his claims earned him the support of Israel's Chief Rabbis, who stated that his extradition would be contrary to *halacha*. Shas, the religious party of the Sephardim, supported Nakash and its legal adviser Rabbi Simcha Meron was regularly consulted by the defendant's wife. Ariel Sharon publicly stated that he strongly 'objected' to handing Jews over to non-Jews.

More important was the support given to Nakash by the former Minister of Justice, Yitzhak Modai'i. His successor – also a member of Likud – Avraham Sharir then declared that Nakash would not be extradited to France and attempted to find a solution by trying him in Israel. This meant the introduction of an amendment to the Israeli Penal Code. Sharir gradually found himself pressurized by his own nationalist camp on one side to allow Nakash to remain and by a growing body of legal opinion on the other hand who insisted that the due process of law be followed. Even amongst people not connected with legal affairs, there was a deep feeling that Israel should not become a haven for Jewish criminals. Finally, Sharir was asked to explain before the High Court of Justice in December 1986 how he vindicated the position of the Ministry of Justice. Sharir detailed his belief that Nakash would be in a perilous situation if he was returned to France. It transpired under questioning that the Minister of Justice had had no apparent contact with either the Israeli Embassy in Paris or the Foreign Ministry in Jerusalem to ascertain the danger facing Nakash. The panel of five judges declared against Sharir, and Nakash was duly returned to France in 1987.

The GSS affair

The intervention of the Executive for patriotic reasons or in the name of national security was not just the prerogative of the Likud and the nationalist camp. The General Security Services (GSS) affair showed that the Labour Party was also willing to suspend the rule of law where political interests were at stake.

In April 1984 Israeli troops succeeded in freeing the remaining passengers from a regular Bus 300 bound for Ashkelon which had been hijacked by four armed Palestinian terrorists. A number of innocent people had been killed in the incident and the news was given out that all four terrorists had been killed during the assault. However, a few days later *Hadashot* published prominently on its front page a photograph of one of the terrorists, Majdi Abu Sham'a, being led away by Israeli soldiers.[9] Sham'a and another terrorist had clearly been killed whilst in captivity. The revelations in *Hadashot* and in the American media that the Minister of Defence, Moshe Arens, had ordered an internal inquiry under Major-General Meir Zorea into the affair splintered the blanket press censorship which had surrounded the incident. The burden of guilt was directed at the commanding officer, Lieutenant-General Yitzhak Mordechai. He later testified that he had personally hit the two remaining terrorists with his revolver to find out whether they had planted any explosive devices on the bus. He then handed the Palestinians over to the border police, who in turn passed them to the GSS. The classified report of the Zorea inquiry concluded that they had been killed by blunt, heavy instruments before they reached the GSS personnel. This prompted the Attorney-General, Yitzhak Zamir, to recommend that Mordechai be prosecuted. A military court-martial subsequently acquitted him. Zamir then initiated an inquiry into the GSS role in the affair. The internal GSS tribunal also acquitted their operatives.

Lieutenant-General Mordechai was in fact telling the truth and was the victim of an intricate GSS cover-up to protect the Services' position. The two terrorists had been killed by a number of outraged GSS operatives in a nearby citrus grove. Yossi Ginossar, a senior figure in the GSS, was even a member of the Zorea inquiry. He had even briefed the GSS people before they testified to the inquiry.

Apparently both Shamir, who was then Prime Minister, and Peres, who became Prime Minister, had *prima facie* support for Mordechai's protestations of innocence during the inquiries but maintained a studied silence. The head of the GSS, Avraham Shalom, who was ostensibly responsible for the cover-up, reputedly informed Peres about the situation in the autumn of 1984 and again in October 1985. According to Shalom, Shamir opposed the Zorea Commission of Inquiry, asking, 'Will those involved stay silent?'

The General Security Service, the main organization used to combat terrorism, is directly controlled by the Prime Minister. The extent to which GSS operatives observe the rule of law is a reflection of its importance in the thinking of the Prime Minister. Unlike Menachem Begin, both Shamir and Peres relegated it to a low rung in their deliberations. Shamir and Peres seemingly preferred to turn a blind eye to misdemeanours committed by the GSS in the name of national security. This approach, however, has both legal and political ramifications. Yitzhak Zamir later alluded to the reasons for the actions of the politicians in the GSS affair:

> The effectiveness of Executive control may also be influenced by the political echelon's reluctance to be personally involved in decisions which may be doubtful from a legal point of view or otherwise objectionable. It may, indeed, be tempting for a politician not to know too much about matters of this kind, and thus, possibly, to escape personal responsibility. A tacit understanding may thus be reached between the Prime Minister and the Head of the Security Service, according to which the Prime Minister would be spared the embarrassment of involvement in unsavoury business. Such an attitude would, of course, impair the effectiveness of the Executive control over the security service. Indeed, whether for this or for some other reasons, the control exercised by the political echelon over the Security Service was not sufficiently tight or effective, as disclosed by some public scandals. [10]

It was rumoured in the Israeli press that Shamir had personally approved Shalom's cover-up.[11] Rather than face an investigation into the security services, both Shamir and Peres permitted Mordechai to be the sacrificial lamb. Reuven Hazak, the deputy head of the GSS, had been ordered to lie by Shalom to the GSS internal inquiry – as had two others. When they requested an explanation, Shalom was not forthcoming. In October 1985 Reuven Hazak informed the Prime Minister Shimon Peres about the cover-up. Peres again did nothing – possibly because he felt that the issue was being used in an internal GSS power struggle. But it was also clear to Peres that any inquiry would involve Yitzhak Shamir, the Prime Minister at the time of the incident. Peres was certainly not willing to risk the disruption and possible dissolution of the National Unity government now that he had attained the premiership. Peres therefore supported Shalom's decision to dismiss all three GSS critics. Hazak then took his information to Israel's chief law officer, Attorney-General Yitzhak Zamir. After months of infighting, in May 1986 Zamir made public new information regarding the Bus 300 incident which clearly suggested that Mordechai had been framed and that GSS agents, including its chief, had systematically lied to the Commissions of Inquiry. There was evidence against four GSS operatives.

The following day the inner Cabinet met and united in hostile opposition to Zamir's desire to order a police investigation or judicial inquiry. The main charge by the politicians was that it would undermine national security if the GSS were investigated. Moreover, both Peres and Shamir could come under suspicion of knowing about the cover-up and could thus be accused of obstructing the course of justice. The politicians regarded Zamir as a political figure with specific views rather than as a judicial one. Zamir therefore came under great pressure not to proceed with his plan for an inquiry. A state of siege ensued, yet Zamir maintained that the GSS had tampered with evidence, suborned witnesses and withheld relevant documents from the two Commissions of Inquiry. Zamir was also opposed by the former and current Ministers of Justice, who were determined to oust him from his position as quickly as possible, especially as some months previously he had announced his intention to resign.

The GSS, however, was under the legal jurisdiction of the Attorney-General and he was determined to see the issue through. 'The law in Israel', he pointed out, 'is designed to assist the security services; for their part they must, of course, carry out their activities within the framework of the law. They are not above the law, nor are they in confrontation with it. The law provides a framework not only to enable them to work, but also to assist them in their work'.

Zamir was swiftly replaced by Yosef Harish, who was thought to be more conservative in his approach, an establishment man with little interest in civil rights. Yet one of Zamir's last acts as Attorney-General was to initiate a police investigation into the affair. After a number of weeks of prevarication, Harish informed a surprised Cabinet that he had no legal authority to halt the police inquiry. When his intention became public knowledge, President Herzog instantly granted an unconditional pardon to the head of the GSS, Avraham Shalom. This had been arranged via the Minister of Justice, Yitzhak Modai'i, who had enlisted the assistance of a partner in Herzog's old law firm. Avraham Shalom applied to Herzog to be pardoned for a crime with which he had not yet been charged, citing in his letter that he had acted 'with permission and authority'. The pardon outraged the legal world. Yosef Harish reportedly knew nothing about the manoeuvre to involve the President and apparently was taken aback by it. A former Minister of Justice, Haim Zadok, called it 'a black day for the rule of law'.

Herzog, who was an old intelligence man himself, pardoned Shalom and four other GSS aides under Section 11(b) of the Basic Law. The option of pardoning someone before they had been tried or convicted had clearly already been considered. Prime Minister Peres had asked Attorney-General Zamir whether the defendants in the case of the Jewish underground could be pardoned – while their trial was still taking place. In consultation with President Herzog's secretary, he formulated the legal opinion that they could not be pardoned while the trial was in progress.[12] As one specialist in presidential pardons pointed out, 'the letter of the law has not been violated but constitutional convention and established norms have definitely been violated'.[13] President Herzog cited the case of *Reuven v. Chairman and the Members of the Law Council* in 1950. However, in that case Justice Agranat had stipulated two reasons for the granting of a pardon: 'The first, to correct the wrong done to a person who has been convicted although he is innocent; and the second . . . to mitigate the sentence imposed upon a convicted person in justifiable circumstances.'[14] Although no one had formally been tried, Herzog pardoned eleven GSS men in all, including its two legal advisers and its representative on the Zorea Commission of Inquiry. He did so for 'the good of the public'. Many pointed to Herzog's contradictory position as the symbol of Jewish unity and as the expression of national consensus. Unlike his predecessor, Yitzhak Navon, who supported the call for a national inquiry after the massacre in the Sabra and Shatilla camps, Herzog made it a hallmark of his terms in office to pardon offenders whose trial or incarceration affected national cohesion.

A few weeks later, the High Court of Justice dismissed appeals against the presidential pardon for the eleven GSS operatives. It ruled that the President was permitted to pardon individuals before a trial, relying on the argument that the British Crown possessed this authority. Yet they indirectly rejected the President's reasons for granting the pardons. Despite Herzog's intention of preventing an investigation, the judges declared that it should go ahead in spite of the pardons. The minority opinion of Judge Aharon Barak in the decision crystallized the conflict between national security and the rule of law in the GSS case:

> If the Attorney-General believes that there is *prima facie* evidence to justify an investigation into very serious offences by someone in the executive branch, then the rule of law requires an investigation . . . considerations of state security do not necessitate another course – there is no security without law. The rule of law is a component of national security.

The price of the pardon was the resignation of Avraham Shalom and the dismissal of Hazak and his two colleagues. The stand of former Attorney-General Yitzhak Zamir earned the support of the legal profession and the press. But, significantly, Zamir's approach was appreciated by only a small minority of public opinion. A straw poll taken by the daily *Yediot Aharonot* showed that 80 per cent of the Israeli public sided with the government in their desire not to investigate the security services.

Yet the affair did have some positive effects. The government was forced to establish a Commission of Inquiry headed by a former President of the Supreme Court. In October 1987 the Landau Commission published its deliberations, which overruled the arguments of the GSS that they were merely performing a 'sacred mission' for the state and that 'cleaning sewers meant dirtying oneself'. Its operatives were not above the law. Furthermore, it recommended a series of measures to ensure tighter control and greater accountability to both the public and to the Knesset, which the government later adopted.

8

Freedom of Association and Expression

Meeting the PLO

At the end of 1989 the veteran peace activist Abie Nathan began a six-month sentence in Eyal prison for meeting Yasser Arafat. He had decided to break a new Israeli law against meetings with the PLO because he felt that such contacts enhanced rather than retarded the chances for peace.

Nathan's activities and the growing contacts between the Israeli peace camp and the PLO in the aftermath of the war in Lebanon were a red rag to many on the Right. They viewed speaking to the PLO as speaking to the enemy. Contact with the organization was seen as undermining the ability of Israel to wage war against the PLO. The Right reacted to the PLO in moral and psychological terms because the Palestinians had committed many atrocities against Israelis and Diaspora Jews. They also reacted ideologically because both the Right and the PLO espoused maximalist positions over the same territory. The Right did not recognize the right of Palestinian self-determination whilst Arafat was incapable of bringing himself unambiguously to accept the existence of the State of Israel. Israeli doves believed – whether privately or publicly – that the PLO was the ultimate negotiating partner with the government of Israel. Some, such as Uri Avneri and Liova Eliav, had been talking to the PLO since the mid-1970s. A number of moderates within the PLO, such as Said Hammami and Issam Sartawi, had paid with their lives for their public stand on dialogue with Israelis. They were said to have spoken in Arafat's name, but the PLO leader rarely took a clear position on where he stood. Marxist rejectionists, such as George Habash, monitored his actions closely. Moreover, Arafat and other senior people in the mainline Fatah group within the PLO were under permanent death threats from the Abu Nidal group and from a variety of Muslim fundamentalists.

167

The opportunity of the Far Right came during the summer of 1986 when a deal was struck between Labour and Likud to support each other's Bills in the Knesset. Likud voted for a watered-down anti-racism Bill designed to outlaw and isolate Rabbi Meir Kahane's Kach movement. In return, Labour was expected to support an amendment to the Law for the Prevention of Terrorism, which delineated the guilt of 'a citizen or a resident of Israel, who consciously carries out, without authorization, contact, either in Israel or abroad, with a person who has a position in the leadership, council, or any other body belonging to an organization which the government has declared to be . . . a terrorist organization, or who represents such an organization'. Only the hawks within Labour voted with the Right and the religious parties. A few voted with the parties of the Left and most absented themselves. Henceforth, contact with the PLO could earn a three-year prison sentence. A few exceptions, such as participation in a non-political academic conference, were defined, but all other contact became illegal. Those of a political nature were unlawful and viewed as a definite threat to national security.

Most peace activists, however, believed that talking to the PLO and urging them to give up terrorism and to recognize the State of Israel improved the prospects for peace. Dialogue, they pointed out, was not negotiation, which was the responsibility of the government of Israel. They argued that a political option was being transformed into a criminal act. If dialogue with the PLO was deemed unlawful, then – in the public mind – it could be construed that unyielding opposition to negotiations with the PLO at a later date was actually a law-abiding position to hold. The Right viewed the PLO as exclusively a terrorist organization dedicated to the destruction of Israel, and those who consorted with them were nothing less than traitors.

Behind this public stance was a determination to wage 'an ideological war of total delegitimization'. Contacts with the PLO legitimized its existence. Indeed, those Israelis who attempted to persuade the PLO to abandon terror for diplomatic initiatives were regarded as ideologically subversive. Moreover, the Right understood only too well that once the PLO overcame the psychological barrier and began to participate in a concerted dialogue with dovish Israelis who regarded themselves as patriots, it would be a small step from there to recognizing the right of the Jews to national self-determination. Even the Labour hawks used the amendment to prevent the dovish wing of the party from meeting the PLO and thus maintained the ascendancy of the hardline approach of the Rabin camp. Their attitude was summed up in the explanatory notes to the Bill:

Recent contact of Israelis with activists and official representatives of terrorist organizations have grown both numerous and frequent. This phenomenon is causing Israel serious harm, both politically and in the area of security and cannot be tolerated. Therefore we propose to outlaw such contacts, if held knowingly and without lawful authority.

Israelis in the peace camp were divided over how to react to this amendment to the law. Some advocated a mass breaking of the law; others believed that the law should not be violated, but that all loopholes in it should be exploited and a campaign for its repeal launched in Israel and abroad.

The very idea of 'contact' was open to interpretation. Israelis who spoke at meetings on joint platforms with members of the PLO outside Israel could not engage in a 'dialogue' with their opponents but had to speak 'through' the chairperson. In February 1989, the Oxford University Union sponsored a public meeting between Bassam Abu Sharif, with other leading PLO members, and members of Knesset. Dedi Zucker, MK, pointed to the absurdity of sitting opposite Bassam Abu Sharif but not being able to speak to him directly as that might be interpreted as 'contact' in a court of law. Did 'contact' mean support? Israeli lawyers argued that if an Israeli made 'contact' with a member of the PLO but was subsequently convinced – in the words of Menachem Begin – that 'the PLO is a bunch of murderers', then he was still liable for prosecution under the law. If the Israeli made 'contact' with a view to persuading the PLO to give up terrorism then this too was unlawful. The mere act of 'contact' was an unlawful act unless authorized by the government. It was irrelevant whether dialogue took place or not, or indeed what kind of dialogue. Avigdor Feldman, who undertook the defence of Israelis charged under the Act, commented that 'if I have a car accident with a PLO official in Honolulu and I ask him for insurance details then I have committed an offence'.

The trial of the four

A few months after the Knesset passed the amendment, twenty-one Israelis met fifteen PLO officials in the Romanian seaside resort of Costinesti to discuss the conflict. The meeting, initiated by the Committee for Israeli–Palestinian Dialogue, deliberately sought to test the law. On their return to Israel, four members of the delegation were handed summons at the airport and charged with breaking the law. Mr Shamir called them 'traitors and PLO supporters' and they consequently became targets for the full opprobrium of the Israeli Right. Rabbi Kahane's Kach Party published the names, addresses and telephone numbers of the delegates in a widely circulated leaflet. Reuven Kaminer, the only member of the four resident in Jerusalem, suffered acute harassment. On one occasion, when he and his family were not at home, a cardiac-arrest unit broke his door down because they had received an urgent telephone call that someone had suffered a heart attack at his home.[1]

The choice of the four had been interesting in itself. The Romanians had diverted the Israelis' plane to the Black Sea resort instead of landing at Bucharest because of fears of a terrorist attack from the Abu Nidal group. No proper explanation had been offered to the Israelis and they began to fear that the exercise of a public dialogue with the PLO would not take place. Four frustrated members of the delegation requested clarification in a half-hour meeting with Romanian officials, who promptly resolved the problem by explaining that the Palestinians and world press would shortly be joining them. On arrival back in Israel, these four were deemed to be leading representatives of the delegation and were therefore charged.

The other seventeen soon wrote to the Attorney-General and requested that they too be placed on trial. When their lawyer asked during their trial why only the four were being prosecuted, the judge disallowed the question. When he then asked why the other seventeen were not being prosecuted, the judge threatened him with contempt of court. As with courts of law throughout the world, this could be attributed to a desire not to overburden the hard-worked legal system, but it also served the political need of the government to project the defendants as merely an unrepresentative unpatriotic minority who had committed criminal offences.

When the trial began in 1986, the public prosecutor pointed out that 'the mere establishment of contact constitutes the offence'. After hearing all the arguments, the judge eventually found them guilty in that they 'had harmed the rule of law' in Israel. The four, Latif Dori, Yael Lotan, Eliezer Feiler and Reuven Kaminer, were sentenced to six months in prison or in community service, and a $2500 fine.

The four then resolved to fight the verdict through the courts on the basis that the PLO Amendment was a major rebuke to the judiciary's often stated commitment to civil rights. Many judges were uneasy about the Amendment, but felt that it was the job of the legislators, not the judiciary, to change the law. Judge Haddasah Ben-Ito of the Tel Aviv District Court rejected the appeal against the sentence and commented that 'even if I agree that it would have been better had it never been adopted, and even if it does constitute an infringement of individual rights – it still does not endanger our democracy and the basic unassailable freedom which the citizens of Israel enjoy even in wartime'.[2] Others were not so sure. Some believed that the amendment paved the path for political dictatorship. It affected the right of a minority with a specific viewpoint to become the majority through democratic means. David Lib'ai, a Labour Member of the Knesset and the former head of the Israeli Bar Association, pointed out that laws were supposed to place limitations on government, not on opposition: 'If an individual is banned from maintaining such contact, why should a political body, like a party, be allowed to maintain contact?'[3]

Freedom of the press

Unlike in the Territories, freedom of the press in Israel is a given basic freedom, a manifestation of the democratic process. The restricting factor here too is the question of national security. Indeed, *Ha'aretz* reported in March 1990 that a quarter of publishable material is banned.[4] The publication of a privileged piece of information might make a good story; theoretically it may be in the public interest that it should be published, but practically it may provide information to Israel's neighbours who seek her defeat and, if possible, her liquidation. Unlike journalists in Western Europe and the United States, Israeli practitioners of the profession have to consider seriously the implications for the State if such a story is published.

The occupation of the Territories in 1967 moved Israel's struggle from an essentially external one with armed Arab states to an internal one against a civilian population, the Palestinians. The Intifada in the late 1980s symbolized the coming-of-age of the post-1967 generation of Palestinians. For Israel, their citizen army became a police force.

These profound changes created a schism within Israel, but also posed dilemmas for Israeli journalists. Should incidents which could be politically damaging to Israel be brought to public attention? Or should the military interpretation of 'national security' be accepted and adhered to?

Since 1967 a new generation of journalists tended to be less convinced of the sincerity of a new generation of politicians. Unlike their predecessors, they did not view themselves as allies of the politicians – a philosophy which was prevalent during the pre-State days in the struggle for independence. The occupation of the Territories and the conflict with the Palestinians provided more and more opportunities for the Executive to misuse the concept of 'national security'. In addition, hawks and doves had different interpretations of the concept. Serious investigative journalism developed after 1967, but so did the pressures placed upon the journalist and the moral complexities of finally publishing the story.

The foundation of the freedom of the press was cemented in the *Kol Ha'am* case in 1953. *Kol Ha'am*, the Communist Party daily, was suspended from publishing for ten days because it had been critical of Ben-Gurion after it had published a false report that Israel intended to send a large number of troops to fight alongside the USA in Korea. The local communists took the authorities to the Supreme Court, which promptly ordered that the ban on the newspaper be lifted. The Supreme Court argued that 'a clear probability standard' had to be shown that there was a genuine link between a statement and 'a substantive evil occuring'. The 'immediacy of harm' had to be demonstrated by the authorities.

No executive likes to be restricted – and especially where a state of siege exists. Under such pressure the difficulty of differentiating between legitimate criticism and hostile propaganda can infect even the most dedicated and hard-working official. The determination of what was or was not 'hostile' or 'incitement' or in 'the interests of national security' was the prerogative of the Executive. In the 1980s especially, the interpretation of this prerogative was increasingly challenged by journalists. There was also criticism of the ease with which editors were willing to accept the word of the Executive: 'Whenever editors automatically accept the [Israeli] government's subjective view of the national interest and consequently suppress information, they are acting irresponsibly by depriving the public of information essential for democratic decision-making'.[5]

In 1949, a committee of editors made a gentlemen's agreement with the government censor on dealing effectively with questions of national security and military secrets. This arrangement substituted for a proposed Act of the Knesset which would have altered the 1945 Defence Regulations of the Mandate. This was in itself a continuation of an arrangement that had existed in the pre-State days. The censor agreed not to apply the Defence Regulations to those newspapers represented on the Editors' Committee. No censorship would be practised unless it impinged on classified military information. Sensitive issues would be submitted for prior appraisal and censorship. In the case of a violation of these principles by either side, a special committee consisting of a military officer, a member of the Editors' Committee and a public official would judge the case. Between 1949 and 1984 there were only 180 appeals to the Editors' Committee – half from the censor and half from the Hebrew press; compared with other countries, 'this figure represents a high degree of understanding between the press and the military'.[6] The accord in 1949 was also designed to place outside the pale of respectability the views of the Communist Party from the Far Left and the Revisionists of Menachem Begin from the opposite side of the political spectrum.

The spirit of the agreement has also been applied to those newly established newspapers which decided not to join the Editors' Committee and whose participation was not wanted by its members. Yet there have been several occasions when they have gone their own way and rejected a consensus view. Shortly after the Bus 300 incident, *Hadashot* published a photograph of one of the terrorists being led away from the site which disputed the official explanation that they had all been killed. It also revealed that the Minister of Defence had ordered an inquiry and requested that its existence should not be disclosed in the press. *Hadashot* was closed down for four days by order of the censor. The newspaper went to the High Court and asked it to rule on the public's right to know; in this case, the judgement went against *Hadashot*. Erwin Frenkel, editor of the *Jerusalem Post* – who was a member of the Editors' Committee – argued at the time that 'the choice for the Israeli Press is not between censorship and its absence. It is between censorship sensitive to the imperatives of freedom and censorship sensitive only to the imperatives of national security'.[7] Although *Hadashot* recently joined the Editors' Committee as a result of internal pressure, its stablemates in the Schoken group, the Tel Aviv-based *Ha'ir* and the Jerusalem-based *Kol Ha'ir*, have remained outside. The liberal Schoken group papers, which include the daily *Ha'aretz*, have maintained high standards of journalism. They will be hard-pressed to maintain such standards as the Israeli press moves from the world of party papers and informative journalism to the sensationalism and exploitative nature of the Western press. The purchase of the daily *Ma'ariv* by the British press baron Robert Maxwell was viewed by many as the first move in this direction.

During the 1980s politicians became increasingly aware of the ability of the press to deliver information to the Israeli public before they themselves had had the opportunity to shape it for public counsumption. Their position as arbiters of the flow of information and opinion-making at home and abroad was thus compromised. Occasionally, news was withheld from the Israeli public so that it could be employed as an instrument of foreign policy. For example, the Israeli media was forbidden to publicize important material relating to the affairs of Jonathan Pollard, the American who spied for Israel, and Mordechai Vanunu, the Israeli who had leaked some of his country's nuclear secrets to the British press, as well as the Irangate scandal, so that it could be leaked to the *New York Times* instead.

In June 1988 President Herzog addressed a Hebrew University symposium on 'Covering Israel on World Television'. He quoted with approval the views of the roving US Ambassador Max Kampelman on the power of the press:

The critical question for our democracy today, however, is not so much the power of the Presidency, which is restrained by the Congress, the opposing political party, the press and the courts; nor so much the power of the Congress, which is restrained by the President, by partisan politics, by the press and by the courts. The relatively unrestrained power of the media may well represent an even greater challenge to our democracy . . . the American Press, however, perhaps the second most powerful institution in the country next to the Presidency, is characterized by few, if any, effective restraints.[8]

Clearly, the press is often an unwanted intrusion as far as the Executive is concerned. In the Israeli context, the belief in a free, unfettered press – despite all its drawbacks – became a matter of public debate. It should also be noted that, as regulators of sources of information and intelligence, the Executive can exert control within the Israeli media.

The war in Lebanon in 1982 revealed much about the Israeli public's 'right to know'. Whilst the government was bent on giving its version of events, many Israeli journalists continued to inform the public of the reality of the situation and the growing doubts about the wisdom of the venture. In part, this was the result of the government's lack of relations with the press. Unlike previous wars, Sharon did not brief correspondents during the two-month duration of the war. He also directed the Chief-of-Staff not to convene the Editors' Committee, or indeed to have any contact with it. This was, in itself, a manifestation of the Begin government's scorn for journalists and general disdain for the Israeli press. Begin did not himself meet with the Editors' Committee for three years. The press, on the other hand, was not overtly sympathetic to his governments – even the right-wing dailies *Yediot Aharonot* and *Ma'ariv* did not support him during the 1981 elections. This led to a belief that they could appeal over the heads of the press direct to the people – a belief that appeared to be vindicated by Likud's astonishing victory in 1981. Yet the lack of contact and the acerbic criticism forced the press to try much harder during the war in Lebanon. They suspended their self-imposed censorship and developed their independent lines of communication with critics within the defence establishment. Indeed, it was investigative journalism that contributed to the revelations of the massacre of Palestinians at Sabra and Shatila and the establishment of the Kahan Commission of Inquiry.

'The Lebanon War was the matriculation certificate of the Israeli press in general and of the military correspondent in particular'.[9] There were instances during the war where the Executive misused 'national security' for its own ends. For example, Minister of Defence Sharon allegedly instructed the censor to alter a report in *Ha'aretz* to suggest that Syrian forces had attacked Israeli troops on the Beirut–Damascus highway, where the exact opposite had in fact occurred. This was because Sharon had already given the false version to David Levy, then acting Prime Minister in Begin's absence, and did not want him to learn the truth from the morning newspapers.

Criticism was not tolerated, even if it reflected widespread unease about the war. The broadcaster Dan Shilon innocuously referred in a question to the Lebanese *plonter* (knot) which resisted untying. He further queried the official approach that stated that there had never been a more just war. Shilon, who had received an award for the high standard of his work during the Six Day War, was summarily dismissed from Galei Zahal, the radio station of the IDF which was within the jurisdiction of the Minister of Defence, Arik Sharon. Shilon paid the price for objective journalism at a time when the Likud government believed that only the authorized interpretation of events should be aired. Some years later, in the name of national security, Galei Zahal literally pulled the plug on the American folksinger Joan Baez minutes before a live broadcast of a concert. A recorded version was transmitted later, omitting her rendition of Si Hyman's popular Israeli protest song about the Intifada, 'Shooting and Crying'. The title crystallized the dilemma of soldiers who participated in actions with which they fervently disagreed. The chorus referred to the incident in which suspected Palestinian youths were buried in the sand by members of the IDF:

> 'Shooting and crying, burning and laughing
> When did we ever learn to bury people alive?
> Shooting and crying, burning and laughing
> When did we ever forget that our children too have been killed?[10]

The Lebanon War created an about-turn in government attitudes towards the press. When it became apparent that the conduct of the war was coming under detailed scrutiny, Likud officials attempted to mend their fences with the press. When Shamir became Premier, he did not follow Begin's approach but assiduously cultivated the press. This led in part to a reimposition of self-censorship by many editors and journalists.

Television and radio

Director-Generals of the Israel Broadcasting Authority (IBA) are political appointees and therefore ideologically coloured. For example, Uri Porat, the incumbent in 1987 at the time of the Intifada and a Likud nominee, had originally been Menachem Begin's press adviser. Begin, like most of the Israeli Right, had little liking for the press, which was often characterized as 'Marxist' or 'PLO sympathizers'. Under Likud sponsorship, the question of language on radio and television became paramount. 'The West Bank' as a descriptive geographical term was not to be used. Neither was the common and relatively neutral 'Territories'. Instead, the land conquered in 1967 was officially referred to as 'Judea and Samaria'. Similarly, the Green Line showing the pre-1967 borders disappeared from Israel Television maps of the country. This implicitly contradicted the status of the Territories in a court of law. When the government is asked to explain before the Supreme Court why it took a specific action in the Territories, the usual statement is that the legal status of the form of government in the Territories is one of 'belligerent occupation'.

Porat's regime at Israel Television was to some extent a throwback to former times, when the press considered itself to be an adjunct of the national struggle against the Arabs. Whilst the concept of a 'mobilized press' may have been understandable in the attempt to establish the State in 1948, was it still the case in the 1980s? Should Israel TV give government policy the benefit of the doubt and fortify 'friendly' relations with the government?

Up until 1965, Israel Radio had been the responsibility of a department in the Prime Minister's office. The ousting of Ben-Gurion and the installation of the more liberal Eshkol administration led to the independence of Israel Radio. The Eshkol government also decided to initiate a national television service and called in the BBC's Sir Hugh Greene to advise on its establishment. While the government was permitted to appoint the Director-General and members of the Board, by law it was not allowed to interfere in its running and general approach. Until 1977 Labour governments appointed people who were generally sympathetic to them, but who also exercised an independent attitude. The Board consisted of writers, people in public life and former journalists who were not afraid to voice their opinions and whose salaries were not ultimately linked to the government. After the ascendancy to power of Menachem Begin in 1977, all this changed. Yosef Lapid was appointed by Likud with a mandate to cleanse Israel Television of the 'leftist mafia'. Yet even he began to develop an independent stance when confronted with the reality of professional journalism. Significantly, he was not appointed for a second term.

The calibre of the Board of the Israel Broadcasting Authority became increasingly poor. Appointees were selected first and foremost for their ideological soundness rather than for their ability to make a contribution. This enabled second-rate politicians to treat the IBA Board as a stepping-stone for their electoral ambitions. This naturally damaged the public image of the Authority. By 1990 individual government ministers even had their own contacts within the television service and on the IBA Board who would fight for extra coverage for their patron's deliberations.

Although there has been much official criticism of foreign coverage of the Israeli–Palestinian conflict, there has also been a concerted effort to mould the news for domestic consumption on Israel Television. Uri Porat restricted coverage of Palestinian opinion in the Territories. Formally, this policy was enacted to reduce the possibility of future Palestinian unrest in the area, but it also deprived the Israeli viewer of full access to information. Reporters were not allowed to interview Palestinian mayors who were 'identified with the PLO'. The war in Lebanon and the demonstrations against it created considerable friction between reporters and the Director-General, who wished to downplay criticism of the war-effort and of the government. The changing political positions of the PLO were similarly ignored; instead, Palestinian terrorism and the pronouncement of extremist statements were given pride of place. Although a Supreme Court judgement in the early 1980s ruled that interviews with the PLO permitted the Israeli public to make an objective appraisal of the organization's attitudes as long as it did not present a 'clear and present danger' to national security, viewers were often given only a partial picture of developments.

Minister of Defence Rabin requested the IBA to limit coverage of Arafat's declaration in Algiers of the State of Palestine in order to prevent unrest in the Territories. Most Palestinians on the West Bank were, however, able to tune in to Jordanian Television. The military authorities solved that problem by cutting off the electricity supply for the duration of the celebrations. The other side of the coin was that the Israeli public was not informed of this important development. Arafat's speech was banned and Porat justified the approach by stating that Israel Television should avoid needless propaganda which would serve the interests of the enemies of the State. During a subsequent Board meeting, the Broadcasting Authority passed a resolution to initiate steps against reporters who 'served the enemy's propaganda'. Porat himself characterized journalists as 'left-wing politicians who are wearing journalists' clothes'. The author David Grossman protested against this policy and was sacked from his job with the Authority. There were also demands to tighten up the use of language. For example, Likud members of the IBA Board suggested that the term 'Palestine National Council' should be replaced by 'Palestinian Terrorist Council'.

Whilst internal morale and the reputation of the IDF were clearly important considerations, the non-broadcasting of uncomfortable scenes permitted the Israeli viewer to gain only a partial picture of the situation in the Territories – a picture based on the official viewpoint. Thus, whereas foreign networks showed Israeli troops beating captured Palestinians, Israel TV refrained from broadcasting such scenes at length. Israeli critics of the coverage of the Intifada by Israel Television have described its approach as 'vegetarian'. Significantly, Israelis who travel abroad are often shocked when they view the confrontations between Israeli soldiers and the Palestinian inhabitants of the Territories. If the Israeli public has become blasé about the Intifada, then undoubtedly Israel Television has played a part in invoking and cultivating this apathy. Shortly before his departure from the IBA – and his replacement by Shamir's press aide – Uri Porat banned a sketch about an Israeli family watching *Dynasty* in the comfort of their living room. Outside a huge fire raged and smoke was beginning to billow into the room. The family burst into song: 'Nothing is burning. There is no need to do anything. No need to rush'. [11]

The press and the public

The debate circles around what is coloured propaganda and what is neutral information – no matter how disturbing. There is a general dislike of reporters, both Israeli and foreign, who describe the Intifada. Indeed, 'The people are against a hostile press' was a common car sticker observed in Israel in 1989–90. A poll of 1000 Israelis, conducted at the end of 1989, indicated a substantial suspicion of the media: [12]

What is your attitude regarding freedom of the press in Israel?

Too much freedom of expression	46.4%
Sufficient freedom of expression	46.5%
Insufficient freedom of expression	7.1%

With which of these two opinions do you agree?

Freedom of expression in the national media contributes to national security	38.8%
Freedom of expression in the media endangers national security	61.2%

With which of the following arguments do you agree?

The Israeli press generally reflects the entire spectrum of public opinion	63.0%
The Israeli press generally reflects the views of the Left	33.7%

The Israeli press generally reflects the views of the Right	3.3%

Significantly, when the respondents were categorized, it was found that a large percentage of the ultra-orthodox, the less educated and those from a Sephardi background believed that there was too much freedom of the press and that it further endangered national security.

Since the psychological barrier in confronting the Intifada was for many a very high one, information was thus potentially a threatening commodity. The feeling that 'if you are not for us, then you are against us' during the last few years has persuaded a considerable number of the best and most experienced journalists to leave Israel TV. Moshe Negbi, a senior editor and legal correspondent for Israel Radio, published a weekly magazine for the station on legal and constitutional aspects of human rights over an eight-year period. Legal analysis of the Kahan Commission, the GSS affair and the situation in the Territories led to attempts to suspend him. Finally, a heightened sensitivity to self-censorship led him to resign from the station after nineteen years.[13]

Foreign journalists, as outsiders, are even more problematic than their Israeli colleagues. For some, they have become figures of hate, irrevocably 'anti-Israel'. Yet journalists often provide only a snapshot of a situation. Their task is essentially to reduce the complexity of events to a logical and faithful simplicity within the context of their short reports. Sometimes the arguments are more sophisticated and once more lean on the doctrine of national security. Yosef Lapid remarked that he did not believe that the international media was hostile to Israel, but

> there are deep-seated prejudices in the soul of Western man which place us in a negative light because of the situation itself. When poor, thin youths emerge from the refugee camps, armed only with stones, and confront well-fed soldiers armed with lethal weapons, the instinct of the observer immediately positions him on the side of the youths, without examining the history of the conflict. In this case, I prefer to be in an uncomfortable situation with the media and in a comfortable situation with regard to the relative strength of the forces in the field.[14]

Even the Israeli press has great difficulty in covering adequately disturbances in all parts of the Territories. Most Israeli journalists work in poor conditions. They must therefore be highly selective in choosing one report from a large number of incidents that will actually appear. The verification of such reports requires travel to the site of an incident, and the journalist arrives after it has actually taken place.

The interpretation of an incident rather than its description is what greets the reporter – an interpretation coloured by both sides of the conflict. IDF press releases report incidents but also offer justification for them. Similarly, Palestinian sources adopt a parallel approach.

On numerous occasions, Israeli reporters have been unable to reach the site of a story to question participants. At the beginning of the Intifada, only a general had the right to declare an area 'a closed military zone'; by 1989 junior officers could implement this definition to bar reporters: 'I have seen such officers the minute they spot a journalist in the field inform him that the area is closed. If the reporter demands to see a signed order to that effect, the order, often blank, is produced, and the relevant details are filled in on the spot: date (today), place (here), period of validity (until further notice)'.[15] This policy was somewhat ameliorated when members of the Twenty First Year group were arrested in 1989 while attempting to meet Palestinians in areas which had been designated 'off-limits' by the military. Their trial was dropped when the court was informed that the closing-off of such areas by junior officers was illegal under Israeli law.

Other Israeli interests also had reasons to document military activities. B'Tselem, the Israeli Information Centre for Human Rights in the Occupied Territories, was established in March 1989. It defined its twin objectives as 'the systematic collection of data on human rights in the Occupied Territories and the dissemination of reliable information', and 'to educate the Israeli public about international human-rights standards and norms and to foster public debate within Israel on the nature and scope of human-rights violations and their impact, both short term and long, on Israeli society and its democratic character'. Within a short time, B'Tselem had attained an authoritative status and its reports were widely quoted in the Israeli press. The organization was trusted by the Palestinians. Significantly, Palestinian witnesses to the Temple Mount tragedy in October 1990 who refused to testify before the government-appointed investigation did offer evidence to B'Tselem. The army was co-operative, for B'Tselem often clarified situations which the military bureaucracy, through overwork, was unable to elucidate. For example, when journalists requested a figure for the total number of Palestinians held under administrative detention, different army sources produced different figures. It thus transpired that the Israel Defence Forces actually did not know how many Palestinian prisoners they were holding. B'Tselem's statistics in many cases proved reliable, for the organization double-checked all its findings before publication. Unlike the Israeli army or Palestinian sources, it did not have to justify statistics; nor did it have any vested interest in the interpretation of information.

Thus, the statistics issued by B'Tselem were sometimes at variance with other sources. For example, B'Tselem reported that there had been 604 'shooting' deaths by the end of March 1990. On 14 May 1990, the IDF reported that there had been 538 fatalities caused by soldiers' gunfire. At the same time, the Palestinian Data Centre for Human Rights reported that 660 had been killed through soldiers' and settlers' gunfire. On 26 May 1990 Arafat told a news conference in Geneva that there had been 1200 martyrs since the Intifada had commenced.

B'Tselem was funded by a grant from the Ford Foundation and received further generous donations from numerous American Jews. As an Israeli organization, it achieved considerable credibility, because it could overcome the automatic prejudice which Arab and foreign sources generated. The Israeli Foreign Ministry, however, was far from pleased when B'Tselem's findings were published abroad and often quoted back by foreign governments. Thus, when the prestigious Jimmy Carter Human Rights Award was conferred on B'Tselem in December 1989, the local Israeli consul boycotted the ceremony. A preliminary B'Tselem inquiry found that the police had overreacted when almost twenty Palestinians were killed during the Temple Mount riot in October 1990. The government Press Office dismissed the report as 'irrelevant' and derided the work of the organization.

The irritation of the Far Left

The Far Left in Israel has also taken an interest in the publication of events in the Territories. Close contacts with the Palestinians, albeit ideological, provided an accessibility to information about incidents which could then be published in Israel and abroad. In November 1989 the Jerusalem District Court sentenced Michel 'Mikado' Warschawski to thirty months in prison and a 10,000 shekel fine for his activities as Director of the Alternative Information Centre in Jerusalem. The office was registered by the Ministry of the Interior and survived financially by offering typesetting services. Although he was cleared of knowingly supporting a terrorist organization, Warschawski was charged for typesetting a booklet which documented the method of interrogation and torture of the GSS in the Territories. The booklet was attributed to a front organization for George Habash's rejectionist Popular Front for the Liberation of Palestine. Warschawski was accused under the Emergency Defence Regulations of providing 'typing services for a prohibited organization'.

Warschawski, a Marxist and formerly a member of the anti-Zionist group Matzpen, had an almost classical Jewish background. The son of a former Chief Rabbi of Strasbourg, he had renounced his *yeshiva* background. Although his politics were shared by few, his information publication *News from Within* was a clear irritant to the military authorities in the Territories, who viewed it as a channel for publicizing the Palestinian version of events. His interrogator told him that although in expressing his views he had been subject to occasional harassment, generally he had been free to do as he wished: 'Do you know why? Because Israel is a democracy and this includes freedom of information and freedom of expression. But there [in the Territories] it's something-different. There it is occupation. If you want to get the rights of democracy, don't work with them. You are walking on no-man's land'.[16] Yet Warschawski viewed himself as just that – someone moving between Jews and Arabs.

The court accepted that he did not know that the pamphlet was attributed to the PFLP but asked why he did not check out its origin before assisting in its publication. Neither could they comprehend why he refused to divulge the name of the person who brought the original pamphlet to him. The information about GSS interrogation techniques had in fact already been published in the Territories. At his trial, Warschawski asked what sort of danger would have been posed if the pamphlet had been published: 'If there is no torture by the Shabak [GSS] this information is fictitious. If there is torture, publishing it is a duty.' Warschawski was in part punished for his views but he earned the support of many in Israel who disagreed with him politically.

Another case which involved the Far Left was that of the editors of the newspaper *Derech Ha'Nitzotz*, who were accused of being a front for Nayef Hawatmeh's Democratic Front for the Liberation of Palestine (DFLP). Like Warschawski's operation, this was a small, peripheral publication that attracted some 600 readers within Israel. *Nitzotz* is the Hebrew for 'spark', which in Russian is *Iskra* – the name of Lenin's publication. The four Israeli Jewish editors of the paper had been longtime activists within the Democratic Front for Peace, which was aligned with the Israeli communists. Following their arrests in the spring of 1988, they admitted that they were members of the DFLP. One of their members had contacted an official of the Democratic Front during a visit to London. The newspaper, in both its Hebrew and Arabic versions, had apparently been financed by the Democratic Front. The four Jewish editors were charged with contacting a foreign agent, membership of a terrorist organization, membership of an illegal organization, and providing a service for an illegal organization. Yet there were clear differences of opinion within the judiciary over the seriousness of their crimes, since they had joined the political wing of the Democratic Front and not its military wing.

On their first application, the defendants were granted bail because they had no previous criminal records and they had not apparently harmed the public good. Even their newspaper had not been initially closed down by the censor. This judgement was overturned when the prosecution successfully petitioned against it. Judge Barak ruled that they had established a civilian arm of a military organization which wished to destroy the State. Moreover, despite the unusual nature of the case, Israeli courts, it was claimed, did not grant bail to those who were accused of membership of terrorist organizations. The editors of *Derech Ha'Nitzotz* entered a second request for bail and once more it was granted, albeit with restrictions. Judge Tal of the Jerusalem District Court ruled that, by definition, membership of a terrorist organization had the aim of endangering national security. This remained the case whether membership of the DFLP was political or military. Yet he concluded that 'nominal membership without the possibility of being active in the organization or on behalf of it, even if punishable, does not necessarily endanger state security'.

Following a bargain in January 1989 to plead guilty to all the charges in exchange for the dropping of the serious charge of contacting a foreign agent, the four were sentenced to terms between nine months and four years. This was partly due to protest against the imprisonment by leftist circles in Israel and the West. The four were adopted as prisoners of conscience by Amnesty International, for the defendants had not been accused of advocating violence. The organization stated that

> Amnesty International acknowledges that the DFLP and other Palestinian organizations advocate armed struggle and have performed acts of violence towards Israel. However, it does not accept that membership of or other forms of association with the PLO or any of its factions constitutes in itself evidence that a certain individual has used or advocated violence. [17]

Part IV

The Military and the Peaceniks

9

The People's Army

Fear of the assailant

The physical protection of its Jewish inhabitants is a central theme in Israeli society and this is reflected in its political life. The security concerns cannot be attributed solely to psychological motives based on centuries of fear. The belligerency of the Arab states and the Palestinians towards Israel during its short history have not engendered a sense of permanent safety. Given the instability of the region, even the most dovish of Israelis would be totally opposed to leaving the country's future to the goodwill of neighbouring Arab leaders. The multitude of casualties in open warfare and the symbolism of terrorist attacks in the light of Jewish history makes every Israeli look carefully at the security of the state and the individual.

Since 1948, approximately 13,000 Israelis have been killed in war, in skirmishes and by acts of terrorism. Some 6000, 1 per cent of the population, died during the War of Independence. Major losses were incurred during the period between 1948 and the Sinai campaign in 1956, and during the surprise attack on Israel during the Yom Kippur War in 1973. Statistically, exceedingly small fractions of the population perished during other periods. During the ill-fated and controversial war in Lebanon in 1982, one-hundreth of 1 per cent of the Jewish population of Israel died. Yet when such a minute statistic is translated into an actual number of people, it amounts to over 600 dead. For the Jews, mindful of their traditions and history, even one death projects a threatening imagery and triggers an ingrained insecurity.

In 1978 a study was carried out by Hebrew University sociologists in which 262 students were questioned about the likelihood of their dying as a result of the conflict. They were also asked about the possibility of being killed in a traffic accident.[1] According to the respondents, the average subjective chance of being killed as a result of the Arab–Israel confrontation was 23.8 per cent. Such perceptions exaggerate a thousandfold the statistical reality of being killed as calculated from past conflicts. Moreover, the average

187

chance of being killed in a traffic accident, 24.4 per cent, was virtually identical. Yet the possibility of death in conflict was certainly perceived as more threatening than death in a car accident. Such comparisons illustrate the psychological barriers erected through a state of no war and no peace with thoughts of potential future destruction always foremost. They also exhibit the deep significance attached to the ideal of living in total security.

Subjective evaluation of the probability	Killed in conflict	Killed in traffic accident
No danger	12.6	13.7
0.1–1	11.9	13.8
2–10	26.7	24.0
11–49	21.0	18.3
50	19.1	23.7
51–75	3.5	1.9
76–100	5.3	4.6

Indeed, an investigation of Israel's policy of instant retaliation to Arab attacks between 1951 and 1969 showed that a central factor was a political need to respond to the public's fears.[2] Ben-Gurion, who was also Israel's first Minister of Defence, reflected the widespread view that the root of the security problem was inextricably tied to the very existence of Israel and its inhabitants. The borders of Israel in 1949 were very precarious from a military point of view. The Green Line separating Israel and the Arab armies was then only 17 kilometres from Greater Tel Aviv and 30 kilometres from Greater Haifa. Jerusalem was divided between Jordan and Israel. The conquest of the West Bank increased those distances:[3]

Distance from forward line to	1949	1967
Greater Haifa	30	50
Greater Tel Aviv	17	64
Jerusalem	0	40

It was recognized that the West Bank had been used to attack Israel in both 1948 and 1967 – and not only by Jordanian forces. Its occupation during the Six Day War provided earlier warning against attack and a forward defence capability. The West Bank provided 'strategic depth' and a topography of high mountain ridges to defend the lowland coastal area where nearly 70 per cent of Israel's population lived. This 'vital area' was only 14–30 kilometres wide and 60 per cent of Israel's industry was situated there.

In contrast, the West Bank occupied an area twice that of Israel's
'vital area' and stretched 55 kilometres from Kalkiliya to the River
Jordan.[4] The mountain ridges which link Jerusalem, Ramallah and
Nablus provide early warning and are thus important intelligence-
gathering positions which no strategist would willingly vacate. The
height of the mountains is the essential factor rather than their
proximity to Jordan, since Israel's electronic vision is blocked from
the lowland coastal plain. Any attack from the east would be directed at
Samaria and the northern Judean hills, for the Dead Sea is an effective
obstacle in the south. There are five major arterial roads leading
into the West Bank, which are then linked internally by north–south
roads. If Arab armies marched through these five roads and captured
these ridges, they would partially blind Israel's electronic vision and
place her at a great disadvantage. The Syrian capture of the Israeli
intelligence stronghold on Mount Hermon in 1973 badly blunted the
military capability of Israel's airforce.

Yuval Ne'eman, a founder of the Far Right Techiya Party, argues that

> whoever occupies Samaria threatens the inner lines of the whole
> centre of the State . . . since the territory allows for the transfer
> of troops on internal lines from North to South and also from
> East to West. Israel must allocate considerable forces to the
> defence of the Sharon so that it is not cut off, and to the area
> of Tel Aviv–Jaffa so that it is not conquered, to Jerusalem and
> the corridor, and also to Haifa and the Jezreel valley. Samaria
> is a classical strategic bridgehead, combining compactness and
> defensibility with direct access to the strategic objectives.[5]

Virtually no Israeli military analyst would dispute the importance of
West Bank topography, but disagreement reigns about its significance
in an overall solution which would satisfy Israel's security requirements. All accept the paramount importance of Ben-Gurion's dictum
that a war must quickly be transferred to enemy territory and away
from Israel's population centres, and that this would be more difficult
from within the Green Line.

The danger to Israel's three major population centres along the
coastal plain would be extremely great if Arab armies moved into
the West Bank. Yuval Ne'eman advocates a dispersal of population
and the colonization of the West Bank for reasons of security to avoid
'another Holocaust'. For Ne'eman, only the annexation of the West
Bank provides the solution.

Military peaceniks

Many Israeli military analysts seem to hold opposite, minimalist views that distinguish between a political border and a security border. Over the years, numerous plans have been advocated which desire the absence of political control over the Palestinians whilst ensuring Israel's security. Indeed, although serving military officers do not propagate political viewpoints, it was clear to most observers that many 'senior officers from [Chief-of-Staff] Dan Shomron down would prefer a partial withdrawal from a demilitarized West Bank.'[6]

In the summer of 1988, the Council for Peace and Security was created. It consisted of 34 generals, 86 brigadier-generals and 116 colonels. In their platform, they argued that 'the *danger* of war is the main threat to national security' and 'Nablus, Hebron and Gaza do not add to our security, they lessen it'. The continuation of the status quo of occupation, they maintained, posed a danger to national security.

Contrary to the popular view of military personnel in Europe and the United States, many senior Israeli commanders were dovish in terms of conceding territory but hawkish when it came to a strong and prepared army. Many former chiefs-of-staff sought a political home in Labour rather than in Likud. Many projected the view that peaceful co-existence with the Palestinians did not constitute a threat to or a weakening of national security – it actually indicated a lack of confidence in the ability of the IDF to repulse any attack. The example of more than a decade of peace with Egypt through the establishment of demilitarized zones was often quoted as an example of what is possible. Despite a widely held suspicion of outside intervention, Shlomo Gazit, a former head of military intelligence, welcomed the presence of an international peace-keeping force and international observers if IDF forces were also present.[7]

Military opposition to Jewish settlement was often cited on security grounds, in that the settlers brought the centres of Jewish population closer to the Arab armies. The idea of early warning and the concept of strategic depth was thus much diminished. Some also considered such a decrease in strategic depth to be an incentive to the Right to implement the Israeli conquest of the East Bank – a purpose still enshrined in revisionist ideology – in order to increase strategic depth. Settlement and the attainment of strategic depth through the acquisition of territory led to diametrically opposite objectives. The control of territory also produced a more critical attitude to Israel by successive US administrations. The more the US perceived that Israel was mortally threatened, the more it would permit Israel freedom of political manoeuvrability. The Bush administration's fierce condemnation of the establishment of new settlements in the Territories when it seemed possible that they would act as a receptacle for the Soviet Jewish emigration was indicative of this point.

There are clearly other components in national-security considerations in addition to the question of territory. In an analysis of

the situation, Lieutenant-General Giora Forman, a former Deputy
Commander of the Israeli Air Force, listed another four considerations:
population, economic resources, technology and the political situation.
He believed that the overall picture of the national-security infrastructure was a dynamic, one, in which a reduction of one factor
could be compensated essentially through an increase of another
component. Significantly, Forman suggests that economic investment
in the territories enhances Israel's security:

> Only rapid industrial development in the Territories can create
> a new society, one that is more democratic, less sensitive to
> compromise, and with 'something to lose' in times of violence.
> An investment of $200 million in industrial development . . .
> would contribute far more to Israel's security today, even
> without a settlement, than a parallel direct investment in the
> military budget.[8]

Aharon Yariv, Chairman of the Council for Peace and Security,
has also pointed out that the distance between the forward line and
the coastal plain is only a partial expression of the understanding
of strategic depth. He included the length of the forward line; the
ratio between the length of this line and the area which has to be
defended from it; the topographic nature of the forward line and the
configuration of the area which has to be defended. Although some,
like Yehoshafat Harkabi, a former head of intelligence of the IDF, have
placed importance on 'technological depth' through new sophisticated
weaponry, Yariv argued, admittedly before the advent of Stars Wars
technology, that strategic depth even in the age of missiles was still
important. Yariv noted that land forces were still required if an area
was to be conquered.[9] Strategic depth was also related to the size
and nature of the invading Arab armies, the time required for the
full mobilization of the Israeli forces, the Arab temptation to launch
a surprise attack and the willingness of the superpowers to accept a
fait accompli.

Yariv and others have argued that only total peace and stability in the
region will eliminate concern over Israel's lack of strategic depth. Withdrawal from the Territories, they have argued, would in varying degrees
increase the possibility for total peace and a decrease in Arab hostility,
which in turn would increase Israel's sense of national security. Even
so, leaving the Territories would reduce the margin of security.

Some commentators have advocated that Israel should distance
itself as far as possible from the Arab armies, substantially shorten
its internal supply lines and surround the State by a wide belt
of demilitarized buffer zones: 'The return of the Territories to
Arab sovereignty under conditions of complete demilitarization, in
accordance with the Camp David model, would not be an act of

goodwill towards the Arabs nor Chamberlainesque appeasement, but first and foremost a favour which Israel would be doing itself'.[10]

Israel Tal, Deputy Chief-of-Staff during the Six War Day and progenitor of the Merkava tank, distinguished between rigid and flexible defence lines. He argued that, whereas the pre-1967 borders were legitimately rigid, it was wrong to transfer such rigidity to the post-1967 forward line:

> We lost our strategic depth and we succeeded only in lengthening our borders. The purpose of a flexible defence is to destroy the enemy without paying attention to territory. In contrast, the purpose of a rigid defence is to preserve territory. We translated the rigid defence of the previous borders to the huge expanses of the new borders. We talked about the new strategic depth for Tel Aviv and Jerusalem, but we pledged fidelity to Kantara and Kuneitra.[11]

There appears to be a wide, although not total, consensus that an unobtrusive Israeli military presence is required on the mountain ridges and on the River Jordan in order not to damage national security. The Israel Air Force also needs to use West Bank airspace for practice. Ephraim Sneh, former Administrator of the West Bank, has suggested that three US AWAC surveillance aircraft would prove as effective in intelligence-gathering as ground stations on the mountain ridges. Yet maximalists such as Yuval Ne'eman have pointed out that ground stations place no restriction on the quantity of equipment and the number of personnel, whereas this is obviously not the case with aircraft and even the most sophisticated satellites.

The question of terrorism, even after a peace agreement, is a central problem for military analysts. Many accept that the PLO is Israel's negotiating partner, but it is also clear that other forces are decidedly opposed to the mainstream policy of Arafat and Fatah. These include Habash's PFLP and Hawatmeh's DFLP within the PLO, the Syrian-backed Ahmed Jibril group and the murderous Abu Nidal group, all of whom bitterly oppose any cessation of the armed struggle. Hovering above all these nationalist groups is the rising Muslim fundamentalist movement, which is beginning to rival the PLO in the allegiance it can command. Hamas is opposed to the existence of Israel on national theological grounds and believes in an Islamic Greater Palestine.

The advent of the age of technology has also meant its individualization. Smaller, more accurate Precision Guided Munitions (PGMs) covering greater distances make the erection of physical barriers around the West Bank as an anti-terrorist deterrent less effective: 'Imagine the effect of a single successful hit by a hand-held anti-aircraft missile fired from a Samarian village against an El Al passenger plane taking off or landing at nearby Ben-Gurion Airport: it could wreck many years of carefully negotiated peace between

Israel and Palestine'. [12] Clearly, there is no absolute answer to this fundamental problem, except that peace and national sovereignty will rapidly diminish the number of potential terrorists. Close co-operation with a Palestinian police force and good intelligence would also be ways of avoiding personal tragedies and political instability.

Shooting and crying

Israelis who concluded that they did not wish to serve in the Territories soon discovered that there was an organization that could advise them. Yesh Gvul (There's a Limit) had come into existence during the war in Lebanon when 2500 reservists signed a petition asking not to serve there. Its activities began in July 1982 when eighty-six reservists signed a letter to Begin and Sharon declaring their refusal to serve in Lebanon and over 150 were eventually imprisoned for short terms. Some soldiers subscribed to *lo le'ot* – 'no to the ribbon' – and refused to accept any military decoration for service during the Lebanon war. Like Peace Now, Yesh Gvul experienced a period of relative inactivity in the aftermath of the war, but this changed dramatically with the onset of the Intifada. By 1 January 1988 – just a few weeks after the outbreak of the Intifada – 160 reservists had signed a declaration of intent 'to refuse to take part in suppressing the uprising and insurrection in the Occupied Territories'. These signatories included three majors, five captains, one medical officer and a Jerusalem municipality councillor. Moreover, a considerable number of these 'refuseniks' were veterans of combat units.

Unlike the younger elements of the army, who were impressionable and worshipped machismo or attached themselves to charismatic figures, the older reservists, who had experienced war and were often married with young families, tended to be more questioning. The Israeli Defence Forces traditionally had a benevolent attitude towards genuine pacifists and those who rejected military service for reasons of conscience. The adherents of Yesh Gvul went beyond conscience and turned their refusal into a political statement. They felt that to serve in the Territories was ideologically supportive of remaining there. There was a strong belief that partly immoral methods were being employed to suppress a partly moral uprising. By the early summer of 1988, the figure of potential 'refuseniks' had risen to 600, because 'in a democratic society which is usually just, there is a moral imperative to obey the law – unless the order or situation is so flagrantly immoral and detrimental to other basic values that there is a higher morality in refusing to obey'. [13] One of the leaders of Yesh Gvul, Tel Aviv lecturer Adi Ophir, distinguished between the defence of Israel and participation in 'the continuing enslavement of another nation' in a letter to Minister of Defence Rabin.

Refusal itself had various degrees of interpretation. For many, it was the purity of not serving in the Territories. For other, it meant serving but refusing to carry out specific instructions. For example, Charles Lenchner, whilst serving his statutory three years in the army, refused to carry out policing in east Jerusalem and was duly sentenced to twenty-eight days in prison.

The official reaction was often mixed. Commanding officers who may have been quietly sympathetic, or who may have wished to avoid embarrassing publicity, would redirect the 'refusenik' to less controversial duties. But Yesh Gvul activities touched a sensitive nerve in Israeli society since the IDF occupied a position of prestige and privilege. Owing to the relatively small numbers, a liberal attitude could be manifested towards refusal without impairing military capability, but what would happen if tens of thousands refused to serve in the Territories? The Palestinians also realized the potential of such a movement: '[The members of the Israeli Peace Movement] are people who protest against the occupation but who pick up a gun and serve in the Occupied Territories when called. The few notable exceptions, such as Yesh Gvul, have tremendous credibility in the Palestinian community'.[14]

Although the IDF General Staff discussed the issue of refusal and decided that it was a peripheral phenomenon, the symbolism of the action antagonized a broad section of the Israeli public, for whom service in the armed forces was something of a sacred cow. The duty of defending one's homeland after centuries of powerlessness was an all-pervading ethic. To refuse was idolatrous. Yet the Intifada brought many patriotic Israelis to the point of selective refusal – and a small number preferred to go to prison for their views.

Many articles from reservists about their experiences appeared in the press. Quite a few were harrowing accounts of the moral dilemmas which some Israelis faced when asked to carry out the Minister of Defence's declared policy of 'might, force and beatings'. Other accounts supporting Rabin's general approach were also published. While some were deeply disturbed at the growing brutalization of Israeli soldiers, others were content to follow military instructions and regarded such actions as a national duty. They looked upon the Intifada as just another stage in the Arab war to dismantle the Jewish State. Tear-gas and rubber bullets against stone-throwing rioters were preferable to live ammunition and countless deaths.

Even so, the IDF were required to act as a riot squad against a civilian population armed with primitive if potentially lethal weapons. There was a lack of precision in the military instructions which the ordinary soldier was expected to obey. What was 'a life-threatening situation' in the context of the Intifada where the Palestinians desisted from using firearms? What reaction was expected when confronted by women and

children hurling stones and rocks? The response of the Israeli solider
on duty was essentially based on an instantaneous personal appraisal of
the situation. Judgement, therefore, varied from individual to individual.
The account of a thirty-nine-year-old reserve officer. Willy Schlapp,
appeared in the Jerusalem newspaper *Kol Ha'ir*. Schlapp and others in
his unit were veterans who had served together for over twenty years.
After their tour of duty in Gaza in the summer of 1988, they resolved
to demonstrate against the situation. The article, entitled 'His private
monster emerged', commented that Schlapp had returned from Gaza a
changed man. According to his mother, 'his eyes are different'. In the
past, Schlapp had been able to exorcise his personal ghosts by writing
poetry. This time, after Gaza, 'he seemed to suffer a kind of paralysis'.

Schlapp served his first tour of duty in Gaza in establishing the Ansar 3
detention camp for Palestinians at Ketziot in the Negev desert. He noted
that

the prisons were overflowing with detainees and the engineering
corps built the camp in double time. We received the first
detainees. We were shocked. They brought in children, blind-
folded and with their hands tied; the regular conscripts were
thrashing them and we had to protect them all the time. Aside
from directives about when firearms may or may not be used, we
had no instructions. . . .

In the course of our service, our relations with the detainees
were bizarre. We were tough but fair. We protected them from
the young soldiers when the latter employed unreasonable force
– they would come running to us to tell us that 'the kids' were
misbehaving.

It was winter. You could hear our guards coughing and blowing
their noses and the same sounds from the other side of the fences.
We had long talks with them and we achieved a certain level of
mutual confidence. There was the trustee for one section, an
adherent of the PLO's central tendency . . . for him Arafat is
a father figure. But he used to tell me that he himself is more
moderate than we could imagine, that if there were an Arab Civil
Rights Movement, he'd vote for them. He claimed that some 10
per cent of the Palestinians are like him. When we left, he gave me
a present wrapped in silver paper: a string of prayer beads, with
a ribbon in two of the PLO colours, red and black. You may ask:
where is the third, the green? The green is symbolized by the dry
olive pits comprising the string.

As you can well understand, we completed that tour of reserve
service with a depressing sense that the system has lost its
sense of direction, but with a certain measure of satisfaction

that we, however insignificant, had done our best under the circumstances.

Our recent tour of duty in Gaza was a different story. We were sent to impose order in two notorious refugee camps, al Buraj and al-Muazi. In al-Muazi, a building block was thrown at me from a rooftop – it struck my leg and put me out of action for a week. Had it hit my head, I would be dead. Towards the end, I got a metal spike in the back and that hurt.

Guys were surprised afterwards that I hadn't become a right-winger. To understand the Palestinian insurgents, you don't have to find national motives. It's sufficient to go through the camp just once and see the overcrowding and the living conditions. There are alleyways 15 inches across. You can't go down them holding your rifle crosswise. The shit flows and there are hundreds of rats wandering around, so fat they aren't scared of you. There are times when a rat comes towards you and there's no room to let it pass. In the whole of the Gaza Strip, which is bursting at the seams, there are 2100 Jews; in al Buraj alone there are 17,000 inhabitants. When you hear the demands of the Israeli settlers, it just blows your mind.

Our first week in al Buraj, we caught an eleven-year-old kid who was throwing stones at us. We went to his home in the middle of the night, we knocked on the gate and hauled his father outside. An officer from the previous unit which we were relieving, asked if this was his son. The father pleaded: 'By Allah, this is my son!' But the officer screeched: 'Beat him!' The father slapped him, but the officer screeched: 'Is that a beating? Hit him!' Possibly out of fear and stress, the father got hysterical and gave his son a murderous beating, knocking him down and kicking him in the ribs with all his might. Later I had a personal experience of my own. One night, I caught a curfew breaker, a youngster of nineteen and I gave him a murderous beating. Afterwards, I felt nauseous. I couldn't eat a thing. Guys wouldn't believe that I had given such a beating. That set off a warning light in my own mind. Here it is, my own private monster, beginning to emerge. That scared me terribly.

Al Buraj is a troublesome camp, often under curfew. Anything can bring on a curfew. On one occasion, they threw rocks at a passing general and he was offended. On the spot, he imposed a four-day curfew.

Its a bizarre place. By day, you see lots of cars, but they vanish at nightfall. It turns out that the inhabitants, fearful of their cars being damaged by the army, take them into their houses. They've opened up wide doorways in the walls, and at night, the car is driven into the living room. You see a car surrounded by rugs, a TV, a ventilator.

There were at least three occasions when we would have been justified in opening fire, but we didn't use live ammunition – not even .22 bullets directed at the feet, in case somebody bent over and got hit in the head. It wasn't fear. We didn't want any fatalities in the area under our responsibility during our term of duty there. In spite of all our precautions, one of the guys fired a rubber bullet down a dark alleyway and took out the eye of a curfew breaker. On 8 August [1988], there were mass demonstrations in al Buraj and we had to veritably storm barricade after barricade. They weren't children, but men aged 17–30. All the same, we were strict about not using live ammunition. After our departure, there were fatalities. One of the absurdities is that we were given a certain weapon, but our firing instructions forbade shots at persons under seventeen. Can you imagine, we were supposed to stand there, facing the mob and shout: 'Anyone under seventeen, go away!' Our company ended its latest tour of duty exhausted and worn out. We're a company with combat training. When you face the enemy, you fire. If war were to break out tomorrow, we'd all come a-running. No sweat. But all of a sudden we were made into a police force. We left with the feeling that this is a government of idiots. Shamir says that for all he cares, the Intifada can go on for nine years. The government has gone astray, it doesn't understand that force is of no use in this instance. The army is pitiable, it's forced to do a job it isn't built for. It's ordered to solve a problem the government is incapable of solving. Nevertheless, this government which I can't trust can rely on me.

There are guys in our outfit who have closed their businesses because of the recent increase in reserve duty. But there have been no refuseniks, nor shirkers. Personal relations in our company are such that if someone needs to go abroad, he calls the company commander who releases him from duty. There is a decision in principle that our men don't apply to the special board which grants deferments in special cases. We are super-patriots, but we completed our last tour of duty in a very bad mood. In the course of our service, we sat in the officers' tent and held a very incisive discussion. We decided that as soon as we are discharged, the entire company would set off for Jerusalem and stand opposite the Prime Minister's office with protest banners. We argued about the usefulness of such a step. We were weighed down by memories of the protest demonstrations led by Motti Ashkenazi after the Yom Kippur War. The first was attended by 40,000, the second by 20,000 and in the third Motti stood alone in a tent in the rain.

Ultimately, our decision was swallowed up by a complexity of other problems, and as ever, the decision was made for us. When we were discharged, we were in a depressed state. We hugged one another and each of us hastened to his own home and job, to pull himself together and to get something done before the next tour of reserve duty.[15]

That sense of frustration manifested itself in intermittent comments from the senior command of the IDF, including its Chief-of-Staff, that the Intifada required a political solution and not a primarily military one. Shamir himself was the public target of some vitriolic attacks when he visited a paratroop unit in Nablus in January 1989. During hours of discussion many soldiers vented their anger on the Prime Minister and told him that he did not know what was going on in the Territories:

To restore order in the casbah, I must behave in a brutal manner with innocent people. I knowingly break military rules in order to make residents afraid of me. . . . I feel humiliated in front of the person I must beat up. These are not the values I was raised on. I feel [the victim] getting stronger while I become weaker. Anyone who tells me not to beat up people simply doesn't understand the reality on the ground. An oppressive regime must oppress. It must live up to its name.[16]

Palestinian children

B'Tselem reported on 1 January 1990 that 136 children had been killed in two years of the Intifada – nearly one-quarter of all Palestinians who had died as a result of Israeli military action.[17] Although military regulations prohibited firing at children, the high percentage reflects not only the degree to which Palestinian children are wrapped up in the 'game' of the Intifada, but also the extent to which Israeli soldiers come to terms with their task by disguising it as a 'game'. Some soldiers have spoken about the task of chasing stone-throwers as 'hide and seek'. Such 'games' can have tragic and fatal outcomes.

We were playing, several children and Kassem, under the soldiers' lookout which is on top of a tall building in the middle of the camp. We saw a soldier come down and we ran – Kassem asked why we were running. . . . The soldier went out of the building and when Kassem was some four metres from the soldier, the soldier shot Kassem from behind, in the head, with a rubber bullet. Kassem fell and the soldier went up again to the lookout. Young men arrived immediately and took Kassem to the Nasser Hospital.[18]

Eight-and-a-half-year-old Kassem Abdallah abu Libdah, from the Khan

Yunis refugee camp, died from his injuries three days later. Military regulations forbid the firing or rubber bullets from a distance of less than 40 metres. Moreoever, the very term 'rubber' bullets is misleading, for the missile is a steel marble coated in rubber or hard plastic.

B'Tselem published further reports about the high percentage of children who were casualties of the Intifada:

On 12 August 1989 at about 7.15 p.m., I was sitting with my neighbours, Mohammed al-Jiliani and Khalil Siyam, playing dominoes near the house of Jiliani, opposite my home. While we were sitting there, several soldiers came on foot accompanied by four youngsters below the age of twenty. The soldiers took the youngsters to the settlement fence, on the other side of the road, near the entrance to the al-Amal neighbourhood and I saw them beating the youths with the butts of their rifles.

After a few minutes had gone by, the parents of the youths arrived, as well as four military jeeps. When the jeeps and the families arrived, I got up and walked over with my neighbour, Subhi Da'alsa, and stood 4 to 5 metres from the jeeps. I heard shouting between the parents of the youngsters and the soldiers. After a few minutes, I heard an officer tell the parents in Arabic to disperse. People dispersed. At that time the youths who had been beaten by the soldiers were also standing near the jeeps and the captain said: 'Go home, I will release the youths.'

I returned with my neighbour, Subhi, and walked towards my house. During the entire incident, my daughter, Buthayna, and her brother, Ramzi [four years old], were standing next to the gate of my house. When I returned, the children approached me and met me about 7 metres from the gate of my house, next to the home of my neighbour Khalil Siyam. When I met the children, I took each child by the hand and glanced in the direction of the jeeps. I saw that three of the jeeps had driven away, but that when the fourth jeep began to drive, one of the soldiers began firing in our direction. I heard gunfire and my daughter, Buthayna, fell. The jeep continued on its way. When my daughter fell, I thought that she had been frightened by the shots, but when I saw that she had fallen on her face without protecting herself with her hands, I knew that she was wounded. The distance between the road and the place where she was injured is 40 metres. When I picked my daughter up, I saw blood and together with my neighbour I took her to the Nasser Government Hospital in Khan Yunis where the doctors declared her dead.

The next day the Governor of Khan Yunis, whose name is Moshe, came to my house. I related the incident and he expressed sorrow at what had happened and promised to keep the soldiers away from the neighbourhood. [19]

The large number of child casualties was not simply the result of a wanton disregard for human life by individual soldiers. Israelis of different viewpoints asked why Palestinian parents permitted their children to become involved in the Intifada, regardless of the rights and wrongs of the struggle. The official Palestinian answer was that it was the duty of all the people to participate in the uprising. The reality was that the Intifada presented a reaction of the post-1967 generation against the quiescence of their parents who had accepted both the Jordanians and the Israelis as their overlords. The Intifada was the creation of teenagers and young men who no longer heeded their parents. Despite fears for their safety, the older generation looked upon their offspring with a definite sense of pride. For them, the new generation had restored a national dignity to the Palestinians – something which they themselves had proved incapable of doing. Yet for some Israelis – particularly those on the Right – it represented a fundamentalist desire for martyrdom and a modern-day version of child sacrifice.

Adjusting to the Intifada

At the beginning of the Intifada, the Israeli Chief-of-Staff Lieutenant-General Dan Shomron attempted to neutralize the philosophy of Defence Minister Yitzhak Rabin, who had advocated non-lethal methods of suppressing the uprising – methods which prompted the Attorney-General to remind Rabin that beating demonstrators in order to punish or humiliate them was illegal. Rabin regarded the Intifada as the continuation of Israel's War of Independence and termed it 'a war of generations'. In an address to the IDF Staff College in August 1989, Rabin commented that the Intifada was simply a new form of confrontation – 'the will of small groups to discover their national identity and demands its realization. The current uprising threatens the future and security of the State of Israel'. Rabin advocated 'patience and steadfastness'. Yet the frustration of the ordinary soldier at being stoned and insulted by Palestinian teenagers was exacerbated in the absence of any real political initiative to solve the problem.

In a letter to his commanders in the Territories in February 1988, Shomron commented that

> under no circumstances should force be used as a means of punishment. The use of force is permitted during a violent incident in order to break up a riot, to overcome resistance to legal arrest and during pursuit after rioters or suspects – all within the confines of the time and the place where the incident occurs.

Force is not to be used once the objective has been attained – for example, after a riot has been dispersed or after a person is in the hands of our forces and is not resisting. In every instance, the use of force must be reasonable and one should refrain as much as possible from hitting anyone on the head or any other sensitive parts of the body. No steps should be taken to humiliate or abuse the local population, nor should property be intentionally damaged.

However, by 10 October 1989, official sources reported that fifty-two indictments against eighty-six soldiers had been filed with the military courts. The offences included manslaughter, causing death through negligence, assault, criminal physical abuse, unbecoming conduct and theft. Forty-three cases were concluded, sixty-three were convicted and nine acquitted. In addition, the Judge Advocate-General reported that between 500 and 600 soldiers had had disciplinary proceedings brought against them. During this time, no officer above the rank of major was tried in a military court for such offences. The heaviest sentences were meted out to those convicted of property crimes. Cases of manslaughter resulted in relatively light sentences and these were often reduced by regional commanders.

Some early abuse reached the international press. The burying of four Palestinians resulted in a two-month sentence and a demotion for the officer in charge. A thirty-minute beating of two Palestinians by four Israeli soldiers was secretly filmed and broadcast by CBS news and thereby witnessed by millions around the world. At a disciplinary hearing two of the soldiers were sentenced to ten days and twenty-one days respectively. The two others were given suspended sentences of three months and two months respectively.

Official explanations denoted these events as *harig* – an aberration of the normally good behaviour of the Israeli army. Much emphasis was placed on Palestinian killings of their own people in the Territories by warring gangs of youths who enforced their own law. Yet in October 1990, a military court convicted four soldiers from the crack Givati Brigade for beating two Gaza Palestinians in February 1988 – one of whom died of his injuries. The senior defendant, Reserve Major Yitzhak Levit, blamed the authority of political circles and, in particular, Defence Minister Rabin for his actions. Unrepentant, he claimed that the court ruling established the precedent that 'only those who do not bear the responsibility do not pay the price.'

An Israeli social anthropologist who reflected on his own time in the Territories concluded that Israeli soldiers enact a masquerade because they are 'not themselves' and do things which they would never consider doing as law-abiding members of Israeli society. The disguises which soldiers developed to cope with a situation cut across the grain of their education and background. It permitted many reservists

> to display 'irregular' *public* behaviour like cursing and swearing, belching and farting, urinating and spitting, or talking dirty. This situation also allows many men to freely exhibit the 'macho' dimensions of their army character. This point is readily evident in regard both to non-verbal behaviour – posturing, hunching of shoulders, or excessive preoccupation with guns and equipment – and verbal behaviour – free use of the imperative, barking words in a forceful manner, or the abandonment of polite forms.[20]

The deeper the soldier reflected on the legitimacy of his actions the more problematic his identification as the stereotypical Israeli male within the social-evaluative system of the society. While the dilemmas thrown up by the Intifada were not glossed over by the IDF, the upper eschelons of the military command also made efforts to deflect a soldier's attention away from a self-examination of the legitimacy of his actions to a consideration of a job well-done. What became important was not the morality of the task itself but how well it was carried out.

The Israeli social anthropologist concluded his examination of himself and his fellow reservists with the observation that such extraordinary behaviour in the Territories may not automatically lead – at least in the short term – to a brutalization within normal society, but to a dual behavioural system:

> Although I was rarely in direct contact with Palestinians while in Hebron, I found myself in a state of turmoil for weeks after my return: I did not sleep well, could not concentrate on my teaching and research, and was short with my children. Above all, I was defensive about any criticism of the army and of the actions of soldiers in the Territories. As I then only vaguely sensed and now more explicitly realize, I took these criticisms and questions personally: that is, as attacks touching on my identity as an army officer and through that as an Israeli, and as assaults upon my commitments to the army and by way of that to my own society. These circumstances were made more difficult by the unfulfilled expectations many people had . . . that stints in the Occupied Territories during the Intifada would effect an immediate political backlash leading to mass movements for change. If anything . . . what I witnessed at that time was the basic resiliency of the situation: in other words, how the application of 'double standards' to behaviours within and across the Green Line could continue.[21]

Refuseniks

Those who felt strongly about serving often found a way around specific problems by manipulating situations or obtaining other postings, but a small minority, for differing reasons, crossed the line and simply refused to serve. Yesh Gvul did not advocate refusal, since that was illegal, but instead provided information for potential refuseniks and support for those who were sent to prison as well as for their families. Yesh Gvul distributed legal information and advice about which orders could legitimately be disobeyed. It also produced a survival kit for potential refuseniks about the mechanics and expectation of refusal. A hot-line was installed for potential refuseniks seeking advice. Although Yesh Gvul was condemned by the Israeli government, no move was made against the organization until the beginning of 1989. This proved to be abortive, for the authorities were unable to define the legal understanding of 'promoting refusal'. If a refusenik or a potential candidate explained his personal position, was he also advocating it for everyone else? Did justification of refusal also mean its general advocacy? Yesh Gvul had intelligently pursued only a line of approach that was strictly within the law. All the organization's documents were checked by lawyers before publication.

The formal activities of Yesh Gvul were opposed by the leadership of Peace Now – and they distanced themselves from the group. The central strategy of the mainstream peace camp was to remain within the national consensus whilst at the same time standing outside it as a movement of protest. In addition, the defence of the country was paramount to its survival. Whilst there should be a dialogue with the enemy, the enemy was still the enemy. Peace Now leaders opposed refusal to serve on a number of levels. They argued that civil disobedience in itself was not wrong, but its application was a matter of judgement. While other means of protest were available, why use 'refusal', which made little impact on a patriotic public? Even Colonel Eli Geva, who refused to lead his troops on an assault on Beirut in the war in 1982, was forbidden by Rabin to return as a reservist a few years later. From the perspective of Peace Now, the activities of Yesh Gvul were peripheral and politically counter-productive.

In a Yesh Gvul anthology published in 1985, a former head of military intelligence, Meir Pail, argued that internal subordination and efforts by commanders and their men to circumvent orders during the war in Lebanon were far more effective and decisive than the open declarations of Yesh Gvul. A common criticism was that the illegality or refusal would simply set an example for the continual breaking of the law by the Right, who often claimed allegiance to a higher authority.

Even so, this difference of approach was not characterized by deep

acrimony. Whilst respecting the moral integrity of those who chose
to go to prison, Peace Now believed it to be politically unwise. Yet
Yesh Gvul often pointed to the lack of logic behind Peace Now's tactical
meanderings:

> One of the things that strengthened me in my decision [to refuse
> to serve] during this period was when I saw a report on Israeli TV
> about a unit – what we call a good unit – serving in the Gaza Strip. It
> showed the problems the soldiers in the unit had in suppressing the
> civil population. There was one shot of a jeep, and inside the jeep a
> very famous Peace Now activist, a man I really appreciate for his
> involvement in education. He sat in the jeep and took part in the
> unit's enthusiasm at that moment of catching two boys throwing
> stones. I said to myself – that's the line I'm not willing to cross. [22]

The differing attitudes within the peace camp towards refusal was
most keenly felt in the Civil Rights Movement (CRM) of Shulamit Aloni.
At the end of July 1990, forty-three CRM municipal councillors signed
an advertisement in *Ha'aretz* in which they declared their solidarity with
one of their colleagues who had been sentenced to twenty-eight days
for refusing to serve in the Territories. [23] This created debate within the
CRM and indeed a split within its leadership. While Ran Cohen and Yossi
Sarid condemned the forty-three councillors, its leader, Shulamit Aloni,
was sympathetic. Indeed, she commented, 'If 500 officers would refuse,
the entire political situation would change'. [24]

Even if working on the inside was advantageous, there was a certain
inconsistency in participating in an event in the Territories one day and
protesting against it in Tel Aviv the next day. Opponents of this approach
believed that service in the Territories made a soldier a victim of the
situation and thereby an indirect supporter of it. Yesh Gvul's activities
emphasized the moral dilemma of serving in such a situation. It was
therefore able to gain the strong support of Yeshayahu Leibowitz, the
moral philosopher, as well as of many others who believed in setting
a clear personal example and living by certain standards. This deeply
concerned Peace Now leaders, who bore the added political burden of
not frittering away its support and influence through a careful reading
of the public psychology. Paradoxically, the leaders of Peace Now may
have been even further to the Left than their radical opponents, but
they understood the futility of such ideological displays. There was a
distinction between the public face of an influential movement and the
moral decision of an individual to refuse to serve. Indeed, some activists
were willing simultaneously to carry through both approaches.

10

The Peace Camp

Diversity and fragmentation

By the mid-1980s, the umbrella organization of the peace movement, Peace Now, was at a very low ebb. Its most heroic phase – the opposition to the war in Lebanon – had passed. Its *raison d'être* appeared to be purely reactive, to deal with any new crisis that might arise. The generality and vagueness of the peace movement as a non-ideological body, embracing Trotskyists and the Far Left as well as Friedmanites and the liberal Right, was both its strength and its weakness. It was able to bring thousands, often hundreds of thousands, together in mass rallies. It could carry out tasks of which political parties were incapable, and indeed filled the vacuum left by Labour as a focus of opposition to Likud policies on the Territories. Yet this also symbolized the movement's inherent contradiction in being both a mainstream body within the Israeli consensus and a protest organization trying to move that consensus.

But Peace Now was not a protest movement on the Western model. It represented a 'consolidation of moods, ideas and experimentation' in Israeli politics since 1967.[1] Peace Now addressed itself to the fact that conventional politics in Israel had been suspended – one did not have to be a Leftist to want a dialogue with the Palestinians. Conversely, it was perfectly possible to be a kibbutznik or moshavnik (a member of a moshav, a communal village consisting of individual farmers) who would support Raful's Tsomet party, which believed in keeping the Territories. In these unconventional circumstances, conventional ideological labels were often misleading.

The only 'ideological' label which Peace Now used was that it deemed itself 'Zionist': 'The movement emphasizes its role as a patriotic interpreter of the true Zionist spirit'.[2] This differentiated it from the Left, which was often post-Zionist or non-Zionist in its outlook. It conversely prevented the Right from projecting itself as the sole interpreter of Zionism. It also indicated a belief in certain fundamentals of Israeli society, such as the Law of Return and the

importance of strong Defence Forces. It did not advocate pacificism or
the exacerbation of factionalism within the IDF through refusal. Peace
Now positioned itself on one side of the conflict and did not pretend to
be an intermediary. Whilst strenuously opposing government policy,
it did not accept that it was simply the villainy of Israel that was
responsible for the contemporary situation. The Palestinians were
neither blue-eyed ideologues of peace and justice nor demonic mass
murderers, but the enemy with whom Israel should sit down and
negotiate.

The importance of appealing to the widest possible audience meant a
virtual de-ideologization of approach and thereby an acceptance of the
lowest common denominator. This meant, essentially, a recognition of
the Palestinian right to national self-determination without defining the
final status of the Palestinian entity; the division of the Land between
the two peoples along the pre-1967 borders; a full recognition of Israel;
and a cessation of terrorism and a solution which satisfied Israel's
security concerns.

Peace Now had originally been formed to ensure that the Begin
government did not renege on the possibility of peace with Egypt. Yet
from the outset there was the realization that a genuine peace could
be achieved only by dealing with the Palestinian problem. This belief
underpinned the early protests against new Jewish settlements in the
Territories and the successful campaign against the war in Lebanon,
which culminated in the huge demonstration in Tel Aviv against the
massacre of Palestinians in the Sabra and Shatilla refugee camps.
During the war in Lebanon, Peace Now's prophecies were gradually
vindicated. A shocked population, which had unaninimously backed
the government in the early days of the war, was forced to confront
unpalatable facts. Avraham Burg, a founder of 'Soldiers against Silence'
and a leading Peace Now activist, commented after the war:

> We knew then what half the population of Israel, including Begin,
> knows now. It's very easy to hide, not to look, to put your head
> down, to ignore the situation and hope it will pass with the wind
> – it didn't. A lot of people who were under fire exhibited real
> courage, but they didn't find the courage to speak out. – What
> will my boss say? Look, everyone supports the war and you are
> only a minority.[3]

Peace Now crystallized the feeling that the people of Israel had not
been told the whole truth and that the government was not morally
omnipotent in times of war:

> You can take every shadow in the street and see gangsters.
> To see an enemy behind every tree. Yes, the PLO had forces

there [in Lebanon] but to compare these with forces that can remotely threaten, not simply the existence of the State, but even to scratch the surface is an illusion. It is demagoguery. What did the PLO have there? Two brigades of rifles against all our tanks! This was not a threat – it was sufficient to expel them from the 45-kilometre security zone and return home after a cease-fire agreement.[4]

The period between the end of the Lebanon War and the start of the Intifada was one of concerted inactivity on the part of Peace Now, and indeed other peace groups. Political grievances were met by the Peres government, which mollified less active members. The departure of Begin lowered the passion of debate. The IDF left Lebanon and remained in a narrow security zone in the far south of the country. Few new settlements were being established in the Territories.

Yet the essential core of the problem – Palestinian national aspirations – remained, and by and large was ignored by both government and the majority of the people of Israel. Although Peace Now activists tried hard to make a dent in this complacency through occasional meetings with Palestinians, a real sense of apathy prevailed. Meetings with local Palestinians, such as the public display of solidarity in Hebron in April 1986, were very much the exception rather than the rule. There were also unsanctioned meetings of Peace Now activists with PLO officials abroad. There was also a distinct reluctance to criticize the Labour Party and its leader Shimon Peres, even though there was a deep desire to detach Labour from its espousal of the Jordanian option towards a recognition that the solution lay with the Palestinians and not with King Hussein. Peace Now therefore often advocated speaking to 'representatives of the Palestinians' – a term which covered both the PLO and Jordan. Following King Hussein's determination in 1988 to relinquish Jordanian claims to the Territories – the West Bank of the Jordan – this compromise was made redundant.

Peace Now's involvement with the dovish wing of the Labour Party deepened, and the expansion of Shulamit Aloni's Civil Rights Movement to incorporate many who were unable to accept Peres's cautious approach signalled developments in other directions. Aloni's party now entitled itself the 'Civil Rights and Peace Movement' and attracted such activists as Dedi Zucker and Mordechai Bar-On from Peace Now, Yossi Sarid from Labour and later Mordechai Virshubski from Shinui. Avraham Burg joined the Labour Party as Peres's adviser on Diaspora affairs and was elected to the Knesset in 1988. Mapam also rejuvenated itself politically as the founding fathers of the party retired or passed away.

Peace Now operated on an Athenian model of activity, in which open meetings were forums of debate and decision. The *ad hoc* leadership was never formally appointed and there were no leadership positions. While there were many aspects of Peace Now's operations – owing to its structure and philosophy – which could be criticized, its longevity showed its importance. It could not be dismissed as a radical flash in the pan, a manifestation of youthful exuberance. Begin's initial attempts to integrate the movement into his interpretation of the consensus during the excitement of the Camp David period failed, as did attempts to find a counterbalancing alternative such as the government-financed 'Safe Peace' movement. Accusations from leading members of the Likud that Peace Now was receiving funds from Saudi Arabia also collapsed through the inherent absurdity of such suggestions.

The emergence of many new and more militant peace groups in the wake of the Intifada led to a revaluation of Peace Now's status as a voluntary protest movement. Yet even before the outbreak of the Intifada, there was a need to place Peace Now on a much more professional level. In October 1989 Peace Now opened its first national office in Tel Aviv and employed a full-time co-ordinator and three part-timers.

Although there were Sephardi organizations within the peace camp, such as 'East for Peace', within some sections of the oriental electorate there was a sense of extreme animosity towards Peace Now, which was perceived as representative of Ashkenazi elitism. In his book *The Land of Israel*, Amos Oz noted the comments of a resident of Bet Shemesh:

> And in what other country in the world would Yossi Sarid wander around free during a war and make propaganda all day for the enemy? In Syria? Or Russia? Or America? Who ever heard of such a thing – that in the middle of a war people would stand up and say it's not our war. Look what you did to this country during the Yom Kippur War. You almost destroyed it. . . . You – you don't have any pride in your country. Only in yourselves, only in your kibbutzim and that Peace Now group. Running all over the world saying 'It's them! This isn't us!' This filthy country is Begin's, but us, we're clean!' You want the world to think that Israel was once a beautiful country but now Begin and his niggers have taken over. That the gentiles should come here tomorrow, today, to help you take the country back into your own hands![5]

Although one criticism from right-wing circles in the Labour Party was that Peace Now cemented the schism within Israel and even undermined a future Labour government's ability to negotiate from a position of strength, many within the peace camp wished Peace Now to move faster, and in particular to develop a dialogue with the PLO. Whilst many believed that this was the inevitable outcome of Peace Now's activities, it was also recognized that to do so before the mainstream of Israeli public opinion could cope with it psychologically would fragment and sectarianize the organization and move it away from the consensus towards the periphery of political influence.

The peace camp was often taunted that there was no Arab equivalent to Peace Now. It was pointed out that the military authorities clamped down on Palestinian political activities in the Territories. Thus, for example, a mass Palestinian demonstration in support of peace in Manger Square in Bethlehem would not be permitted to go ahead. Palestinian activities in support of an accommodation with Israel were driven underground and often into unproductive channels.

In addition, while the movement acted to place the issue of talking to the Palestinians on the agenda, the PLO had started to take a more positive view of a dialogue with Israelis and, more specifically, with those who labelled themselves 'Zionists'. Between the Six Day War and the Yom Kippur War, there was virtually no Israeli–Palestinian dialogue. After the twelfth session of the Palestine National Council in Cairo in 1974, there was an apparent renunciation of the concept of a Greater Palestine and a willingness to meet Israelis. During the 1970s, Issam Sartawi, Said Hammami and others – apparently with Arafat's blessing – had privately met members of Peace Now. During the siege of Beirut in 1982, Arafat and even Habash had noted and welcomed the demonstrations against the war in Lebanon. These developments coalesced in the summer of 1988 when both the PLO and Peace Now made their dialogue direct rather indirect, public rather than private. In July 1988 Peace Now welcomed Bassam Abu Sharif's trial balloon, which called for a recognition of Israel and a cessation of violence. A few weeks later, when King Hussein pulled out of the West Bank, politically, administratively and financially, Peace Now finally called for official talks with the PLO as the representative of the Palestinian people. In turn, this was followed by Arafat's proclamation of the State of Palestine and the declarations and clarifications in Algiers, Stockholm and Geneva.

In parallel, there had been a growing dialogue with leaders of the pragmatic wing of the Palestinian nationalist movement in the Territories, such as Faisal Husseini and Sari Nusseibeh. This had originated in contacts between dovish academics at the Hebrew University and Palestinian communists who taught at institutes of higher education in the Territories. The communists facilitated contacts between Israeli peace activists and Palestinian nationalists. Palestinian intellectuals in the Territories began to take a more courageous stand in advocating dialogue with Israelis.

The evacuation of the PLO from Beirut in 1982 and the débâcle of the internecine conflict with the Syrian-backed Abu Musa group in 1983 induced a self-analysis within the Palestinian camp – and particularly within the mainstream Fatah. This influenced a decline in consensus politics and a tendency towards coalition building[6] – a situation which in some fashion mirrored developments in Israel. The overt opposition of the Palestinian rejectionists, the PFLP and the DFLP, was also somewhat softened when they returned to the PLO. In addition, more and more Palestinians had come into contact with Peace Now and took note of their numerous protests and demonstrations. By the late 1980s all major Palestinian groups in the PLO were willing to conduct a dialogue with Israelis, with the exception of Habash's Popular Front for the Liberation of Palestine.

These developments took place in the shadow of the Intifada. It provided a catalyst for political and practical development within the broad Israeli peace movement, but it also brought increased criticism of Peace Now's circumspect approach from within the organization and from its traditional critics on the ideological Left. The Intifada vindicated many calls from peace activists that the status quo in the Territories was on the verge of fragmentation. Yitzhak Rabin had initially referred to the outbreak of the Intifada as 'passing events' and refused to rush back from the United States. The Labour Party's response to the outbreak no doubt disappointed many in Peace Now, including many party members. Even the dovish members of the Party were muted – no doubt mindful of the selection process for the 1988 electoral list. The apparent indifference of the Labour Party, together with the events themselves, propelled many Peace Now activists towards a more radical stance, so that those in RATZ, the party of Shulamit Aloni, became more influential in the peace movement.

The practice of serving in the Territories now became supremely important, since the focal point of discontent was the 'Iron Fist' policy. Peace Now refrained from condemning the ordinary soldier, or indeed the IDF commanders, but instead focused on Minister of Defence Rabin as the architect of all the troubles. It also supported the Shultz Plan, as well as Peres's proposals for an international conference, despite reservations. It hoped to encourage the Labour Party whilst opposing the rejectionism of Likud.

The logic of peaceniks participating in the suppression of the Intifada was once more based on Peace Now's insistence on remaining within the mainstream of Israeli society:

The Intifada is directed against all of us. Any stance which ignores the fact that we are on one side of the struggle and that we shall refuse to lose the battle as long as it is conducted by violent means, is liable to place us outside any general consensus and damage our ability to seek a non-violent solution. It must be clear now and in the future that the centrist peace camp is not prepared to 'give up the fight', though we are obliged to continue with the complex and delicate task of condemning the continuing oppression, as long as there is no parallel effort to solve the problem by political means.[7]

Not surprisingly, the first protests against the Intifada came within days of its outbreak in the form of a vigil outside the Defence Ministry in Tel Aviv. Its participants were the ideological Left – Hadash (communists), Shasi (Israeli Socialist Left) and the Progressive List for Peace (PLP). Yet the protests which followed were organized by a multitude of new peace groups which were governed less by socialist ideology than by a determination to find new approaches. By 1 April 1988, a few months after the start of the Intifada, *Ha'aretz* was able to publish a list of forty-six protest organizations – and this was less than comprehensive.[8]

The emergence of new groups

The belief that a movement has more influence by working on the inside did not appeal to those who demanded a more activist and indeed ideological approach. There was a frustration with the 'Peace Now culture'. Many argued that more stringent measures were required to meet the urgency of the times, the sharp challenge of the Intifada: 'Peace Now's Ashkenazi, educated, liberal following is not so much a group of activists as it is a Greek chorus reacting with horror and anguish – and offering no real alternatives'.[9]

Reacting to Peace Now's semi-establishment image rather than to the logic of its tactics, the peace movement diversified rather than fragmented. New groups espousing new directions were spawned which often did not defer to the consensus or respect mainstream opinion. Yet all used the umbrella of Peace Now to work together for large events such as the 'Time for Peace' demonstration at the end of December 1989. A seasoned supporter of Peace Now commented that 'the road to peace is a rather wide freeway with different models going in separate lanes at different speeds. What counts is that they aim in the same direction and that they do not allow themselves to be sidetracked'.[10]

The advent of new groups was also influenced by the decline of the traditional Left as an organized force is Israel and within the peace movement in general. Primarily, this was an instance of socialist rejection of Stalinism and Moscow-sponsored communism. The advent of *glasnost* and *perestroika*, and the revolutions of the winter of 1989 in Eastern Europe, accelerated the trend to leftist individualism as opposed to an organized collective. Many individual Leftists worked in peace groups alongside newcomers, but in an almost non-ideological sense. Their approach in terms of their participation did not differentiate them from those of a liberal or apolitical disposition. When Peace Now began to advocate talking to the PLO and effectively a two-state solution, some left-wingers applied to join the organizations since few differences now remained.

Groups tended to work around specific issues. Yesh Gvul provided advice to soldiers who refused to serve in the Territories. Women's groups formed – the best known were the 'Women in Black', who demonstrated each Friday lunchtime in Jerusalem. 'Dai L'Kibush' (Down with the Occupation!), which initiated the Friday vigil in January 1988, began with a few dozen people and rapidly became a staple feature. Women in Black evoked an image of widows and death. Indeed, over 5000 women dressed in black marched to the Western Wall from the Friday vigil during the 'Time for Peace' rally to welcome the 1990s. Although the activities of Dai L'Kibush were directed primarily at influencing Israeli public opinion, it boasted Jewish and Arab members:

> Our group expresses a clear message of solidarity with the Palestinian struggle for national self-determination. We work to influence Israeli public opinion to accept a just solution to the Israeli–Palestinian conflict and to build a democratic society in Israel. We particularly address ourselves to those numerous Israelis who are repulsed by the methods used to suppress the civilian uprising, concerned about the implications of continuing the occupation but, either through ignorance or fear, hold back from supporting a real and meaningful programme for peace.

Although many women protested during the war in Lebanon, there had been no specific movement of women. After the war, however, a widespread campaign, 'Parents Against Silence', attempted to secure the return of Israeli troops from Lebanon and to ensure that those who were responsible for the war were held publicly accountable. Although it was supposedly a movement of parents, in reality it consisted of mothers only. No doubt they had noted the increasing involvement of women in the world of politics, from Mrs Thatcher's election to the silent protests by the mothers of the *desaparecidos* in Argentina's Plaza del Mayo.

The weekly protest of the Women in Black in Jerusalem and other cities provoked hostility from the Far Right and indeed there were incidents of attacks by outraged males: 'People curse, spit, throw eggs and tomatoes, threaten us and constantly remind us that we are only women, that our place is in the kitchen, that we are traitors'.[11]

The blossoming of several women's groups arose out of a growing sense of the inequality of women within Israeli society, as well as out of a desire for peace. In particular, the absence of peace and the continued placing of Israel on a military footing put women at a disadvantage in society. The almost automatic transition of men from the military into civilian life – and especially into senior positions – effectively blocked the advancement of women into appropriate posts:

> For forty years women have been told that security is the country's main concern, and women's issues must be relegated to a subordinate position. The military has a place of pride in the public agenda. Military values are carried over into civilian life. Heroism, the 'benevolent' fighter, loyalty to comrades-in-arms: these male codes present a problem of values for women, who have not been at the front and who only make a supportive contribution.[12]

The complex identification of some Israeli women with the plight of the Palestinians may have reflected disenchantment with their own situation. The sense that women had a unique contribution to make to the peace movement became quite widespread. Not only did they participate in large numbers in the organization of umbrella movements such as Peace Now, but they also formed a number of women's groups. Shani (the Israeli Women's Alliance against the Occupation) was formed a few weeks after the commencement of the Intifada. Its founding members consisted of feminist activists, women well integrated into political movements and those with no previous involvement in the Israel–Palestine conflict:

> Had circumstances in our country been different, it is unlikely that such a diversified group of women would find itself working together towards a common goal. . . . As women we see clearly the impact of these policies on Palestinian women and children: the closing of schools and nurseries; the increasingly difficult economic situation; and the absence of husbands and sons who have been arrested, detained or seriously injured. We are grieved and appalled by the growing number of deaths.

Another women's group, the Tel Aviv-based Israeli Women for Women Political Prisoners, began to adopt imprisoned female Palestinians. Their activities personalized the cases of numerous Palestinian women and drew attention to conditions of incarceration, prolonged imprisonment without trial, treatment of prisoners, and regulations and behaviour during family visits.

The use and indeed the rediscovery of the Diaspora became useful and important. There was little reticence in using opposition to Israeli government policy to raise funds and to inform Diaspora Jews. Although there was a greater reluctance in the Diaspora to establish competing peace organizations, Jews on the political Left, who were often uninvolved in formal communal networks, responded enthusiastically to calls from these newer Israeli peace organizations which took a more radical stance. 'Zionism' as a positive codeword was never mentioned and there was no pandering to the complex psychology of Diaspora Jews. There were fewer qualms about working with the political Left in a host country or working closely with PLO sympathizers. Thus the International Jewish Peace Union was happy to meet Arafat in Paris in 1989. The Jewish Socialist Group in London organized the first public meeting between British Jews and PLO representatives in London in 1988 – and before the Algiers Declaration.

In contrast, Diaspora groups such as the Friends of Peace Now, like their parent organization in Israel, were more mainstream in their approach. Their members were often active in other spheres of communal activity and thus commanded a much wider audience. Public meetings in London of Israeli Knesset members and official PLO representatives drew packed audiences from a wide cross-section of Anglo-Jewry.

In January 1990, the Tel Aviv-based International Centre for Peace issued an invitation from sixty prominent Israelis to convene a World Jewish Leadership Peace Conference. The Centre, which had developed over many years an impressive mainstream Israeli and Diaspora network of peace activists, was able to persuade Shimon Peres to speak to the Conference. Peres's vagueness did not go down well with these Diaspora Jews and they strongly applauded Shulamit Aloni's scathing attack on him for his inability to be 'the leader of the peace camp'.

An organization of new immigrants, 'Israelis by Choice', also became active with the start of the Intifada:

> Our message to our fellow Israelis is that the sustained occupation is a betrayal of the ideals which brought us here. Detentions without charge, house demolitions, deportations, beatings and the killing of civilians demean the Jewish people and cannot quell the national uprising of the Palestinians.

A central feature of such organizations was an emphasis on dialogue with the Palestinians in the Territories. The growing realization that a lack

of contact served Likud policy and permitted the demonization of the
other side catalysed these contacts particularly after the start of the
Intifada and even more so after the Algiers Declaration. Peace Now
organized day trips to visit Palestinians in their homes in Tulkarm.
Others organized visits for Diaspora Jews to Palestinian villages and
particularly to the remnants of demolished homes. A group of religious
Jews celebrated the Jewish Sabbath in the Bethlehem suburb of Beit
Sahour.

Israeli support groups for Palestinians were formed. For example,
the Committee for Beita, a village where buildings had been demolished
as a result of a settler hike and the resultant accidental death of a fifteen-
year-old girl by a guard, attempted to help inhabitants rebuild their lives
and their homes. 'Immigrants by Choice' circumvented army roadblocks
and visited Beit Sahour, which had been declared a closed military zone
by the army because its inhabitants refused to pay taxes to the Israeli
administration. The villagers received their guests with gratitude and
appreciation. The Committee for Israeli – Palestinian Dialogue, which
had initiated a campaign against the 'PLO law', brought together Israeli
and Palestinian parents who had lost children as a result of war and
conflict in a public but poignant discussion.

This trend towards dialogue and support inevitably resulted in
Israeli–Palestinian political co-operation. The Time for Peace demonstration witnessed the spectacle of tens of thousands of Israelis and
Palestinians linking arms in the hope that the 1990s would bring
harmony to the region. At the end of 1988, the Israeli–Palestinian
Human Rights Committee came into existence, its activities co-
ordinated by Israelis and Palestinians working together. Its first
public activity was a public hearing in Jerusalem on the status of
the human rights of Palestinian children. The hearing examined topics
such as children in prison, victims of physical violence, effects of
collective punishment, extreme disruption of family life and aspects
of child development.

Spiritual protesters

The importance of dialogue was felt keenly by some traditional religious
Jews – many of whom came originally from the United States. Oz
V' Shalom (Courage and Peace) was formed in the mid-1970s and
attracted many religious intellectuals and academics, primarily from
the Hebrew and Bar-Ilan Universities. Their main purpose was to
show the existence of an alternative to the Gush Emunim philosophy,
but also to create a dialogue with them. They were disturbed by the
resistance of religious Jews to the evacuation of Yamit, and particularly
by the lack of sensitivity and concern for human life during the war in

Lebanon. Following the terrible news of the massacre of Palestinians in the Sabra and Shatila refugee camps on Rosh Ha'shona (Jewish New Year), many religious Jews were deeply shocked at the condemnation by Rabbi Chaim Druckman of the National Religious Party of the *yefei nefesh* (bleeding hearts).

> After we had just spent the whole morning praying, trying to do *tshuva* [repentance], and talking about God's universal concern that a rabbi on *motsei Rosh Ha'shona* [the evening after the Jewish New Year] could be so insensitive and not have one word to say about the hundreds of men, women and children who had been killed. The next day, the fast of Gedalya, we organized a demonstration outside Hechal Shlomo [a central synagogue in Jerusalem] and *dovened mincha* [recited the evening prayer].[13]

Netivot Shalom (Paths to Peace), the organization which grew out of this sense of outrage at the massacres, initially attracted large numbers of religious Jews who were severely disturbed by the episodes of the war in Lebanon. Compared to Oz V'Shalom, it had a much broader appeal, which attracted younger and more devout people. It attracted in particular the *hesder yeshivot*, religious seminaries whose students divided their time between serving in the IDF and religious learning, which had been disproportionately affected by considerable numbers of fatalities in the war. In particular, the heads of *yeshivot* in Gush Etzion, Rabbis Amital and Lichtenstein, put their full authority behind Netivot Shalom. While it considered itself part of the peace camp, there were basic differences between it and Peace Now. The latter would demonstrate on the Jewish Sabbath since it was the only free day – a holiday for the secular Jews, a holy day for the religious ones. Secular doves tended to characterize the settlers in the Territories as religious fanatics and followers of Meir Kahane, whereas the religious doves had closer ties through dialogue with Gush Emunim and did not accept this monolithic stereotype. The essential difference was that Peace Now's philosophy had been shaped by the Haskalah and the French Revolution, whereas Netivot Shalom was guided by the dictates of the Torah and Jewish tradition in general. A booklet about the Territories, published by Peace Now in the early 1980s, contained no allusion to Jewish sources, only a reference to 'The Little Prince' by Saint-Éxupéry.

The Rabbinic Human Rights Watch, which included orthodox, conservative and reform rabbis, monitored violations of human rights. An interdenominational group, Clergymen for Peace, was also formed. This brought together Jews, Christians and Muslims. Palestinian Christians, in particular, played an important role in trying to bridge the gap between Muslims in the Territories and traditional Jews in

Israel. The difference in approach of some rabbis was dramatically highlighted when they visited the family of a Palestinian bystander who had been killed when Rabbi Moshe Levinger, a central but controversial figure in Gush Emunim, opened fire in strange circumstances. The court sentenced Levinger to five months' imprisonment. The group of rabbis and other clergymen visited the family of the deceased on the day when Levinger was carried shoulder-high by young *yeshiva* students into prison in a celebratory protest at the sentence.

Professional groups, such as photographers, mental-health workers, sculptors and painters, all formed groups after the commencement of the Intifada. At the end of January 1988, 489 psychologists, psychiatrists, psychoanalysts, social workers, occupational therapists and psychiatric workers protested against the acceptance of the status quo: 'We have learned over the years to shut our ears, blunt our feelings, as if all this was not happening to us or issuing from us. We are being swept into a life of fear, violence and racism. We are losing our sensitivity to human suffering'. This was followed by a conference of 600 professional workers on the psychological ramifications of the Intifada on both Jews and Arabs. In February 1988 an academic organization formed at Tel Aviv University, 'Ad Kan' (Up to Here!), co-ordinated the signing by 20 per cent of Israel's university lecturers of a petition against the continuing occupation. Ad Kan put much activity into a campaign to reopen schools and institutes of higher education in the Territories. 'Kav Adom' (the Red Line) organized a peace march of Jews and Arabs from the north of the country to Jerusalem in the south. Many figures in the world of entertainment joined this march. The Tsavta Club in Tel Aviv continued its long tradition of being a venue for dissent and innovation.

The philosophy of no compromise

The 'Twenty First Year' was another new organization which promoted adoption. The Tel Aviv committee adopted the Jelazoun refugee camp. The Twenty First Year group came into existence at the end of 1987 to commemorate the twenty-one years of Israeli presence in the Territories. Its genesis lay among academics at the Hebrew University who were attracted by the ideas of the French philosopher Michel Foucault on the misuse and manipulation of language. In one sense, the organization was an extension of Yesh Gvul, in that 'refusal' was extended to areas of Israeli life other than military service.

The Twenty First Year focused on the corrupting influence and gradual acceptance of the inevitability of the Israeli presence in the Territories: 'The real moral and political question at issue today is not the price of peace, but the price of the Occupation'. A 'Covenant of Struggle against the Occupation' succinctly spelled out the problem:

> The Occupation has become an insidious fact of our lives. Its presence has not been confined to the Occupied Territories. It is, alas, among and within us. Its destructive effects are in evidence in every aspect of our lives.
>
> The Israeli economy benefits from the blatant exploitation of Palestinian labour; it has developed a distorted colonialistic structure. The educational system is based on a double message: while promoting 'democratic values' it condones a repressive regime which controls the lives of disenfranchised subjects. . . .
>
> The Israeli culture is pervaded by a self-satisfied glorification of its tortured posture; its political involvement is by and large sterile. The Hebrew language has undergone a process of contamination; it has been harnessed to the imperatives of the Occupation. It has been called upon to provide a misleadingly benign vocabulary to anaesthetize the repression and flagrant violations of human rights. Israeli political thought is preoccupied and impoverished by the debate over the future of the Occupied Territories; it has locked itself into stereotypical conceptions of the Palestinian enemy and a demonological perception of its acts of resistance.
>
> Expressions of protest against the Occupation are circumscribed by the national consensus; protests do not transgress the boundaries deemed permissible by the Occupation regime. The Israeli of good conscience expresses his or her anguish, remonstrates and demonstrates, but by accepting the terms and norms of political conduct set by the regime implicitly collaborates with the Occupation. The presence of the Occupation is total. Our struggle against the Occupation must therefore be total.

This absolutism manifested itself in specific aims. Members of the organization refused to visit the Territories unless invited by local Palestinians. They promised to publicize and boycott institutions, places of entertainment and the products of companies 'whose Palestinian employees are denied human dignity and decent working conditions'. The Twenty First Year also determined not to purchase goods manufactured by Jewish settlements in the Territories.

Their attitude to the Intifada and its effects was uncompromising. They stated that they would not obey military commands which ordered them to participate in 'acts of repression or in policing in the Occupied Territories': 'We shall not allow these ignoble deeds to be pushed from our consciousness; we shall not harden our hearts. We shall remain vigilant and accordingly protest against such deeds in every possible way, including being physically present where and when they take place.'

The statement of the Twenty First Year did not categorically demand that its members would actually refuse to serve in the Territories. This would have been illegal under Israeli law, since there is no provision for exemption from military service on grounds of conscience. The Twenty First Year thus employed the philosophy of Yesh Gvul in a much wider context.

Another area which differentiated many Peace Now people from fundamentalists in other peace groups was their attitude to Jerusalem. Since the Six Day War, eight new suburbs had been constructed, thus enlarging the city's area from 38 square kilometres in 1967 to 108 in 1990:[14]

New suburb	Number of inhabitants
Ramat Eshkol and Ma'alot Dafna	11,600
French Hill	9,600
Neve Ya'akov	17,000
Ramot	29,000
Greater Sanhedria	4,500
Pisgat Ze'ev	6,500
East Talpiot	15,000
Gilo	28,000
Jewish quarter of the Old City	3,000
	124,000

The suburbs effectively surrounded Arab East Jerusalem, thus preventing a physical division of the city once again. It also complicated the possibility of East Jerusalem as the future capital of a Palestinian State, since few Israelis wished to renounce sovereignty over any part of Jerusalem – and especially the Old City with its historic and religious associations. While some in the peace camp viewed the suburbs as no more than new settlements in the Territories beyond the 1967 Green Line, others saw this as simply an extension of Jewish West Jerusalem. When President Bush convolutedly spoke about 'the establishment of settlements in East Jerusalem' at the beginning of 1990, he once more raised a source of division in the peace camp.

Peace plans and peace groups

There are numerous suggestions for annexing parts of the West Bank in the name of national security. Widening the coastal plain, developing strategic corridors and absorbing areas with no Palestinian population are cited as reasons. The Allon Plan (1970) envisages the annexation of 50 per cent of the West Bank and it was the basis of Labour policy in successive elections. The Sharon Plan (1980) required the absorption of 75 per cent of the West Bank. A minimalist plan put forward by Brigadier-General Arieh Shalev, involving deployment of Israeli forces on the mountain ridges and on the River Jordan, required between 1 and 2 per cent to be under Israel's jurisdiction. [15]

A central problem that broad organizations such as Peace Now faced was the lack of a clear-cut solution to the Middle East conflict. Essentially, Peace Now did not put forward a detailed peace plan, but rather laid out guidelines for a solution. Its wide, non-ideological approach mitigated against specific peace proposals, and indeed it saw its role as bringing the opposing sides together to face each other at the negotiating table. The peace movement may have put forward the general idea of a two-state solution through negotiating with the PLO, but its central role was to break down the stereotypes and imagery that pervaded a nervous Israeli public.

A final agreement, it was argued, should be secured by the elected representatives of both peoples. Yet few concentrated on the prospect of an Israeli–Palestinian meeting collapsing immediately because both sides were so far apart in their perceptions. Even if the Labour leadership met with Arafat and other PLO leaders, no agreement could be reached on the basis of the Allon Plan or variations which forced the Palestinians to surrender large parts of the West Bank. Clearly, before any meeting with even the slightest chance of success could be envisaged, it would be important to proceed in a general direction where there was a good measure of consensus beforehand.

Shmuel Toledano, a former adviser to three Israeli Prime Ministers on Arab affairs and a former Member of the Knesset for Shinui, addressed this issue. He produced a 'mutual test' plan in the mid-1980s which integrated all the questions raised by both sides. Although primarily directed towards the Israeli public, it aimed at breaking down the psychological barriers erected by both sides. The plan stated the following:

1(a) The government of Israel will name a specific date, five years following said decision, when Israel will vacate, with minor modifications, the territories that were occupied in the 1967 war. The government of Israel will announce that it will not object to the creation of a Palestinian State in those territories, if the parties concerned will fulfil the conditions detailed below in Paragraphs 2 and 5.

(b) The above decision will receive the approval of the Knesset. The decision will then be transmitted to the UN with the request that it be granted the status of an international document. Necessary steps will be taken to ensure that this decision will not be cancelled or altered.

(c) The US and the USSR will act as guarantors for the implementation of the agreement. They will also serve as arbitrators; in case of disagreement between the two powers, the US will have the right of veto.

(d) The minor modifications will include the neighbourhoods built around Jerusalem since 1967.

2(a) The Arab countries bordering Israel, i.e. Jordan, Syria, Lebanon and Saudi Arabia, will declare an end to the 'state of hostilities' against Israel. This will include cessation of the boycott, recognition of the right to existence of the State of Israel, no support of terrorism, and the termination of the campaign to delegitimize Israel in international forums. This declaration will replace the cease-fire agreement of 1967 with Jordan, the cease-fire agreement of 1982 with Lebanon, and the separation of forces agreement with Syria from 1974.

(b) The PLO will declare an end to the Intifada and the Intifada will actually come to an end.

(c) The PLO will declare an end to acts of terror against the State of Israel and against Israelis and Jews abroad. The terror will cease in practice. (Isolated acts of terror committed by Arab or Jewish extremists will not be considered a breach of the agreement.)

(d) The PLO will recognize the State of Israel.

(e) Free tourism will exist between Israel and its neighbouring countries, Jordan, Lebanon, Syria and Saudi Arabia. Trade agreements will be signed between these countries and Israel.

(f) The PLO will revoke the 'right to return' to the area within the Green Line (Israeli territory prior to the 1967 war).

(g) Land confiscated from individual owners, but not in use, will be returned to the original owners, one year after the implementation of Paragraphs 2a–f.

(h) One year after the implementation of the conditions included in Paragraphs 2a–f no new settlements will be erected. During the first year of the agreement there will be no massive settlement policy: the present settlement policy will continue.

(i) A team of experts from neutral countries will evaluate the sum of money to be paid as compensation for the property (buildings, land, etc.) owned by Arabs before the War of Independence and confiscated by the State of Israel. The government of Israel will pay these amounts in instalments over a period of five years with the help of the USA and international bodies.

(j) A team of experts from neutral countries will evaluate the sum of money to be paid as compensations for the property (buildings, land, etc.) owned by Jews who lived in Arab countries which was confiscated. The governments of the countries concerned will pay these amounts in instalments over a period of five years and with the help of the USA and international bodies.

3 Two years prior to the date agreed upon in Paragraph 1a and subject to the fulfilment of the conditions included in Paragraphs 2a–f, free democratic municipal elections will be held in the Territories which will mark the beginning of the process of the foundation of the new Palestinian State.

4 One year prior to the date agreed upon for the foundation of the new State, discussions will take place between the State of Israel, the representatives elected in the territories and PLO members in as much by virtue of the agreement, during the previous four years, the PLO did not commit any act of terror, stopped the Intifada, recognized the State of Israel and revoked the 'Right of Return'. Simultaneously discussions will commence between Israel and Syria on the Golan Heights.

5 The agreement between Israel and the Palestinian representatives must include the following points:

(a) Israel will have the right to send her army into the Palestinian State in the event that a foreign military power attempts to enter the Palestinian State, with or without the consent of the Palestinian State.

(b) Common defence measures will be taken in the event of terrorist attacks on Israel from hostile bodies within the Palestinian State.

(c) The Palestinian State will establish a symbolic (ceremonial) army only, during the first ten years of its existence.

(d) A limited number of military personnel will be stationed at a number of points along the Jordan River during the first five years of the existence of the Palestinian State to act as an 'early warning system' in case of infringement.

(e) Israeli military planes will have the right to conduct manoeuvres and reconnaissance flights in the air-space of the Palestinian State during the first five years of its existence.

(f) An economic agreement will be signed between the two countries.

(g) The settlements will not be dismantled. The settlers in each settlement will decide whether:

–   to continue living there as Israeli citizens;

  – to continue living there as Palestinian citizens;
  – to evacuate the settlements.

(h) Jerusalem: separate municipal elections will be held, one for Western Jerusalem whose Mayor will be a Jew, and one for Eastern Jerusalem, whose Mayor will be an Arab. The Holy Places will be managed by all three faiths, each site to be supervised by its respective faith. The sovereignty of Jerusalem will remain Israeli.

(i) International bodies, particularly the US and Japan, will take responsibility for, and guarantee the solution of the Arab refugee problem. Resettlement locales will not include the pre-1967 territory of the State of Israel.

(j) International bodies, particularly the US, will commit themselves to grant financial aid to help resolve the economic difficulties facing the new Palestinian State.

(k) The Jordanian government will sign a special agreement of mutual defence with the State of Israel.

(l) Jordan, Syria, Lebanon and Saudi Arabia will enter into a peace agreement with the State of Israel.

6 Golan Heights: if Syria will not be ready to fulfil the conditions included in Paragraphs 2a and h, the above proposal will still be valid but the Golan Heights problem will not be discussed until Syria accepts the above proposal.

The beauty of the Toledano 'mutual test' plan was that it avoided the prospect of face-to-face negotiations before a measure of trust between the opposing sides had been achieved. It also circumvented the naming of the Palestinian representatives at an initial stage. To sit or not to sit with the PLO would be of diminished importance. It commenced with a statement of intent by the government of Israel to permit the establishment of a Palestinian State in five years. Certain trust building measures had to be adhered to within a four-year period before any discussions could begin. Then, the plan surmised that each side would feel that more was to be lost than to be gained if progress was not made.

The plan projected certain advantages for the Palestinians: a solid commitment to a state; a sovereign state within five years, with some limitations to protect Israel's security needs; a state with no limitations after fifteen years.

The advantages for Israel would be: serious evidence over a five-year period that both the Arab countries and the Palestinians were genuinely moving along a path to peace; peace treaties with the Arab States at the end of the five-year period; military limitations on the new State to prevent the entry of foreign armies during the ten years from statehood.

Toledano submitted his 'mutual test' plan to 1184 Israeli Jews in December 1989. Kibbutz members and Jewish inhabitants of the West Bank were excluded. The respondents were asked whether they were in favour or were opposed to the plan:

The results of the general poll were as follows:

Definitely in favour of	21%	} 60%
In favour	39%	
Against	23%	} 35%
Definitely against	12%	
No response	5%	

A breakdown of the politics of those who supported the plan revealed the following results:

Supporters of Likud	51%
Supporters of Labour	78%
Supporters of religious parties	33%

Significantly, 51 per cent of Likud supporters agreed with the plan. Toledano pointed out that when asked the question 'If the demand for a Palestinian State in Judea, Samaria and the Gaza Strip will be the last obstacle to peace, should Israel agree or not agree to the creation of a Palestinian State?' only 20 per cent accepted the creation of a Palestinian State. The 'mutual trust' plan raised the proportion to 60 per cent. Clearly, this turn-around was not due to any dramatic change in public opinion. Toledano for the first time appealed to the psychological fears of Israeli Jews and assuaged them by offering a detailed remedy.

Toledano was able to separate those who opposed territorial concession into those who did so for reasons of national security and those who did so for ideological reasons.

The Palestinians also reacted favourably to the plan, albeit with certain reservations. Two Palestinian newspapers, *Al Thawra* – the official mouthpiece of the PLO – and *Al Quds*, welcomed the plan. Even Nayef Hawatmeh's DFLP noted its positive points. In addition, 50 per cent of Israeli Arabs also welcomed it. Toledano believed that the influence of the Palestinian rejectionist camp would simply wither as the Palestinian people themselves believed that it was in their fundamental interests to carry it through. The example was cited of

Lehi in 1948, who willingly laid down their arms once the State of Israel was established and effectively renounced their hardline rhetoric and policies.

The sticking-point which interrupted a coalescence of Israeli and Palestinian positions was the status of Jerusalem. Toledano attempted to distinguish between control and sovereignty. The Palestinians would have control over their areas and the Jews likewise. Israel, however, exerted sovereignty over Jerusalem, thus precluding even East Jerusalem as capital of a future Palestinian State. Significantly, the response of the Israeli respondents fell to 45 per cent when questioned specifically on the status of Jerusalem. Faisal Husseini, perhaps the leading Palestinian nationalist in the Territories, agreed with the plan in general but rejected Toledano's formulation on Jerusalem.

The symbolism of a united sovereign Jerusalem was deeply felt by a wide spectrum of Israeli opinion. Significantly, the problem of Jerusalem was relegated to a later stage in the Toledano plan – perhaps in the hope that the importance of the peace momentum would then overcome the emotional attachments of both peoples to the Holy City and so resolve itself to the satisfaction of both parties.

11

Reactions to the Gulf Crisis: The Drift away from Dialogue

Hawks and Doves

When Saddam Hussein's forces invaded Kuwait on 2 August 1990, the destruction of the broad coalition that had argued for nearly two years for an Israeli–PLO dialogue seemed assured. With the PLO and most Palestinian groups aligned with Iraq on one side and the White House and Israelis of virtually all persuasions on the other, it appeared that the time for moderation and reconciliation was truly at an end. On the day of the Iraqi invasion, the main preoccupation for Israelis was the course of action to be taken if Jordan were also threatened by Iraq. Even Yossi Sarid, a leading peace campaigner, stated that if Saddam moved his war machine into the Hashemite kingdom, then this would certainly be a cause for war. Ironically, little was said about the possible repercussions concerning relations between the Israeli peace movement and the Palestinians.

Three days after the attack, a group of dovish Knesset members and Palestinian leaders from the Territories assembled for a pre-arranged meeting whose purpose was to breathe some life into the flagging peace dialogue. A joint platform was agreed, but inevitably the question of the invasion of Kuwait was raised. Amnon Rubinstein, the leader of Shinui, wanted to know where the Palestinian leadership stood on the issue. The Palestinian response was confused. Ultimately, they decided that the best answer was no answer since the current PLO position seemed to be alignment with Iraq. Clearly, they were bewildered by the turn of events.

In addition, during the first week of August, tensions between Israelis and Palestinians reached new heights with random killings of Jews, followed by anti-Arab rioting. The rampage of Jewish youths was exacerbated by Kach activists and others from the far Right who were adept in guiding emotions at scenes of violence and funerals of victims. When Palestinian support for Saddam in the Territories became apparent, Kach also initiated a campaign of personal harassment against dovish Israelis. In particular, the 'Women in Black' were singled out. On the first weekly demonstration after the invasion, some of the women protesters were physically attacked and abused. The movement's leaders received a stream of threatening telephone calls. The 'Transfer' Party, *Moledet*, reiterated its policy of moving out the inhabitants of the Territories using their support for Saddam as a new justification. Geula Cohen of *Techiya* expressed the hope that if Israel were forced to invade Jordan, then it should not be returned to King Hussein, reviving the original Zionist hope that a Jewish State should extend to both sides of the Jordan.[1]

The reaction of ordinary Palestinians in the Territories was one of unmitigated delight at Saddam's opposition to the Americans and to all things Israeli. To the majority of Israelis, the protests and demonstrations by the youth of the Intifada in favour of Saddam Hussein were indicative of the hollowness of the PLO's claim that they occupied a neutral position. Their cries of vengeance made it seem that nothing had really changed; their exhortations to Saddam to use his chemical weapons against Israel were evidence that the Palestinians still wanted the destruction of the Jewish State. It mattered not that Saddam had killed many of his own people and led them into a disastrous war with Iran, he appeared to them as a latter-day Saladin who would maintain a balance of terror against the Zionist State with new weapons of untold destructive power.

Although Palestinian solidarity with Iraq developed initially as a response to US intervention, it deepened further with Saddam's subsequent linkage of withdrawal from Kuwait to the Palestinian problem. Despite all the propaganda victories the hardships of the Intifada had brought a Palestinian State no nearer. The PLO abroad had been unable to deliver the political fruits of their struggle. As belief in the efficacy of their new approach waned, Saddam Hussein had simply stepped into the political vaccuum and given the Palestinians new hope. There was also widespread belief that any attempt to convince the Israeli public was a waste of time and effort. Only brute strength, it was argued, would pressurize Israel into making concessions. This outpouring of Palestinian frustrations manifested itself in a poll in an East Jerusalem weekly, *Al-Nadwa*, shortly after the invasion. Eighty-four per cent of West Bank Palestinians considered Saddam a hero. Unlike the PLO, a majority, 58 per cent, actually supported the invasion of Kuwait.

Many Palestinians viewed Saddam's attempt to link his plight to the Palestinian problem not merely as a public relations ploy, but as a potential route towards resolving the question of the Territories. Even for those Palestinians who were originally sceptical about support for the Iraqi cause, Saddam's initiative provided new hope. Despite private reservations about the Iraqi leader they reasoned that Saddam's crude methods might work where more sophisticated, more reasonable approaches had failed. They were further encouraged in this belief when Presidents Bush and Mitterand hinted that an Iraqi withdrawal would be followed by a renewed attempt to resolve the problem of the Palestinians and Arab–Israeli relations. Moderate Israelis were deeply shocked at the strength of the Palestinian response to the Gulf crisis. They viewed it as undermining everything they had worked for and a cruel blow to hopes for a peaceful resolution of the conflict. For some days after the invasion there was a stunned silence, a visible depression. This was in large measure due to sheer frustration, but many Israelis were also stunned at the willingness of the Palestinians to let go of the gains of the last few years. Both morally and pragmatically, they could not understand why the Palestinians should indulge in such a counter-productive exercise. Some argued that the PLO simply did not grasp that a joint US–Soviet move against Saddam was actually in their own interests. Elazar Granot, a leader of Mapam, commented 'I could understand it if Arafat had told the Cairo Arab summit – "Look, the Palestinians are a people without a homeland, dispersed all over the Arab world. We're Saddam Hussein's political hostages. We have to keep a low profile in this conflict . . ." Yet this didn't happen'.[2]

For dovish Jews there was also a moral question, as Saddam had cared little for human rights in Iraq and earned international notoriety for his use of chemical weapons against the recalcitrant Kurds. He had also been implicated in the hanging of Iraqi Jews in 1969, shortly after the Baathists came to power. After the execution tens of thousands of Iraqis were bussed to Baghdad to witness the lifeless bodies in Liberation Square, presumably to underline the regime's ruthless intent to crush any opposition, real or imaginary. Tariq Aziz, the present Foreign Minister of Iraq, commented in 1972 that 'the event was a monument of confidence staged by the revolution . . . to prove to the people that what had been impossible in the past was now a fact that could speak for itself.'[3] Many liberal Israelis expected the Palestinians, as victims themselves of human rights violations, to share their abhorrence of Saddam's regime. The debate in the Arab world over whether nationalist or democratic values should take precedence cut no ice in Israel.

Edy Kaufman, a long-time Israeli human rights activist, appealed through the medium of the Arabic press. Writing in *Al Fajr*,[4] he addressed his 'dear Palestinian neighbours and friends: As far as I am concerned, if you approve or disapprove of Iraq's acts in Kuwait, that is your own business. What concerns me is that you unequivocally stand up and condemn any threat against me and my family. I have been on your side when demanding the end of occupation and your right to establish a state of your own in the West Bank and Gaza. Please do not let me down when I and you see my survival threatened'. Elazar Granot called upon the Palestinians not to 'be fooled by catch-words of deceit, extremism and blood'. Such catch-words, he warned, 'can dig chasms'.[5]

The anger of the Israeli peace camp reached its apogee with a bitter condemnatory article in *Ha'aretz* by Yossi Sarid.[6]

Had I supported the establishment of a Palestinian state only because the Palestinians, too, deserve a state – I would now withdraw my support. But I continue to demand their right to self-determination and an independent state because it is my right to get rid of the occupation and all the harm it brings. Perhaps they deserve the occupation but we don't. I insist, in spite of all, on maintaining my human dignity but I don't need Arafat, Husseini and Daroushe for this supreme effort. It is all mine and it is almost inhuman in its humanity. Until a further announcement, if they want to talk to me, they can look for me.

It was that last phrase – 'sheyechapsu oti' – 'they can look for me' which was seized upon. The Right began to treat their arch-enemy Yossi Sarid as a wayward child returning to the fold. His colleagues on the Left attacked him for his virtual abandonment of the process of dialogue. Yet Sarid was not alone. Indeed, some believed that he had restored the credibility of the Left amongst the Israeli public. The poet, Yehuda Amichai, viewed the Palestinians as being neither serious nor sincere when they condemned violence. 'They merely used that approach because they thought it would get them somewhere.'[7]

In essence, those who interpreted the dialogue with the Palestinians in a moral sense had quite different expectations from those who defined it in purely pragmatic terms. Shulamit Aloni asked, if Saddam turned to Israel with a peace offer, 'would we refuse it?'[8] The author A.B. Yehoshua also recalled that Israel had established diplomatic relations with both Stalin and Ceaucescu – relations which were not based on moral considerations.[9] The author David Grossman asked, 'do you only make peace with a "rational" enemy or with the enemy?' Grossman clearly believed that Sarid's article had damaged those 'tens of thousands of Israelis who in recent years mustered the will power, self-restraint and composure to give peace a chance – who have now been given an eloquent excuse to give up, to fall back on the temptation of a simplistic and stereotypical point of view. To the fatalism which says: "there's no one to talk to and we'll live by the sword forever".'[10]

PLO Policy and its effects

Although the PLO's approach to the Gulf crisis was something of a bombshell for the Israeli Peace camp, it was not totally unexpected. Throughout 1990, Arafat had gradually moved away from the position which he had espoused in December 1988. Indeed, his open acceptance of a two-state solution, his apparently unambiguous recognition of Israel and his guarantee of a cessation of cross-border raids seemed to have brought the Palestinians little by the end of 1989. Thus, although Arafat had made considerable political headway in the West, he was unable to move an Israeli government paralysed by too many diverse political interests. Neither had the efforts of the Israeli Peace Movement and many Diaspora Jews achieved any real progress. Although Shamir held out the prospect of talking to the Palestinians, he was always able to postpone that eventuality by raising new objections. The final blow came when Shimon Peres failed to form a government on a 'peace' ticket. During the first few months of 1990, Arafat began to follow a more hard-line approach which he hoped would appease the growing number of Palestinian critics. At the same time, he continued the policy of encouraging dialogue between Israelis and Palestinians. This inconsistency in policy clearly showed itself when Saddam Hussein threatened to attack Israel with chemical weapons while Arafat was independently extending an invitation to Peres to meet him at 'the earliest possible moment' to discuss an Israel–Palestine peace agreement. By pursuing a twin-track policy, Arafat believed that he could please all factions within the PLO.

In February 1990, the Popular Front issued a statement in Damascus urging Palestinians in the Territories to use arms against Israeli troops even though the very fact that firearms were not used during the Intifada had made a considerable impression in the West. Moreover, after a period of relative quiet, primitive pipe bombs planted in public places in Israel became almost a regular occurrence. Arafat desperately needed a diplomatic breakthrough which he hoped would vindicate his Geneva policy. But the collapse of the Eastern bloc in the winter of 1989 removed a traditional pillar of support for the PLO. In addition, the Soviet Foreign Ministry adopted a much more even-handed approach to the Israel–Palestine issue than hitherto.

The willingness of the beleaguered Gorbachev regime to permit more or less unrestricted emigration for Soviet Jews, and the imposition of a strict quota by the United States, was translated into a huge influx of new immigrants into the country. While the Israeli Right was overjoyed since this would counter the demographic argument by offsetting the higher Palestinian birthrate, the Palestinians themselves were dealt a profound psychological blow. All their anxieties and insecurities were wrapped up in the spectre of Jewish emigration to Israel – it brought back memories of the defeat of 1948 and, for some, the flight from their homes. Within the reality and mythology of those fears, Shamir tied Soviet Jewish emigration to his dream of a 'greater' Israel in an address to old Revisionists in Tel Aviv. Although he later claimed that such a 'Greater Israel' should not be given a territorial interpretation, the Palestinians believed that this was a signal for full-blooded Jewish settlement of the Territories. Shamir's remark, whether deliberate or otherwise, had converted a psychological fear into a practical reality.

Arafat's ever-diminishing emphasis on the importance of Israeli public opinion showed itself in a blurring of goals with regard to the emigration issue. It often appeared not so much as a Palestinian campaign against settlement in the Territories, but as a campaign against Jewish emigration to Israel per se. In addition, the open-ended nature of the Israeli government reply to international criticism that Soviet Jews were free to settle anywhere did not calm fears, despite official claims that only a fraction of a percentage of Soviet Jewish emigrants actually settled in the Territories. Even so, a report by the West Bank Data Base project at the beginning of March 1990 showed that, in most cases, the Israeli Government offered more incentives to Israeli citizens to move to the Territories than to relocate to small towns within Israel itself.[11] Despite this, few Soviet Jews wished to exchange the insecurity of a disintegrating Union of Soviet Socialist Republics for the difficulties of a settler life. Few were attracted by the promotional campaigning of settlements such as Ariel. The overwhelming majority preferred the urban jungle of central Tel Aviv.

Arafat's flirtation with Iraq thus came amidst a rising tide of Palestinian frustrations and his own inability to assuage them through clearly tangible diplomatic gains. Reports that discussions were taking place between Hamas, the PFLP and the Islamic Jihad on the possibility of establishing a rival Unified National Command in the Territories simply increased the pressure on Arafat to put his Geneva policy into cold storage.

When hostilities with Iran came to an end in 1988, Saddam Hussein gradually began to revert to the pan-Arab posture that had endeared him to Palestinian rejectionists in the 1970s. His anti-imperialist rhetoric became more strident and he clearly perceived himself as the ascendant leader of Arab nationalism. In essence, he was thus much closer to the pan-Arab aspirations of George Habash than to the Palestino-centric Arafat. Saddam's ideological rejuvenation coincided with the realization of Arafat's diplomatic failure. Saddam was thus keen to harness the Palestinian revolution under his own wing. In April 1990, a meeting of the PLO Executive took place in Baghdad and adopted 'a new Palestinian military strategy that provides for gathering all Palestinian forces to enable them to restore their combat abilities'. A considerable part of the PLO relocated to the Iraqi capital. The most rejectionist of the Palestinian groups were pressurized by the Iraqis to base themselves in Baghdad. Many of those who had hitherto been dependent on Syria now looked to Iraq. Three hundred members of the Abu Nidal Group moved to Iraq for training and Abu Nidal himself was reported to have returned to Iraq where he had access to a $11 million bankroll. [12] Ahmed Jabril who had loyally worked for Syria for three decades was also asked to relocate to Baghdad. In addition to Abul Abbas' PLF, the PFLP-Special Command was situated in the Iraqi capital. Abu Ibrahim of the Arab Organization of 15th May who was reputed to be the designer of suitcase and stereo bombs of the type involved in the Lockerbie disaster also lived in the city. True to form, Arafat did not want to close the door finally on the prospect of dialogue. As late as the end of June, he sent a letter to Menachem Rosensaft who had met Arafat with other American Jews in Stockholm. Arafat again reiterated the familiar stand of his fading Geneva policy. [13]

A few days before the invasion of Kuwait, Arafat acknowledged the emergence of Iraqi imperial ambitions and their relevance to the Israel–Palestine issue. 'The time when Israel had the upper hand in the region is now in the past. Right now, there is an Arab upper hand that is equal to the Israeli hand, if not exceeding it.'[14] Yet Arafat was placed in an invidious situation by Iraq's invasion of its tiny oil-rich neighbour. On the one hand, he had agreed to an effective alliance with Iraq in his retreat from his Geneva policy – an alignment which limited his political manoeuvreability. On the other hand, he attempted to continue his role as the independent mediator, a middleman in the vortex of Arab politics. Although he believed that this strategy promoted the cause of Palestine, the invasion showed up the contradiction of his position. In this case Arafat's policy of never committing himself totally to the hegemony of a particular Arab ruler, and the double-edged interpretation of his policies, drastically backfired. Arafat's warm embrace of the Iraqi President at a meeting three days after the invasion was repeatedly broadcast in the Western media. It did not matter that he went on to Cairo the following day to mediate with President Mubarak; the dominant image projected was of the PLO as a loyal ally of the Iraqi leader. The refusal of the PLO to condemn Iraq at numerous Arab and Islamic summits during August 1990 was not perceived in the West as a sign of benevolent neutrality in order to seek an all-Arab solution to the crisis, but as strong support for Saddam Hussein.

In addition, Arafat had seemingly relinquished his economic base for the continuation of the Intifada. Saudia Arabia had given the PLO

$1 billion since 1979.[15] In 1990, Kuwait had donated £45 million to the PLO. The 300,000 Palestinians who worked in Kuwait gave 5 per cent of their salaries to the Palestine National Fund. This source of income now ceased. Moreover, 100,000 inhabitants of the West bank were dependent on remittances from the Gulf. In Hebron, the building of the largest hospital in the Territories was suspended because Kuwait had financed its construction. Operating hospitals such as Jerusalem's Makased hospital depended for three quarters of their funding from the Gulf States. Indeed, some 30 per cent of the GNP of the Territories came from aid or remittances from the Gulf. Moreover, some 30–50,000 Palestinians in the Gulf possessed Israeli ID cards and were eligible to return – at a time when there was a 30 per cent unemployment rate in the Territories. Ironically, the vociferous support which ordinary Palestinians in the Territories spontaneously gave to Saddam further restricted Arafat's ability to manoeuvre. It also marginalized the pragmatic policies of pro-PLO leaders such as Faisal Husseini. Faisal Husseini's approach was attacked both by Palestinians and Israelis. The Popular Front published a leaflet in the Territories which attacked Husseini for his pro-Western attitudes while the right wing editorial-writer in the *Jerusalem Post* associated him with the riot on the Temple Mount which led to nearly a score of Palestinian dead and over a hundred injured.[16] Finally, Shamir's Far Right government blamed Husseini for the continuing Palestinian violence and temporarily placed him in administrative detention.

There was a throwback to less sophisticated political tactics. Following the deaths on the Temple Mount, Fatah issued a leaflet which called for the use of 'more serious weapons'. A leaflet issued by the United National Leadership of the Uprising returned for the first time to the old definition of Israel as 'the Zionist entity'. The Muslim fundamentalist organization Hamas described all Jews as legitimate targets after the Temple Mount killings. Shortly afterwards, a nineteen-year-old member of Islamic Jihad stabbed to death three Israelis in Baka, a middle-class, liberal neighbourhood of Jerusalem. This in turn was followed by attacks on Palestinians by enraged Jews and calls for stronger measures by the Far Right. The tit-for-tat tribalistic violence became a tragic symbol of the accelerating polarization between Israelis and Palestinians. Although such well-meaning projects as the Israeli-Palestinian Dialogue Centre opened in Beit Sahour in Bethlehem, the pragmatists on both sides of the conflict were unable to restrain their maximalists and extremists. The voices of reconciliation were shunted into the political sidings and the advocates of retribution gained the upper hand.

Official Responses

The Israeli government's response was decidedly low-key. Apart from Arik Sharon, no member of the government was going to dismember Mr Bush's alliance in the Gulf and separate such strange bedfellows as Assad's Syria and the sheikdoms. Mr Shamir only replied in response to direct Iraqi threats against Israel. Likud clearly delighted in the political mess which the Palestinians had created for themselves. Foreign Ministry policy was to identify all Palestinian positions with Iraq. If Saddam had been their unwitting ally in uncoupling the US–PLO dialogue in the summer, then his invasion of Kuwait assisted them in further undermining the peace camp in Israel and in accentuating the demonization of the Palestinians. Indeed, Bibi Netanyahu so much approved of Sarid's article in *Ha'aretz* – 'if they want to talk to me, they can look for me' – that he even commissioned a Foreign Ministry English translation and authorised its international distribution through Israeli embassies.[17]

The Gulf crisis and the increased random killings of Jews increased support for the Likud and the Far Right amongst the Israeli electorate. An opinion poll conducted in November 1990 by the Smith Research Centre found that 42 per cent of its respondents declared themselves more hawkish towards Palestinians since the onset of the Intifada. The same percentage registered no change in their attitude, while only 6 per cent became more dovish in their views.[18] Another opinion poll of 1,200 Israelis for the *Davar* newspaper showed that only 21 per cent of the electorate would vote for Shimon Peres's Labour Party – a 10 per cent drop below its vote in the 1988 Election.[19]

Yet while the Americans were at pains to soothe Arab fears that this government of the Far Right would utilize the crisis to invade Jordan – the 'East Bank' in the Revisionist heritage – the White House was clearly much more sensitive to the political wishes of its Arab allies. While he denounced Saddam's attempts at linkage, President Bush reminded the Israeli government that Mr Shamir's own initiative to hold elections in the Territories was still on the agenda. Mr Shamir, however, announced his intention to look for pliant – and probably non-existent – Palestinians as negotiating partners. While the Gulf crisis did indeed distract world attention from the Palestinians, the West's desperate need to secure Arab allies to oppose Saddam in turn weakened Israel's leverage with the United States.

In the Diaspora, the Jewish organizations continued to support any action the Israeli government took. The Conference of Major Jewish Organizations told President Bush that US Jewry fully supported him. Yet a score of Jewish philanthropists cancelled a UJA trip on Concorde to Israel. Many Diaspora doves reflected the self-questioning of Israeli

doves which followed the invasion of Kuwait. Many concluded that
their approach had been the right one, but that the forces of extremism
on both sides had just been too strong. Others, like the British writer
Chaim Bermant, came to a different conclusion. 'Those Jews who
called for the restoration of most of the occupied territories to Arab
hands and the creation of a Palestinian state – and I was one of them
– must now be grateful that their voice went unheard, for such a
state would have been a fervent ally of Saddam Hussein.' If the PLO
were happy to change its allies frequently in the spirit of realpolitik,
wouldn't this also be the case if it governed a Palestinian state on
Israel's doorstep?[20] A.B. Yehoshua predicted the toppling of Arafat
as an outcome of the crisis and his replacement with more pragmatic
figures. Arthur Hertzberg, writing in the *New York Review of Books*,
came to a diametrically opposite conclusion. 'Even now, when he has
allied himself with Iraq and is thus in particularly bad odour, both in the
United States and Israel, he remains a pragmatist, shifting positions
from day to day, and he is still the Palestinian leader with whom peace
might be made, if it ever can be made.'[21]

Notes

Introduction

1 BBC Monitoring SWB ME/0840, 11 August 1990.
2 Ettinger's cable was leaked in *Ha'aretz*, 22 May 1990; Arad's five-page classified evaluation was reported in *Yediot Aharonot*, 27 May 1990.
3 *Yediot Aharonot*, 14 March 1990.
4 'Paradise Postponed', editorial, *Jewish Quarterly*, vol. 35, no. 1 (129) 1988 (London).

Chapter One

1 Joseph B. Schechtman, *The Jabotinsky Story: The Early Years 1880–1923*, vol. I. (New York, 1956) p. 319.
2 Sasson Sofer, *Begin: An Anatomy of Leadership* (Oxford, 1988), p. 35.
3 Ya'akov Shavitt, *Jabotinsky and the Revisionist Movement: 1925–40* (London, 1988), p. 40.
4 Yehoshaphat Harkabi, *Israel's Fateful Decisions* (London, 1988), p. 70.
5 Erich and Rael Jean Isaac, 'The Impact of Jabotinsky on Likud's Policies' *Middle East Review*, vol. x, no. 1 (fall 1977), pp. 31–48.
6 Eric Silver, *Begin: A Biography* (London, 1984), p. 21.
7 Ze'ev Jabotinsky, *The Meaning of Adventurism* (*Rasswyet*); quoted in Schechtman, *The Jabotinsky Story*, vol. II. (New York 1961), p. 453.
8. Ibid., p. 437.
9 Record of Jabotinsky's conversation with Golomb, 10 July 1938; quoted in Schechtman, *Fighter and Prophet*, p. 451.
10 Susan Zuccotti, *The Italians and the Holocaust* (New York, 1987), p. 27.
11 Ze'ev Iviansky, 'Individual Terror: Concept and Typology', *Journal of Contemporary History*, 12 (1977), p. 63.
12 Emmanuel Katz, *Lehi: Freedom Fighters of Israel* (Tel Aviv, 1987), p. 7.
13 Meir Ben-Horin, 'Max Nordau: A Study of Human Solidarity' (PhD thesis, Columbia University, 1952), p. 260.
14 Joseph Heller, 'Avraham ("Yair") Stern 1907–1942: Myth and Reality', *Jerusalem Quarterly*, 49 (winter 1989).
15 Amnon Rubinstein, *The Zionist Dream Revisited* (New York, 1984), p. 70.
16 Benny Morris, *Jerusalem Post*, 23 June 1989.

17 Bernard Wasserstein, 'New Light on the Moyne Murder', *Midstream*, March 1980.
18 Yaakov Eliav, *Wanted* (New York, 1984), p. 127.
19 Morris, op. cit., fn. 16.
20 Joseph Heller, *The Stern 'Gang' 1940–9: Ideology and Politics* (unpublished English translation of book published in Hebrew).
21 Harkabi, *Israel's Fateful Decisions*, p. 140.
22 James Cameron, *Guardian*, 6 March 1978.
23 Nahum Goldman, *Memories* (London, 1970), p. 180.
24 Rael Jean Isaac, *Israel Divided: Ideological Politics in the Jewish State* (Johns Hopkins University, 1976), p. 52.
25 Ibid., p. 13.
26 Milton Viorst, *Sands of Sorrow: Israel's Journey from Independence* (London, 1987), p. 160.
27 Ephraim Togornik, Party Organization and Electoral Politics: The Labour Alignment in *Israel at the Polls, 1981*, ed. Howard R. Penniman and Daniel J. Elazar (Washington, 1986), p. 49.
28 Amos Oz, *In the Land of Israel* (London, 1983), pp. 34–7.

Chapter Two

1 Sasson Sofer, *Begin: An Anatomy of a Leadership* (Oxford, 1988), p. 137.
2 Rael Jean Isaac, *Party and Politics in Israel* (New York, 1981), p. 136.
3 Milton Viorst, *Sands of Sorrow: Israel's Journey from Independence* (London, 1987), p. 216.
4 *Jerusalem Post*, 24 April 1979.
5 Ilan Greilsammer, The Likud in *Israel at the Polls 1981*, ed. Howard R. Penniman and Daniel J. Elazar (Washington, 1986), p. 96.
6 Ehud Sprinzak, 'The Emergence of the Israeli Radical Right', *Comparative Politics*, vol. 21, no. 2 (January 1989), pp. 171–93.
7 Ephraim Inbar, 'The "No Choice War" Debate in Israel', *Journal of Strategic Studies*, vol. 12, no. 1 (March 1989), p. 31.
8 Shulamit Hareven, 'Eyewitness', *New Outlook* (March/April 1983).
9 Joseph B. Soloveichik, 'The World is not Forsaken', in *Reflections of the Rav*, ed. Abraham R. Beidin (Jerusalem, 1979).
10 Shmuel Sandler, 'The Religious Parties', in *Israel at the Polls 1981*, ed. Howard R. Penniman and Daniel J. Elazar (Washington, 1986), p. 116.
11 Ehud Sprinzak, 'Fundamentalism, Terrorism, and Democracy: The Case of Gush Emunim', *New Outlook*, (September/October 1988).
12 Ehud Sprinzak, 'From Messianic Pioneering to Vigilante Terrorism: The Case of the Gush Emunim Underground', *Journal of Strategic Studies*, vol. 10, no. 4, 1987.
13 Abraham Rabinovich, *Jerusalem Post*, 4 August 1989.
14 *Yediot Aharonot*, 8 November 1985.
15 Ephraim Ya'ar and Yochanan Peres, 'Democracy as a Matter of Demography', *Israeli Democracy* (winter 1988).
16 *Jerusalem Post*, 4 March 1988.
17 Ibid.

18   Joseph Gorney, *The British Labour Movement and Zionism* (London, 1983), pp. 178–9.
19   *Ma'ariv*, 10 July 1987.
20   *Ha'aretz*, 15 November 1988.
21   David Ben-Gurion, *Zichronot*, vol. IV (Tel Aviv, 1980), pp. 297–8.
22   Shabtai Teveth, *Ben-Gurion and the Palestinian Arabs: from War to Peace* (Oxford, 1985), pp. 190–1.
23   Yossi Amitai, *Ahvat-Ahim Bemivhan* (Tel Aviv, 1988) – an analysis of Mapam's internal dilemmas about the expulsions. See also *Jerusalem Post*, 18 November 1988.
24   Benny Morris, *The Birth of the Palestinian Refugee Problem 1947–49* (Cambridge, 1988), p. 140.
25   Shabtai Teveth, 'The Palestine Arab Refugee Problem and its Origins', *Middle East Studies*, vol. 26, no. 2 (April 1990), p. 243.
26   *Ha'aretz*, 3 August 1988.
27   Ibid., 26 June 1990.
28   *Hadashot*, 19 July 1987.
29   Asher Arian and Raphael Ventura, *Public Opinion in Israel and the Intifada: Changes in Security Attitudes* (Tel Aviv 1989).
30   *Jerusalem Post*, 23 October 1988.
31   Ibid., 21 December 1987.
32   Ibid., 4 March 1988.
33   *Al Hamishmar*, 6 November 1987.
34   Aharon Yariv, *Ha'aretz*, 26 May 1980.
35   *Kol Ha'ir*, 20 November 1987.
36   *Davar*, 1 November 1987.
37   Hanan Porat, 'Hanan Porat Returns to Politics: Hanan Porat Interviewed by Ehud Dor', *New Outlook* (September/October 1988).
38   Avie Walfish, *Arab and Jewish Co-existence: Teaching and Living It*, (Pardes Institute, Jerusalem 1988).
39   *Hadashot*, 6 June 1988.

Chapter Three

1   Jacob Neusner, *Self-Fulfilling Prophecy* (Boston, 1987), pp. 138–9.
2   *Jerusalem Post*, 6 October 1989.
3   Eliezer Don-Yehiya, 'Jewish Messianism, Religious Zionism and Israeli Politics: The Impact and Origins of Gush Emunim', *Middle Eastern Studies*, 23 (1987).
4   Lilly Weissbrod, 'Gush Emunim Ideology – From Religious Doctrine to Political Action', *Middle Eastern Studies*, 18 (1982).
5   *Jerusalem Post*, 4 March 1988.
6   Janet O'Dea, 'Gush Emunim: Roots and Ambiguities: The Perspective of the Sociology of Religion', *Forum*, 2 (25) (1976), p. 45.
7   Hanan Porat, quoted in O'Dea, 'Gush Emunim', p. 42.
8   Martin Buber, *On Zion: The History of an Idea* (London, 1973), p. xx.
9   Joshua Prawer, *The History of the Jews in the Latin Kingdom of Jerusalem* (Oxford, 1988), pp. 152–61.

10 Maimonides, *The Commandments*, ed. Charles B. Chavel (London, 1967), p. 263.

11 Prawer, *The History of the Jews in the Latin Kingdom of Jerusalem*, pp. 156–7.

12 Ezra ben Solomon 'A new document on the beginning of the Kabbalah' (Tel Aviv, 1934), pp. 161–2; quoted in Moshe Idel, 'The Land of Israel in Medieval Kabbalah', in *The Land of Israel: Jewish Perspectives*, ed. Lawrence A. Hoffman (Bloomington, 1986).

13 Avi Ravitsky, *Kol Ha'ir*, 24 September 1982.

14 *Jerusalem Post*, 4 March 1988.

15 Ibid., 6 October 1989.

16 Ibid., 20 May 1988.

17 *Ha'aretz*, 9 May 1976.

18 *Jerusalem Post*, 18 August 1989.

19 Sol Roth, *Halachah and Politics* (New York, 1988), p. 38.

20 *Jerusalem Post*, 6 October 1989.

21 Uriel Tal, 'Contemporary Hermeneutics and Self-Views on the Relationship between State and Land', in *The Land of Israel: Jewish Perspectives*, ed. Lawrence A. Hoffman (Indiana, 1986).

22 Interview with Mordechai Soussan, *New Outlook* (October 1979).

23 *Kol Ha'ir*, 24 September 1982.

24 Isaac Newman, *Jerusalem Post*, 1 May 1990.

25 Yoseph Shilhav, 'Interpretation and Misinterpretation of Jewish Territorialism', in *The Impact of Gush Emunim: Politics and Settlement in the West Bank*, ed. David Newman (London, 1985), pp. 117–8.

26 Herbert Danby, 'The *Mishna*', pp. 379–80.

27 Author's personal interview with Isaac Newman.

28 *Jerusalem Post*, 13 July 1984.

29 Avishai Margalit, 'Israel: the Rise of the Ultra-Orthodox' *New York Review of Books*, 9 November 1989.

30 Julien Bauer, 'Religious Parties in Israel: Reality versus Stereotypes', *Middle East Focus*, vol. 11, no. 2, p. 10.

31 Shmuel Sandler, 'Israel's 1988 Knesset Elections and the Transformation of the Israeli Polity', *Middle East Review*, vol. XXII, no. 2 (winter 1989–90).

32 *Newsweek*, 4 October 1982.

33 Rabbi Moshe Levinger in David J. Schnall, *Beyond the Green Line* (New York 1984).

34 Yehoshua Zuckerman in *Nekuda*, 43 (21 May 1982), pp. 18–22, quoted by Uriel Tal, op. cit., pp. 326–7.

35 Rabbi Levi Lauer, Principal of the Pardes Institute at the Hebrew University, lecture, 23 January 1990.

36 David Weisburd, *Jewish Settler Violence* (Pennsylvania, 1989), p. 66.

Chapter Four

1 Gabriel Sheffer, 'The Elusive Question: Jews and Jewry in Israeli Foreign Policy', *Jerusalem Quarterly*, 46 (1988).

2 Ibid. Nahum Goldman, *Memories* (London 1970), p. 313.
3 David Ben-Gurion, Where There Is No Vision, the People Perish in *Unease in Zion*, ed. Ehud ben Ezer (Jerusalem, 1974), p. 71.
4 Stephen S. Wise, *Challenging Years* (London, 1951), p. 218.
5 Richard Marienstras, 'The Jews of the Diaspora, or the Vocation of a Minority', *European Judaism*, vol. 9, no 2 (London, 1975), p. 6.
6 Charles S. Liebman, Diaspora Influence on Israeli Policy in *World Jewry and the State of Israel*, ed. Moshe Davis (New York, 1977), p. 314.
7 Samuel Halperin, *The Political World of American Zionism* (Detroit, 1961), appendix IV.
8 Charles S. Liebman, *Pressure Without Sanctions* (New Jersey, 1977), p. 151.
9 Ben Halperin, *The Idea of the Jewish State* (Harvard, 1969), p. 241.
10 Abraham Joshua Heschel, 'The Individual Jew and His Obligations: An Address to the Jerusalem Theological Conference, August 1957', in *The Insecurity of Freedom* (Philadelphia, 1988,), p. 210.
11 Hanoch Smith, *Attitudes of Israelis towards America and American Jews* (New York, 1983).
12 *Ha'aretz* 18 January 1973; quoted from Liebman in *World Jewry and the State of Israel*, pp. 327–8.
13 Immanuel Jakobovits, A Reassessment of Israel's Role in the Contemporary Jewish Condition in *World Jewry*, ed. Davis (New York, 1977), p. 285.
14 Gershon D. Cohen, From Altneuland to Altneuvolk in *World Jewry*, ed. Davis, (New York, 1977), p. 241.
15 *People's Daily* (Beijing), 27 June 1989.
16 Albert J. Sullivan, *Towards a Philosophy of Public Relations:Images in Information, Influence and Communication*, ed. Otto Lerbinger and Albert J. Sullivan (New York, 1965), p. 249.
17 Ra'anan Gissin, Discussion on Middle East Propaganda and Terrorism, sponsored by the Rothberg School for Overseas Students (Hebrew University) and the Institute for Studies in International Terrorism (SUNY), Jerusalem, 21 August 1989.
18 Ibid.
19 Elad Peled, Nineteenth America–Israel Dialogue, *Congress Monthly*, vol. 51, 2/3.
20 Moshe Gilboa, ibid.
21 Henry Siegman, ibid.
22 Leon Wieseltier, ibid.
23 Britain – Israel Public Affairs Committee, *Lebanon: The Facts* (London 1982).
24 *Jewish Chronicle*, 5 October 1990.

Chapter Five

1 Theodore R. Mann, 'Mission to the Middle East', *Congress Monthly* vol. 55, no. 3, (March/April 1988).
2 Jerome M. Segal, 'Forging the State of Palestine Begins with a Simple Declaration', *Washington Post*, 27 May 1988.

3   Stanley Sheinbaum, 'Stockholm Encounter', *New Outlook* (March/April 1988), pp. 29–31.

4   The former President of the Board of Deputies of British Jews stated that there were 360,000 members of the community and half as many again unaffiliated: *Jerusalem Post*, 23 November 1988.

5   For a discussion on British Jews, see the fourth Jacob Sonntag Memorial Symposium on 'The Shape of Jews to Come', *Jewish Quarterly*, 133 (spring 1989).

6   Steven M. Cohen, 'Ties and Tensions: an Update', *The 1989 Survey of American Jewish Attitudes Towards Israel and Israelis* (New York, 1989).

7   Leonard Fein, *Where Are We? The Inner Life of America's Jews* (New York, 1988), pp. 121.

8   Peter Y. Medding, 'Segmented Ethnicity and the New Jewish Politics', in *Jews and Other Ethnic Groups in a Multi-ethnic Society, Studies in Contemporary Jewry Vol. III*, edited by Ezra Mendelsohn (New York 1987), pp. 38–9.

9   Arthur Hertzburg, 'This Elaborate Dance', *Jewish Quarterly*, vol. 35, no. 1 (129) (1988).

10 Milton Goldun, 'Politics and Philanthropy: The State of American Jewish "Giving"', *Congress Monthly*, vol. 56, no. 6, (September/October 1989).

11 *Jerusalem Post*, 13 October 1982.

12 *The Times*, 6 July 1982.

13 Manfred R. Lehman, *Jerusalem Post*, 21 October 1982.

14 *New York Times*, 25 January 1988.

15 Steven M. Cohen, *Are American and Israeli Jews Drifting Apart?* (New York, March 1989).

16 Stanley B. Horowitz, 'Fundraising in the Future', *Judaism* (spring 1987).

Chapter Six

1   *Jewish Chronicle* 12 February 1988.

2   Ibid., 13 June 1989.

3   Ibid., 15 March 1989.

4   Walter Ruby, *Jerusalem Post*, 23 March 1988.

5   Arthur Hertzberg, 'The Illusion of Jewish Unity', *New York Review of Books*, 16 June 1988.

6   Ibid.

7   Albert Vorspan, 'Jewish Umbrellas and Dissent', *Tikkun*, vol. 3, no. 3, (May/June 1988)

8   *Jerusalem Post*, 4 January 1989.

9   Ibid., 20 March 1988.

10 Ibid., 10 November 1989.

11 Ibid., 12 November 1989.

12 Ibid., 30 November 1989.

13 Ibid., 27 December 1989.

14 Ibid., 23 March 1990.

15 Benjamin Netanyahu, *Terrorism: How the West Can Win* (New York, 1986), introduction.

16 Ariel Merari, Tamar Prat, Sophia Kotzer, Anat Kurz, Yoram Schweitzer, *Inter 85: A Review of International Terrorism*, (Tel Aviv 1986) p. 51.
17 Ibid., p. 52.
18 *Jerusalem Post*, 24 November 1986.
19 Phil Baum and Raphael Danziger, 'A Regenerated PLO? The PNC's 1988 Resolutions and Their Repercussion', *Middle East Review*, vol. XXII, no. 1 (fall 1989), p. 17.
20 *Independent*, 25 January 1989.
21 *Tikkun*, vol. 4, no. 3 (May/June 1989).
22 *Jerusalem Post*, 30 December 1988.
23 *Time*, 9 January 1989.
24 *Jerusalem Post*, 3 January 1989.
25 Robert Spiro, 'Speaking for the Jews', *Present Tense*, vol. 17, no. 2 (January–February 1990).
26 *Jerusalem Post*, 16 December 1988.
27 Ibid., 30 December 1988.
28 Ibid., 10 February 1989.
29 Ibid.
30 Author's personal interview with David Tal.
31 Ariel Merari, Tamar Prat and David Tal, 'The Palestinian Intifada', *Terrorism and Political Violence*, vol. 1, no. 2 (April 1989), p. 187.
32 *International Herald Tribune*, 2–3 June 1990.
33 Israel Radio Arabic Service, 5 June 1990.
34 Yossi Melman, *The Master Terrorist: The True Story behind Abu Nidal*, (London, 1987), pp. 113–9.

Chapter Seven

1 Yitzhak Zamir, 'Media Coverage of Military Operations', *Israel Yearbook on Human Rights* (Faculty of Law, Tel Aviv University, 1988), p. 63.
2 Ruth Gavison, 'Israel's Bill of Rights', *Israel Yearbook on Human Rights* (Faculty of Law, Tel Aviv University, 1985), pp. 118–9.
3 Shulamit Aloni, 'Colonial Laws in the Service of the New Government', *New Outlook* (January/February 1983).
4 Rita J. Simon, Joan M. Landis and Menachem Amir, 'Public Support for Civil Liberties in Israel', *Middle East Review*, vol. xxi, no. 4 (summer, 1989).
5 H. C. 448/85, *Dahar Adv. v Minister of the Interior* 40(2), Piskei Din 701; *Israel Yearbook on Human Rights* (Faculty of Law, Tel Aviv University, 1987), pp. 301–2.
6 Shimon Shetreet, 'Judicial Review of National Security: the Israel Perspective', *Israel Yearbook on Human Rights* (Faculty of Law, Tel Aviv University, 1988), p. 44.
7 Yehudit Karp, Extract from the Karp Report, *New Outlook* (March/April 1984).
8 Myron J. Aronoff, *Israeli Reality in the Begin Era*, ed. Steven Heydemann (London, 1984), p. 65.
9 *Hadashot*, 29 May 1984.

10 Yitzhak Zamir, *Rule of Law and Control of Terrorism*, Tel Aviv University Studies in Law, vol. 8 (Tel Aviv, 1988), pp. 86–7.
11 *Yediot Aharonot*, 1 June 1986.
12 Author's personal interview with Yitzhak Zamir.
13 *Jerusalem Post*, 26 June 1986.
14 Baruch Bracha, 'The Constitutional Position, the Pardoning Power and Other Powers of the President of the State of Israel', *Israel Yearbook on Human Rights* (Faculty of Law, Tel Aviv University, 1979).

Chapter Eight

1 Author's personal interview with Reuven Kaminer.
2 Reuven Kaminer, 'Challenging the Courts', *New Outlook* (January/February 1990).
3 Hillel Schenker, 'The Anti-peace Amendment', *New Outlook* (March 1987).
4 *Ha'aretz*, 7 March 1990.
5 Moshe Negbi, *Jerusalem Post*, 8 January 1988.
6 Article 19, 'World Report: Information, Freedom, Censorship' (1988), p. 262.
7 *New York Times*, 5 May 1984.
8 Chaim Herzog, Information Department of the Israel Embassy, London, 16 June 1988.
9 Moshe Negbi, 'Paper Tiger: The Struggle for Press Freedom in Israel', *Jerusalem Quarterly*, 39 (1986).
10 *News from Within*, 31 May 1988.
11 Leon Hadar, 'Israeli TV Coverage of the Intifada', *Middle East Insight* (January/February 1990).
12 Ephraim Ya'ar, 'Who's Afraid of a Free Press?', *Israel Democracy* (winter 1989).
13 Author's personal interview with Moshe Negbi.
14 Joseph Lapid interviewed by Gila Ya'ar, 'The Media and the Territories', *Israel Democracy* (summer/fall 1988).
15 Zvi Gilat, 'The Intifada and the Israeli Press', *New Outlook* (November/December 1989).
16 *Kol Ha'ir*, 10 November 1989.
17 Amnesty International Report, *The Case of the Editors of Derech Ha'Nitzotz*, April 1989.

Chapter Nine

1 Baruch Kimmerling, *Making Conflict a Routine in Israeli Society and Its Defence Establishment*, ed. Moshe Lissak (London, 1984) pp. 17–19.
2 Shlomo Aronson and Dan Horowitz, 'The Strategy of Controlled Retaliation', *State and Government* (summer 1971).
3 Aharon Yariv, 'Strategic Depth', *Jerusalem Quarterly*, 16 (1980).
4 Meron Benvenisti, *The West Bank Handbook* (Jerusalem, 1986), p. 40.
5 Yuval Ne'eman, quoted in ibid., p. 43.

6   Ephraim Sneh, *Newsweek*, 6 June 1988.
7   Shlomo Gazit, *Jerusalem Post*, 25 December 1988.
8   Giora Forman, 'The Security Lie', *New Outlook* (July 1988).
9   Aharon Yariv, 'Strategic Depth', *Jerusalem Quarterly* 16 (1980).
10   Asher Yaniv, 'Something Happened to the Israeli Deterrent', *Politika* (May 1989), and *Israel Democracy* (summer 1989).
11   Israel Tal, 'To Live in Friendship', *New Outlook* (July 1988).
12   Joseph Alpher, 'A Palestinian Mini-State: the Security Challenge for Israel', *Tikkun*, vol. 3, no. 5 (September/October 1988).
13   Ruth Gavison, *Jerusalem Post*, 3 June 1988.
14   Jonathan Kuttab, 'A Palestinian View of the Israeli Peace Camp', *New Outlook* (March 1990).
15   *Kol Ḥa'ir*, 26 August 1988.
16   *Newsweek*, 30 January 1989.
17   B'Tselem, Annual Report, 1989, pp. 119–23.
18   'Cases of Death and Injury of Children', *B'Tselem Information Sheet* (Jerusalem, 1 January 1990).
19   Ibid.
20   Eyal Ben-Ari, 'Masks and Soldiering: The Israeli Army and the Palestinian Uprising', *Cultural Anthropology*, vol. 4, no. 4 (1989), p. 378.
21   Ibid., pp. 384–5.
22   Sinai Peter, quoted in Danny Gur-Arieh, 'Refuseniks', *New Outlook* (August 1988).
23   *Ha'aretz*, 26 July 1990.
24   Ibid., 3 August 1990.

Chapter Ten

1   Author's personal interview with Mordechai Bar-On, 1982.
2   Edy Kaufman, 'The Intifada and the Peace Camp', *Journal of Palestine Studies*, vol. 17, no. 4 (summer 1988).
3   Author's personal interview with Avraham Burg, 1982.
4   Ibid.
5   Amos Oz, *In the Land of Israel* (London, 1983), p. 40.
6   Yezid Sayigh, 'Struggle Within, Struggle Without: the Transformation of PLO Politics since 1982', *International Affairs*, vol. 65, no. 2 (spring 1989), p. 254.
7   Mordechai Bar-On, 'The Peace Movement after Algiers', *New Outlook* (May 1988).
8   Reuven Kaminer, The Protest Movement in Israel in *Intifada: The Palestinian Uprising against Israeli Occupation*, ed. Zachary Lockman and Joel Beinin (London, 1990), p. 231.
9   Aaron Back and Gordon Fellerman, 'Peace Soon? Israeli Protest Politics and the Intifada', *Tikkun*, vol. 3, no. 6 (November/December 1988).
10   Edy Kaufman, op. cit.
11   Rachel Ostrowitz, 'Dangerous Women: the Israeli Women's Peace Movement', *New Outlook* (June/July 1989).
12   Naomi Chazan, 'The Israeli Woman – Myth and Reality', ibid.

13   Author's personal interview with Debbie Weismann, 1982.
14   *Ma'ariv*, 8 March 1990.
15   Arieh Shalev, *The West Bank: Line of Defense* (New York, 1985).

Chapter Eleven

1   *Ha'aretz*, 16 August 1990.
2   *Jerusalem Post*, 24 August 1990.
3   Samir al-Khalil, *Republic of Fear*, (London 1990), p. 55.
4   *Al Fajr*, 7 October 1990.
5   *Al Hamishmar*, 12 August 1990.
6   *Ha'aretz*, 17 August 1990.
7   *Jewish Echo*, 24 August 1990.
8   *Yediot Aharanot*, 27 August 1990.
9   *Ha'ir*, 24 August 1990.
10   *New Outlook*, September 1990.
11   West Bank Data Project, March 1990, as quoted in the *New York Times*,
     4 March 1990.
12   *Independent*, 14 April 1990.
13   *Forward*, 27 July 1990.
14   BBC Monitoring SWB ME/0829, 30 July 1990.
15   Saudi Press Agency, 26 February 1990.
16   *Jerusalem Post*, 9 October 1990.
17   *Ha'aretz*, 19 August 1990.
18   *Jewish Echo*, 14 December 1990.
19   *Jewish Echo*, 21 December 1990.
20   *Observer*, 26 August 1990.
21   *New York Review of Books*, 25 October 1990.

Glossary of Hebrew Terms

Achdut Avoda   pioneering left Socialist Zionist Party, characterized by maximalist policies towards the Arabs. Now part of the Labour Party.

Af Sha'al   not an inch

Agudat Yisrael a-Zionist ultra-orthodox party influenced by Hassidism. Five seats in the 1988 election.

Al Hamishmar   left-wing daily newspaper.

Aliya   emigration to Israel, literally 'going up'.

Am Israel   the People of Israel.

Ashaf   PLO.

Ashkenazim   Jews from Central and Eastern Europe.

Avoda Ivrit   Hebrew labour.

Banai   acronym for the Covenant of Eretz Israel Loyalists, predecessor of the Techiya party authority.

Betar   Revisionist youth, later affiliated to Herut.

B'nei Akiva   National Religious Party youth.

Brit Ha'Biryonim   Union of Zealots or Hooligans, neo-fascist group, active in the early 1930s.

B'Tselem   Israel Information Centre for Human Rights in the Occupied Territories.

Davar   Labour movement daily newspaper.

Degel Ha'Torah   non-Zionist ultra-orthodox party, influenced by the Lithuanian school of *mitnagdim*. Two seats in the 1988 election.

Ein Vered group   maximalist Labour activists.

Eretz Israel   the Land of Israel.

Galut `exile.

Galuti   of a Diaspora mentality.

Ger Toshav   resident alien.

Ger Tsedek   convert to Judaism, a righteous alien.

Gush Emunim   religious settlers' movement in the Territories.

Gush Etzion   a group of Jewish settlements which fell to the Arab Legion in 1948, retaken by Israel in 1967.

Ha'aretz leading intellectual, liberal daily newspaper.

Hadash Political Front of Communists and assorted progressives.

Hadashot campaigning Israeli daily newspaper.

Hagana Jewish Defence Force in the Yishuv, predecessor of the IDF.

He'Hazit the publication of Lehi.

Ha'Kibbutz Ha'Meuchad kibbutz movement of Achdut Avoda.

Ha'Medina Ha'Enoshit the humane state.

Ha'Poalei Ha'Mizrachi religious Labour-oriented Zionist movement, now part of the National Religious Party.

harig aberration.

Hasbara explanation of events.

Hassidim adherents of a popular ultra-orthodox movement, characterized by devotion to its rabbinical leader and fervent concentration on the relationship with God.

Havlaga policy of self-restraint.

Herut party formed by Menachem Begin in 1948 and successor to the Revisionists; now part of Likud.

Heshbon Ha'nefesh self-examination.

Hester Panim the hiding of God's face.

Hillul Ha'Shem the profanation of God's name.

Im ba l'horgach hashkem l'horgo if someone comes to kill you, rise up to kill them.

Informatzia information.

Irgun Zva'i Leumi National Military Organization led by Menachem Begin in the struggle against the Mandatory authorities.

Kabbala the Jewish mystical tradition.

Kach Far Right party, led by the late Rabbi Meir Kahane, outlawed by the Knesset.

Keren Hayesod Palestine Foundation Fund.

Keren Kayemet l'Israel the Jewish National Fund.

Kibbutz Ha'Galuyot the ingathering of the exiles.

Lehi 'Fighters for the Freedom of Israel', formerly the Stern Group.

Likud right-wing bloc, inheritor of Revisionism. Dominant party in the 1990 government; forty seats in the 1988 election.

Ma'arach Labour alignment with Mapam, 1969 until the formation of the National Unity government with Likud.

Mafdal National Religious Party. Five seats in the 1988 election.

Malchut Yisrael the sovereignty of the Land.

Mapai centrist Labour Party led by Ben-Gurion. Dominant party in early Israeli governments.

Mapam dovish Marxist–Zionist party. Three seats in the 1988 election.

Meimad   dovish religious Zionist party formed to fight the 1988 election.

Mesirut Nefesh   the utmost devotion.

Milchemet Hova   war of duty.

Milchemet Mitzva   obligatory war.

Milchemet Reshut   elective war.

Mishna   first subject-ordered codification of the oral law.

Mishpachat ha'lochamim   the family of Irgun fighters.

Mitnagdim   ultra-orthodox opponents of the Hassidim.

Mitzva   commandment, good deed.

Mizrachi   religious Zionist movement, central component of the National Religious Party.

Moledet   Far Right party, characterized by the policy of 'transfer'. Two seats in the 1988 election.

Netivot Shalom   religious peace movement.

Nitzotzot   divine sparks.

Palmach   the leftist assault companies of the Hagana.

Pikuach Nefesh   the saving of Jewish lives, the principle of the primary importance of the saving of life.

Poskim   religious authorities who rule on the practical application of the Halacha.

Rafi   Mapai breakaway party, 1965–8, led by Ben-Gurion.

Ratz   Civil Rights and Peace movement.

Rodef   assailant.

Sephardim   Jews from oriental countries.

Shas   ultra-orthodox Sephardi party. Six seats in the 1988 election.

Shechina   the Divine Presence.

Shefichut damim   the shedding of blood.

Shinui   dovish centrist non-socialist party. Two seats in the 1988 election.

Shiurim   religious study sessions, usually given by a rabbinical authority.

Shlemut ha'Moledet   the 'completeness' of the homeland.

Shoah   the Nazi Holocaust.

Shtadlanim   unelected Jewish representatives of communal interests who petitioned the ruling authorities in the Diaspora.

Sitra Achra   the camp of the other side.

Ta'amula   propaganada.

Talmud Bavli   Babylonian Talmud.

Talmud Yerushalmi   Jerusalem Talmud.

Tami   Sephardi breakaway party from the National Religious Party. Three seats in the 1981 election.

Techiya   Far Right party, formed after Camp David through a split in Likud. Three seats in the 1988 election.

Tenach   acronym for the three sections of the Jewish Bible: Torah, Prophets, Writings.

Tenua l'Ma'an Eretz Israel   movement for the (Greater) Land of Israel.

Teshuva   spiritual renewal.

Tohar Ha'neshek   the purity of arms.

Torah   the five books of Moses. In a wider sense, the entire body of religious precepts, learning and life.

Torah Va'Avoda   Torah and Work

Tosafot   collections of medieval commentaries on the Talmud.

Tsomet   Far Right party of former Labour movement people. Two seats in the 1988 election.

Yahad   Party formed by Ezer Weizmann to fight the 1984 election, now part of the Labour Party.

Yediot Aharonot   popular Israeli daily newspaper.

Yefei Nefesh   do-gooders.

Ye'Hareg ve'al Ya'avor   'one should rather be killed than transgress'.

Yeshiva   religious seminary.

Yishuv   the Jewish settlement in Palestine before 1948.

Yishuv Ha'aretz   settling the Land.

Yordim   Israelis who have left Israel.

Select Bibliography

Al-Khalil, Samir, *Republic of Fear: The Inside Story of Saddam's Iraq* (Hutchinson Radius, London, 1990).

Alexander, Yonah, and Sinai, Joshua, *Terrorism: The PLO Connection* (Crane Russack, New York, 1989).

American Friends Service Committee, *A Compassionate Peace: A Future for the Middle East* (Hill and Wang, New York, 1982).

Arian, Asher, *Politics in Israel: The Second Generation* (Chatham House, Chatham, 1989).

Aronoff, Myron J., *Israeli Visions and Divisions* (Transaction, New Brunswick, 1989).

Aronson, Geoffrey, *Israel, Palestinians and the Intifada* (Kegan Paul International, London, 1990).

Aronson, Ronald, *The Dialectics of Disaster* (Verso, London, 1983).

Avineri, Shlomo, *The Making of Modern Zionism: The Intellectual Origins of the Jewish State* (Weidenfeld and Nicolson, London, 1981).

Avineri, Shlomo, *Moses Hess: Prophet of Communism and Zionism* (New York University Press, New York, 1987).

Avishai, Bernard, *The Tragedy of Zionism: Revolution and Democracy in the Land of Israel* (Farrar, Straus Giroux, New York, 1985).

Avishai, Bernard, *A New Israel: Democracy in Crisis* (Ticknor and Fields, New York, 1990).

Beit Hallahmi, Benjamin, *The Israeli Connection: Who Israel Arms and Why* (I.B. Tauris, London, 1987).

Ben Ezer, Ehud, *Unease in Zion* (Quadrangle, London, 1974).

Benvenisti, Meron, *The West Bank Handbook* (Jerusalem Post, Jerusalem, 1986).

Benziman, Uzi, *Sharon: An Israeli Caesar* (Robson Books, London, 1987).

Bethell, Nicholas, *The Palestine Triangle* (André Deutsch, London, 1979).

Blundy, David, and Lycett, Andrew, *Qaddafi and the Libyan Revolution* (Weidenfeld and Nicolson, London, 1987).

Buber, Martin, *On Zion: The History of an Idea* (East and West Library, London, 1973).

B' Tselem Reports: *Demolition and Sealing of Houses* (September 1989); *The System of Taxation in the West Bank and the Gaza Strip* (February 1990); *The Use of Firearms by the Security Forces in the Occupied Territories* (July 1990).

Cameron, James, *The Best of Cameron* (New English Library, London, 1981).

Cameron, James, *Cameron in the Guardian 1974–1984* (Hutchinson, London, 1985).

Chomsky, Noam, *Peace in the Middle East?* (Fontana, London, 1975).

Chomsky, Noam, *The Fateful Triangle: The U.S., Israel and the Palestinians* (South End Press, Boston, 1983).

Cohen, Michael J., *Palestine and the Great Powers 1945–1948* (Princeton University Press, Princeton, 1982).

Cohen, Michael J., *Truman and Israel* (University of California Press, Berkeley, 1990).

Cohen, Aharon, *Israel and the Arab World* (W. H. Allen, London, 1970).

Cohen, Mitchell, *Zion and State* (Basil Blackwell, Oxford, 1987).

Crossman, Richard, *Palestine Mission* (Harper and Brothers, New York, 1947).

Crossman, Richard, *A Nation Reborn* (Hamish Hamilton, London, 1960).

Curtis, Michael, *The Middle East Reader* (Transaction, New Brunswick, 1986).

Davis, Moshe, *World Jewry and the State of Israel* (Arno, New York, 1977).

Dayan, Moshe, *Breakthrough* (Weidenfeld and Nicolson, London, 1981).

Drezon-Tepler, Marcia, *Interest Groups and Political Change in Israel* (SUNÝ, New York, 1990).

Eban, Abba, *An Autobiography* (Random House, New York, 1977).

Efrat, Elisha, *Geography and Politics in Israel since 1967* (Frank Cass, London, 1988).

Eisentadt, S. N., *The Transformation of Israeli Society* (Weidenfeld and Nicolson, London, 1985).

El-Asmar, Fouzi, *To Be an Arab in Israel* (Francis Pinter, London, 1975).

Eliav, Liova, *New Heart, New Spirit: Biblical Humanism for Modern Israel* (JPS, Philadelphia, 1988).

Elon Amos, *The Israelis: Founders and Sons* (Bantam, London, 1972).

Farouk-Sluglett, Marion, and Sluglett, Peter *Iraq since 1958* (I. B. Tauris, London, 1990).

Fein, Leonard, *Where Are We? The Inner Life of America's Jews*, (Harper & Row, New York, 1988).

Fisch, Harold, *The Zionist Revolution* (Weidenfeld and Nicolson, London, 1978).

Findley, Paul, *They Dare to Speak Out* (Lawrence Hill, Westport, 1985).

Flaphan, Simha, *When Enemies Dare to Talk* (Croom Helm, London, 1979).

Flaphan, Simha, *The Birth of Israel: Myths and Realities* (Pantheon, New York, 1987).

Frankel, William, *Israel Observed: an Anatomy of a State* (Thames and Hudson, London, 1980).

Ghilan, Maxim, *How Israel Lost its Soul* (Penguin, London, 1974).

Gorney, Joseph, *The British Labour Movement and Zionism* (Frank Cass, London, 1983).

Gorney, Yosef, *Zionism and the Arabs 1882–1948* (Clarendon Press, Oxford, 1987).

Gowers, Andrew, and Walker, Tony, *Behind the Myth: Yasser Arafat and the Palestinian Revolution* (W. H. Allen, London, 1990).

Grossman, David, *The Yellow Wind* (Jonathan Cape, London, 1988).

Ha'am, Ahad, *Nationalism and the Jewish Ethic: Basic Writings of Ahad Ha'am* (Herzl Press, New York, 1962).

Halabi, Rafik, *The West Bank Story: An Arab's View of Both Sides of a Tangled Conflict*, (Harcourt Brace Jovanovich, New York, 1982).

Halpern, Ben, *The Idea of a Jewish State* (Harvard University Press, Harvard, 1969).

Halperin, Samuel, *The Political World of American Zionism* (Wayne State University Press, Detroit, 1961).

Harkabi, Yehoshafat, *Arab Attitudes to Israel* (Valentine Mitchell, London, 1972).

Harkabi, Yehoshafat, *Israel's Fateful Decisions* (I. B. Tauris, London, 1988).

Heikel, Mohammed, *Autumn of Fury: The Assassination of Sadat*, (André Deutsch, London, 1983).

Heller, Mark A., *A Palestinian State: The Implications for Israel* (Harvard University Press, London, 1983).

Hertzberg, Arthur, *Being Jewish in America: The Modern Experience* (Schocken, New York, 1979).

Hertzberg, Arthur, *The Zionist Idea* (Atheneum, New York, 1982).

Hiro, Dilip, *The Longest War: The Iran–Iraq Military Conflict* (Paladin, London, 1990).

Hirst, David, *The Gun and the Olive Branch* (Faber and Faber, London, 1977).

Hoffman, Lawrence A., *The Land of Israel: Jewish Perspectives* (Indiana

University Press, Bloomington, 1986).

Isaac, Rael Jean, *Israel Divided: Ideological Politics in the Jewish State* (John Hopkins University Press, Baltimore, 1976).

Isaac, Rael Jean, *Party and Politics in Israel* (Longman, London, 1981).

Jaffee Centre for Strategic Studies, *The West Bank and Gaza: Israel's Options for Peace*, (Jaffee Centre for Strategic Studies, Tel Aviv, 1989).

Jakobovits, Immanuel, *If Only My People: Zionism in My Life*, (Weidenfeld and Nicolson, London, 1984).

Jansen, Michael, *Dissonance in Zion* (Zed, London, 1987).

Kaufman, Gerald, *Inside the Promised Land* (Wildwood House, London, 1986).

Keller, Adam, *Terrible Days* (Amstelveen, Cyprus, 1987).

Kienle, Eberhard, *Ba'th v Ba'th: The Conflict between Syria and Iraq 1968–1989* (I. B. Tauris, London, 1990).

Kimmerling, Baruch, *The Israeli State and Society: Boundaries and Frontiers* (SUNY, New York, 1989).

Langer, Felicia, *An Age of Stone* (Quartet, London, 1988).

Liebman, Charles S., *Pressure without Sanctions* (Fairleigh Dickinson, New Jersey, 1977).

Lissak, Moshe, *Israeli Society and its Defence Establishment* (Frank Cass, London, 1984).

Lockman, Zachary, and Beinin, Joel, *Intifada: The Palestinian Uprising against Israeli Occupation* (I. B. Tauris, London, 1990).

Lucas, Noah, *The Modern History of Israel* (Weidenfeld and Nicolson, London, 1974).

Maoz, Moshe, and Yaniv, Avner, *Syria under Assad* (Croom Helm, London, 1986).

McDowall, David, *Palestine and Israel: The Uprising and Beyond* (I. B. Tauris, London, 1989).

Medding, Peter Y., *Israel: State and Society 1948–1988* (Institute of Contemporary Jewry, Oxford University Press, Oxford, 1989).

Medding, Peter Y., *The Founding of Israeli Democracy 1948–1967* (Oxford University Press, Oxford, 1990).

Melman, Yossi, *The Master Terrorist: The True Story behind Abu Nidal* Sidgwick and Jackson, London, 1987).

Merhav, Peretz, *The Israeli Left*, (A. S. Barnes, San Diego, 1980).

Mishal, Shaul, *The PLO under Arafat* (Yale University Press, New Haven, 1986).

Morris, Benny, *The Birth of the Palestinian Refugee Problem 1947–1949* (Cambridge University Press, Cambridge, 1987).

Morris, Benny, *1948 and After: Israel and the Palestinians* (Clarendon Press, Oxford, 1990).

Nahas, Dunia, *The Israeli Communist Party* (Croom Helm, London, 1978).

Newman, David, *The Impact of Gush Emunim: Politics and Settlement in the West Bank* (Croom Helm, London, 1985).

O'Brien, Conor Cruise, *The Siege* (Weidenfeld and Nicolson, London, 1986).

Organski, A. F. K., *The $36 Billion Bargain: Strategy and Politics in U. S. Assistance to Israel* (Columbia University Press, New York, 1990).

Oz, Amos, *In the Land of Israel* (Fontana, London, 1983).

Penniman, Howard, J., *Israel at the Polls: Knesset Election of 1977* (American Enterprise Institute for Public Policy Research, Washington, 1979).

Penniman, Howard, R., and Elazar, Daniel J., *Israel at the Polls, 1981* (Indiana University Press, Bloomington, 1986).

Peretz, Don, *Intifada: The Palestinian Uprising* (Westview, London, 1990).

Peri, Yoram, *Between Battles and Ballots: Israeli Military in Politics* (Cambridge University Press, Cambridge, 1983).

Perlmutter, Amos, *Israel: The Partitioned State* (Charles Scribner's Sons, New York, 1985).

Porat, Dina, *The Blue and Yellow Stars of David: The Zionist Leadership in Palestine and the Holocaust 1939–1945* (Harvard University Press, London, 1990).

Porath, Yahoshua, *The Palestinian Arab National Movement 1929–1939: from Riots to Rebellion*, (Frank Cass, London, 1977).

Prawer, Joshua, *The History of the Jews in the Latin Kingdom of Jerusalem* (Clarendon Press, Oxford, 1988).

Pryce-Jones, David, *The Closed Circle: An Interpretation of the Arabs* (Weidenfeld and Nicolson, London, 1989).

Rabin, Yitzhak, *The Rabin Memoirs* (Little Brown, Boston, 1979).

Reinharz, Yehuda, *Chaim Weizmann: The Making of a Zionist Leader* (Oxford University Press, Oxford, 1985).

Rose, Norman, *Chaim Weizman: A Biography* (Weidenfeld and Nicolson, London, 1986).

Roth, Stephen J., *The Impact of the Six Day War* (Macmillan, London, 1988).

Rubenstein, Sondra Miller, *The Communist Movement in Palestine and Israel 1919–1984* (Westview, London, 1985).

Rubinstein, Amnon, *The Zionist Dream Revisited* (Schocken, New York, 1984).

Sacher, Howard M., *A History of Israel*, vol. II (Oxford University Press, Oxford, 1987).

Sadat, Anwar, *In Search of Identity* (Collins, London, 1978).

Sahliyeh, Emile, *In Search of Leadership: West Bank Politics since 1967* (The Brookings Institution, Washington DC 1988).

Said, Edward, *The Question of Palestine* (Routledge and Kegan Paul, London, 1981).

Schechtman, Joseph B., *The Jabotinsky Story: The Last Years 1923–1940* (Thomas Yoseloff, London, 1961).

Schenker, Hillel, *After Lebanon* (Pilgrim, New York, 1983).

Schiff, Zeev, and Ehud, Ya'ari, *Israel's Lebanon War* (Allen and Unwin, London, 1985).

Schiff, Zeev, and Ehud, Ya'ari, *Intifada* (Simon and Schuster, London, 1990).

Schnall, David J., *Radical Dissent in Contemporary Israeli Politics* (Praeger, London, 1979).

Schnall, David J., *Beyond the Green Line* (Praeger, New York, 1984).

Schweitzer, Avram, *Israel: The Changing National Agenda* (Croom Helm, London, 1986).

Segre, V. D., *Israel: A Society in Transition* (Oxford University Press, Oxford, 1971).

Segre, Dan V., *A Crisis of Identity: Israel and Zionism* (Oxford University Press, Oxford, 1980).

Shavitt, Yaakov, *Jabotinsky and the Revisionist Movement: 1925–1948* (Frank Cass, London, 1988).

Sheffer, Gabriel, *Modern Diasporas in International Politics* (Croom Helm, London, 1986).

Shipler, David *Arab and Jew: Wounded Spirits in a Promised Land* (Times, New York, 1986).

Shlaim, Avi, *Collusion across the Jordan* (Clarendon Press, Oxford, 1988).

Silver, Eric, *Begin: A Biography* (Weidenfeld and Nicolson, London, 1984).

Simon, Leon, *Ahad Ha'am: A Biography* (East and West Library, London, 1960).

Sinclair, Clive, *Diaspora Blues: A View of Israel* (Heinemann, London, 1987).

Sofer, Sasson, *Begin: An Anatomy of a Leadership* (Basil Blackwell, Oxford, 1988).

Stone, I. F., *Underground to Palestine* (Hutchinson, London 1979).

Swirski, Shlomo, *Israel: The Oriental Majority* (Zed, London, 1989).

Sykes, Christopher, *Crossroads to Israel* (Indiana University Press, Bloomington, 1973).

Talmon, J. L., *Israel Among the Nations* (Weidenfeld and Nicolson, London, 1970).

Teveth, Shabtai, *Ben-Gurion and the Palestinian Arabs* (Oxford University Press, Oxford, 1985).

Thomas, Hugh, *The Suez Affair* (Weidenfeld and Nicolson, London, 1967).

Timerman, Jacobo, *The Longest War* (Picador, London, 1982).

Tivnon, Edward, *The Lobby: Jewish Political Power and American Foreign Policy* (Simon and Schuster, New York, 1987).

Viorst, Milton, *Sands of Sorrow: Israel's Journey from Independence* (I. B. Tauris, London, 1987).

Weisburd, David, *Jewish Settler Violence* (Pennsylvania State University Press, London, 1989).

Wolfsfeld, Gadi, *The Politics of Provocation and Protest in Israel* (SUNY, New York, 1988).

Yaniv, Avner, *Dilemmas of Security: Politics, Strategy and the Israeli Experience in Lebanon* (Oxford University Press, New York, 1987).

Index

257